THE AIR CONTROLLERS' CONTROVERSY

We have two ways to face the future. Either face it with a defeatist attitude and accept whatever it holds for us, or we can design the future, and I choose the latter.

Hubert H. Humphrey, PATCO Convention, 1975.

THE AIR CONTROLLERS' CONTROVERSY
Lessons from the PATCO Strike

Arthur B. Shostak, Ph.D.

Drexel University
Philadelphia, Pennsylvania

David Skocik, M.A.

Temple University
Philadelphia, Pennsylvania

 **HUMAN SCIENCES PRESS, INC.**
72 FIFTH AVENUE
NEW YORK, N.Y. 10011-8004

Printed in the United States of America
987654321

Library of Congress Cataloging-in-Publication Data

Shostak, Arthur B.
   The air controllers' controversy.

   Includes index.
   1. Air Traffic Controllers' Strike, 1981.
2. Professional Air Traffic Controllers Organization
(Washington, D.C.) I. Skocik, David. II. Title.
HD5325.A4252   1981   331:89′28138774042   86-411
ISBN 0-89885-319-2
ISBN 0-89885-320-6 (pbk.)

For those former controllers and their families
who "lived" PATCO, walked the picket line,
supported USATCO and PATCO LIVES, and dreamed a better dream . . .

Our struggle must not go unheeded, but rather, it should be allowed to have as much publicity as possible for the sake of future generations of Labor. We are an important facet of American history, and our story needs to be preserved, no matter if we are seen as right or wrong . . .
Letter, *PATCO LIVES* January/February 1985 p. 8 (written by a "fired PATCO controller").

CONTENTS

Bill Taylor—PATCO LIVES organizer and sole staffer, in Washington office.

ACKNOWLEDGEMENTS

While many former PATCO activists helped the book come together, two in particular stand out: Jack Maher and Bill Taylor made all the difference. Jack, a co-founder in 1968 of PATCO, was the first to encourage the idea of this book, and he went on to arrange introductions to key personalities, critique every chapter, and add an indispensable perspective. Bill Taylor, an officer of PATCO and USATCO, and the founder of PATCO LIVES, volunteered hours of interview time, generously shared material from his files, critiqued many chapters, and brought to bear the unique point of view of someone who has never given up the struggle, and who continues to believe history will vindicate and honor the 1981 effort.

Other PATCO activists without whom the chapters would lack much behind-the-scenes detail, color, and tone include Stan Gordon, John F. Leyden, Bob Meyers, Bob Poli, Jack Seddon, and Dave Siegal. Steven O'Keefe gave permission to use his 900 surveys of former controllers, a one-of-a-kind resource that made possible some informed analysis of the strike's aftermath. USATCO officers, especially Gary Eads and Mike Fermon, were patient, cordial, and informative during my many visits to the "bunker."

Non-PATCO respondents who helped fill in vital aspects of this complex tale included Leo Perlis, one of the intermediaries between PATCO and the White House; David L. Kushner, Director of Organizing for the AFL-CIO's American Federation of Government Employees (AFGE), a key figure in the on-going effort to unionize working controllers; and John Thornton, now with MEBA (and earlier, PATCO)—once a leading organizer in the AFGE 1984-1985 campaign.

Academics who shared research and ideas of their own included Katherine S. Newman, a Columbia University anthropologist; Britta Fischer, Chairperson of the Sociology Department at Emmanuel College; and Rick Hurd, an economist at the University of New Hampshire (the last two of whom are represented by essays especially prepared for this volume).

A former student of mine at the AFL-CIO's George Meany Center for Labor Studies, John W. Pinto, critiqued much of the book from the perspective of a non-PATCO unionist, and provided valuable ideas in points of clarity and emphasis. Another Meany Center student, Jeanne Belkin, interviewed controllers in New York, and sent me informative tapes of the sessions. Similarly, a Philadelphia friend, Edie Kligman, conducted a midwest interview that adds another dimension to the array of interviews included at the close of the volume.

While my associate and I worked separately on our contributions, I learned much about controller work realities from Dave Skocik, and was buoyed by his enthusiasm for this project from the outset. Although neither of us can be held responsible for possible drawbacks in the other's chapters, we read and shared constructive criticisms of one another's writing throughout—reserving by joint agreement the right to hold independent views in certain complex and gray areas.

Betty Shostak, my mother, diligently clipped newspaper articles on PATCO and controller issues from 1980 to date, a resource that helps explain the New York City/Florida citations in chapter footnotes, and meant much personally to me. Lynn Seng and her sons, Matt and Dan, gave me the time and space this sort of project requires, even as Lynn listened, exchanged views, and labored alongside me with a sensitivity that helped sustain my belief in the task.

My typist, Sharon McDonnell, was as diligent, swift, and responsible as a writer could hope, and met my secretarial needs splendidly. Drexel University granted me half-time leave for the research and writing of the book, a generous type of support without which this (self-funded) project might never have been completed. As often before over my 17 years at Drexel the staff of the library was exceedingly helpful, and Richard Binder, in particular, secured materials of special value to my research.

Above all, however, my debt is greatest to scores of former controllers who gave freely of their time and most personal thoughts in lengthy interviews conducted in Boston, Chicago, Cleveland, Ft. Lauderdale, Fremont (CA), Los Angeles, New York City, Philadelphia, and Washington, D.C. I hope I have done justice to their story, and assume full responsibility for any shortcomings that accrue. While I have known from the outset this presentation may upset and even hurt some I count as friends, and many others I admire, I offer my interpretation and conclusions in the best spirit of the 1981 strike itself; that is, on behalf of the vision championed by PATCO, the vision of a profession serving the nation and its practitioners better than ever before in aviation history.

Arthur B. Shostak, Ph.D.

Unlike Art Shostak's tremendous research investment, much of my material came directly from recollections and personal files. His commitment to this project was the impetus I needed to consolidate what I knew of the events that led to August 1981. Organization is the key to any work, but Art's ability to collate, analyze, and distil literally thousands of documents into a coherent account was the key to this one.

My wife Roseann assisted me by allowing me the luxury of her unquestioned support coupled with the time and understanding I needed to compose my thoughts into an orderly format. That support began long before my involvement with PATCO and continued through the trauma of the strike. In this immediate work, she also assisted Art and me through many hours spent retyping portions of the manuscript to accommodate additional material. Our three children, Eric, Karen, and Kristin, contributed by their quiet acceptance of many hours without a father.

Four people who have put up with much since 1981 are my parents and in-laws. My parents, Edward and Rosemarie, after having raised nine children, again began helping a grown son to meet his expenses as he continued working unpaid for a banished union into 1982. My in-laws, Tony and Lillian Miscavige, also contributed financially and morally, never raising doubts nor questions. The greatest thing these four people gave me was respect and trust. Their support allowed me to "go down fighting," rather than passively accepting defeat. I thank them for their belief in me which transcended the issues of the strike and has continued through my graduate studies.

Dr. Ray Miller, a professor and friend dating back to my undergraduate days at Delaware's Wilmington College, provided much encouragement for this work. Having earlier collaborated on a screenplay documenting the strike in 1983, we had begun working on a book of our own. He kindly offered me the material we had jointly produced for this effort.

The goal of this book, as I see it, is simply to provide insights into the actions of good people who made the mistake of colliding head-on with a popular president. Rather than the story of a dismantled union, it is about the individual people who participated in the collective action of August 1981, and lived through its consequences.

The following pages resurrect for examination some items dimmed by the laminations of time; for the majority, the wounds have healed, though the scars will always remain. It is said that adversity creates a sense of belonging with those who share it. In that respect, this account belongs to all those who lived it.

David Skocik, M.A.

FOREWORD

I have always been fascinated by the glass booth atop the tall tower out at the local airport, and by the silhouettes of tiny figures inside handling giant responsibilities. But the people up there had remained distant unknown shadows until a Spring day in 1980 when I offered to help an adult student obviously perplexed by an assignment.

We were out at the AFL-CIO George Meany Center for Labor Studies in Silver Spring, Maryland, a residential education center where I have guest-taught for 2 weeks a year since 1975. The student turned out to be Jack Maher, a cofounder in 1968 of the Professional Air Traffic Controllers Organization (PATCO), and his assignment involved preparing a questionnaire for use with the union's 14,500 members.

PATCO was gearing up for tough negotiations in 1981, when its third contract since 1972 expired with the Federal Aviation Administration (FAA). The union wanted to know how its members ranked alternative contract demands, and how they felt about the possibility of a major job action in 1981 (the union had conducted six such acts since 1970, albeit the controllers did not, as federal employees, have a legal right to take any such steps).

My casual collaboration that day led to a year-long contractual relationship with the union. I made numerous trips to PATCO headquarters in Washington, D.C., and, with research associates Richard Parenti and Dr. John Colamosca, eventually prepared five lengthy reports analyzing rank-and-file answers to our five lengthy questionnaires. As we secured over 12,500 re-

15

turns to our last survey of PATCO's 14,500 members we came to possess a fairly high-powered, timely, and valuable body of information, one that I helped explain to PATCO activists at special meetings in 1981 in Boston, Chicago, Philadelphia, and elsewhere.

What finally convinced me to undertake this book, entailing 4 years of research, was the devastating shock of both loss of the strike and the very union organization itself. Nothing over my 1980-1981 association with PATCO had prepared me for the rapidity and thoroughness of the August 1981 defeat. While I had heard warnings that some firings, and even a short-lived decertification of PATCO, were possible, I was incredulous when President Reagan's instant intervention led to the firing of 11,345 PATCO backers, and in short order, to the public pillorying, court-induced bankruptcy, and permanent decertification of the union.

Now I had many difficult questions to wrestle with:

> Why the loss? How could PATCO have miscalculated so badly? How could $2^{1}/_2$ years of strike preparation have produced so little, and failed to prevent so stark an outcome?

> How were the ex-controllers taking their defeat? What sort of adjustments were necessary in their standard of living? What views did they have of the strike, of PATCO, of the labor movement, the FAA, and the government? How had the strike influenced their quality of life, and what lay ahead for them?

> How had the strike influenced the American labor movement? Had the unions done everything possible on PATCO's behalf, and, if not, why not? How did PATCO activists assess labor solidarity, and what insights could labor draw from the entire experience?

> What had become of PATCO's successor organization, the United States Air Traffic Controllers Organization (USATCO)? And in what ways did it meet the pressing needs of ex-controllers? Why did USATCO shut down after two years of operation, and what might be expected from its successor, PATCO LIVES?

Above all, I wanted to know what were the most essential *lessons* the labor movement, Congress, and the FAA might learn from the rise and fall of PATCO—the better to avert such an enormous human toll—in another epic labor-management clash in the years immediately ahead.

In pursuit of insights I went coast-to-coast, and overseas to London, to interview key respondents. I marched on a PATCO picketline at the Philadelphia International Airport a week after the strike began; spoke at PATCO strike rallies; and visited the homes of ex-controllers in Chicago, Philadelphia, and elsewhere, to discuss adjustment challenges with strikers, spouses, and their children. I culled the literature identified by computer-based library search techniques, and made numerous field research visits to USATCO, and, after its demise, to PATCO LIVES. I also conducted my own analysis of 900 ex-controller surveys gathered in February 1984, by striker Steve O'Keefe; circulated first-draft copies of the chapters in this book to a dozen PATCO activists for constructive criticism; and sought out a collaboration in the person of an ex-controller and PATCO activist (Dave Skocik) to lend authenticity, color, and behind-the-scenes insights to the volume.

Had time and personal funds permitted, there was much more research I would have liked to have done, including the interviewing of key FAA personnel—only two of whom I sought out.[1] Similarly, I would have liked to interview a representative sample of several thousand strikers who chose to ignore USATCO and PATCO LIVES. But, with the strike's fifth anniversary approaching in 1986, I chose to suspend my field research long enough to prepare this first book-length exploration of the (tentative) answers I have thus far found to some of my questions.

Should this volume somehow help all the concerned parties . . . ex-controllers *and* working controllers; PATCO stalwarts *and* FAA careerists; strikers who joined USATCO/PATCO LIVES *and* others who did not; labor leaders who backed PATCO *and* others who failed to—PATCO's legacy may still bolster the profession and the air traffic system for which 11,345 dedicated men and women gave their all in 1981.

Arthur B. Shostak, Ph.D.

PREFACE

I have few, if any, regrets about my decision to oppose the powers-that-be. History cannot be changed. Nor is this book an attempt to gain sympathy. It seeks to explain the forces (rather than contract issues) which motivated more than 11,000 federal employees to walk off the job in anger. It was a phenomenon which has no precedent nor equal, yet, to many of its participants, still seems justified. The intensity we shared on the job carried over into the months and even years following the strike. I shall never forget those days with my former colleagues, who will always be my brothers and sisters.

I wrote the bulk of my material prior to exploring the feelings of my former colleagues. To my initial surprise, I found my thoughts echoed time and again in those of my former colleagues.

Then it occurred to me that the action we took more than 4 years ago, though collective, was very much individually inspired. It reiterated to me that the much maligned PATCO was truly a vehicle for our very real solidarity.

PATCO is no more. Neither is its successor, USATCO. But the air traffic system of this nation continues to be handled by human beings. And these same fallible creatures hold the safety of the system in their grasp. Safety is, by law, mandated to be the paramount concern of the FAA. But of all the components of safety (i.e., state-of-the-art computers, advanced radars, windshear warning devices and ground and airborne navigational aids) the key remains the human being. Every successful private sector employer has discovered that human relations consists of much more than threats of disciplinary action.

My hope in contributing to this work (as painful as it was at times), is that management of the human element may be accorded as high a priority by the FAA as that of traffic management. Only then will the conditions exist for any planned rebuilding of the system. Air traffic controllers are independent thinkers. That is why they were sought out and hired by the FAA. Unless they are permitted to participate in decisions which affect them and their working lives, they will revolt again: In a line from a PATCO strike newsletter, "it's just a matter of time . . ."

David Skocik, M.A.

INTRODUCTION

Controllers—"The Proud Professionals"

How many of us would be able to meet the kinds of demands that are made of air traffic controllers? How many of us could bear that particular pressure and responsibility on a regular basis? I am sure that the number is small indeed.
Congressman William H. Brodhead, *Hearings*, April 30, 1981.

. . . we are dealing with a situation that has been building up for many years. Indeed, it has been unfolding like a Greek tragedy, and if something constructive isn't done soon, we can expect a tragic climax to this drama in the near future.
C.F. von Kann, President, National Aeronautic Association (3 months before the strike). *Hearings*, U.S. Congress, 1981.

5:48:06 P.M.—Pilot: Getting kind of hot in the oven with this controller. See, that's what the lack of experience does. I'm glad we didn't have to go through that mess. I thought sure he was going to send us through it.
Excerpt from transcript of cockpit conversation before Delta Airline crash that cost 135 lives, August 2, 1985.

Controllers—in Profile. What was the job like? A thirty-year-old Texan who worked a tower chief's position from 1971 through August 3, 1981, remembered the tension vividly:

You could never admit you had any limitations. If you did, and they got reported, you were in *bad* trouble . . . What's much worse were the errors you didn't know about, because when you learned about them you got a

21

negative adrenalin surge. . . . You had to feel you were the *best* in the tower! Old-timers used to reminisce about Berlin in '48 when the airlift meant bad winds and avoiding Russian airspace: that was *the* real test of a controller, and it left several of them burned out, but proud, *real* proud . . .

You got scared, even when you had parachutes and the whole nine yards. If you want to know the truth, we were *always* running scared. You had to believe in the inevitability of a mistake; otherwise, you got too gung ho . . . and, after an incident, you were never any good afterwards. You worked traffic, you stayed cool, and you puked your guts out in the bathroom afterwards . . .

All of this accumulated as the years went by, and the traffic grew denser, more varied, and more error-prone:

I miss it, sometimes a lot, because I really enjoyed working airplanes . . . even though I had reached my proficiency peak years ago. It was like being a juggler; you just can't stay as sharp as when you began. I developed a smoother style, and knew more and more about my limitations. I came to do a more consistent job, and did not bobble as many as before. But I felt the downside of the curve beginning . . . the FAA should have had a *good* evaluation process to help you realize this, but they didn't, damn 'em! . . . Now, life without that job is just too sedate, too damn ordinary and sedate for my taste.

Over and again in interviews conducted coast-to-coast for this book ex-controllers returned to this theme—"The job could be a killer! But oh, what a grand way to go!!"

Among the many proud claims high-spirited members of PATCO used to enjoy making was the boast they were "a breed apart," professionals distinct from all others in the government's employ. When the wife of a striker sought in 1983 to explain this distinctiveness she offered a most remarkable analogue:

You say you want to know what were they like, before they got murdered. Well, I'll tell you . . . *they were like gods.* They were like "Marlboro cowboys;" they were like giants; they were like nobody else; they were like *real* men . . . macho, crazy, eager, proud, dedicated . . . they *loved* the job, the same crazy job that was killing them much of the time . . . the same job that drove them up a wall, but that also made life exciting and dangerous and *real*, the way they liked it . . .

At the time of the 1981 strike certain behavioral scientists who had completed a 5-year, $2.8 million FAA-sponsored study of 416 controllers, told reporters their study showed them as a group to be

. . . strong, emotionally normal, dominant, independent, highly motivated, conscientious, sociable and self-confident people with significantly
higher intelligence levels than the national average.[1]

Their research, however, also found that controllers in the 1973 to 1978 period had *very* low morale. Many had an intense and chronic feeling of alienation from their FAA managers, and hated the supervisory system. Many believed the FAA would scapegoat them if anything went wrong, but, as "people
who take pride in their job," the researchers explained, "they take pride in
not being intimidated."[2]

Controller Qualifications

In 1980, the last full year of operation before the strike changed everything, the FAA received more then 25,000 applications.

1) Each had to be a high school graduate with 3 years of "general experience," which meant any kind of work.

2) In the past, nearly 50 percent had been former military controllers. And, in 1980, nearly 15 percent were females.

3) About 9,000 scored 70 or more on a scale of 100 in an all-
   day battery of aptitude tests. (These were designed by FAA
   staffers to measure such qualities as ability to think in three
   dimensions, respond quickly, and maintain awareness of
   many events occurring at the same time.)

4) Of the 9,000, about 1,800 were accepted into the FAA's
   Oklahoma-based academy, and those were applicants who
   had scored in the high 80s or 90s.

5) Eventually, after 17 to 20 weeks of schooling, about 30 percent of those who entered were dropped. And another 10
   percent to 12 percent were dropped after graduation, and
   were assigned instead to a radar center.

Only about 5 percent of the original 25,000 applicants actually achieved their
ambition and served as FAA controllers (at a starting base salary in 1981 of
$15,123 to $18,500 a year). With only about 1,800 new recruits drawn into
the program annually, many otherwise qualified applicants were turned away
each year—even as it took about 3½ years for a newly graduated controller
to qualify as a journeyman, with solo responsibility for guiding aircraft.[3]

Controllers in Trouble.   Even when much was going well, the daily demands of the job could still undermine personal well-being:

> Over a long period of cumulative exposure the combination of inade-
> quate facilities, insufficient rest, intense concentration, rapid decisions,
> tension, and the awful awareness that sooner or later the laws of probabil-
> ity will win a round, that even a relatively minor error can quickly cumu-
> late into disaster, become greater than most men can or should be ex-
> pected to bear.[4]

Not surprisingly, therefore, a $2.8 million research study (1973-1978) found
controllers had a risk of hypertension two or three times the average, drank a
considerable amount in their off-hours, and had problems with self-control
and minor scrapes with the law.[5]

Another type of problem concerned the reluctance of white males to accept the legally forced integration of nonwhites and women into the close
"family" of facility coworkers. Black controllers organized a Black Caucus in
self-defense, while a bloc of about 3 percent of female controllers often har-
bored much resentment against sexist opposition. Revealing is this recall of a
male West Coast controller:

> We had two women out of 38 in the L.A. Tower, and both were among
> the best controllers in the whole bunch. I never paid much attention to
> them, and they just kind of blended in—but once, after both had gone
> out with us on strike, I got to listening while one of them talked about how
> the FAA and PATCO had *both* treated women poorly. Both kind of de-
> meaned females, and did not take them serious, and never considered
> them promotion material. Both took their complaints lightly, and neither
> was really fair, or so I was told . . . One of the two women joined USATCO,
> however, and sent money back to help other controllers; the other sort of
> disappeared . . . the more I've thought about what she was saying, the
> more I'm inclined to agree, though I was not picking it up at the time. . .

No more, though no less prejudiced than defensive white males in general,
the dominant block of controllers put *special* pressure on "different" new-
comers—and thereby undermined the vital camaraderie upon which system
safety and controller well-being depended.

Family life suffered when controllers inevitably took job pressures home,
as in the case of this 1981 complaint from a striker's wife:

> By the fourth day of a work week, he has no patience, and it's almost as
> though his head is going to explode. Our whole family runs according to
> Kennedy tower's traffic . . . The oldest man the FAA has ever listed on the
> tower bulletin board [as recently deceased] was 51. They all die young. My
> husband doesn't tell me anymore when a controller dies.

An 8-year veteran of FAA employ, the thirty-seven-year-old husband noted
that he had 50 or more planes in the air at the same time on his hardest days,
and if the strike didn't improve the situation, he wasn't going back to the job.[6]

Other family problems could be traced to mandatory overtime and rotating shift work, two controversial practices that undermined parenting and neighboring roles. Looming larger, however, than all the rest was the rare stress entailed in an air industry catastrophe:

"I know what his shift's been like the minute he walks in the door," says Pauline Bernard, whose husband Robert is a controller at the New York area en route center. "After a bad night he'll head straight for the refrigerator or the liquor cabinet. Then he'll talk my ear off for 3 hours."

... "The worst part," she says, "is when you hear there's been a crash. You eat your heart out until you find out whether he was the controller in charge."[7]

Much to its credit, the controllers' union retained a specialist, Leo Perlis, to design a major program to help reduce the toll of alcoholism, marital disputes, separations, and divorce; but, before it could be implemented, the 1981 strike wrote an end to everything.

Summary. What was it like being an air traffic controller before August 3, 1981? A veteran of 10 years tower duty insists nothing could match it:

It was like being *inside* a video game, a new and exciting video game. It was always something different! When I worked the airplanes, swishing them in and out, I'd have problems I had to pose instant solutions for, and they *had* to work ... We used a sixth sense, one that computers will never have. We had to learn to flow with it, flow with the traffic, as if we were in an art form or part of some piece of music ...

It was one helluva macho experience. You had to be *the* best goddamn controller in the facility, or well on your way to claiming the title. The "Clint Eastwood" syndrome was alive and well where we worked. ...

Another former controller with 15 years' ATC experience was similarly upbeat in his recall:

When you had worked some *deep* traffic, and worked it well, it was quite a boost to your self-esteem. Sometimes you'd even get a letter of appreciation, and that was even better ... When I worked it was like I had memorized a roadmap for 100 miles around. When I worked, when I handled a string of pearls out there, maybe 20 airplanes, all relying on me, and when I'd run them in without a single problem it felt good, *real* good ...

Other ex-controllers interviewed for this book also cheered the flattering responsibility, bracing challenge, and vital affirmation of the job. Given the popularity of a revealing country music ditty like "Take this Job and Shove

It!," the affection of former controllers for what they had lost remains all the more impressive.

How significant are the background characteristics of these 11,345 men and women in making sense of the 1981 strike and its aftermath? While the chapters that follow will explore the linkage in depth, suffice it here to offer one provocative illustration from 4 months after the strike:

> Dr. C. David Jenkins, a behavioral epidemiologist at Boston University, and an author of a Government study of controllers, said they are, in large part, independent people with extreme self-confidence. Refusing to concede errors of tactics, he said, and continuing to talk of winning the strike when it would appear they have lost, is consistent with these attitudes. . . .[8]

Much, in sum, of the turbulent and costly campaign detailed in the following chapters is better understood if the distinct background, personality, and job attitudes of the pre-1981 air traffic controller is kept sensitively in mind.

Part I

AIR TRAFFIC CONTROL

. . . we're committed to looking back for only one reason: to be reminded of what not *to do. If we don't, we'll just continue to cause ourselves even more pain . . .*
Editorial, *USATCO Newsletter*, November 1983.

If a man happens to find himself . . . if he knows what he can be depended upon to do, his courage, the secret reserves of his determination, the extent of his dedication, the distance of his feelings for honesty and unpostured goals . . . then, he has found a mansion which he can inhabit for all the days of his life.
James Michener, quoted in *USATCO Newsletter*, September 1983.

Changes. We've had plenty. Painful ones. And still we have a long way to go. We strive to continue as companions, brothers and sisters who decided 17 long months ago that the battle was worth fighting, the struggle, if need be, for a lifetime. It is our effort, our march. Maybe someday, someone will pay attention.
USATCO Newsletter, January 1983.

Chapter 1

FROM COW FIELDS
TO CONTROL TOWERS

1920-1968

The strike is a result of frustration that's been building up for years. We're not on strike over money. Not 10 percent or 20 percent of these people would have walked out over money. People are tired of being dumped on, and they want to make it to retirement.
Robert M. Devery, PATCO Striker, *Business Week*, August 24, 1981, p. 38.

If I was impressed with any one thing about controllers whose work I followed each day for nearly 6 months, it was their absolute dedication to their work. The personal price they pay is too great for their commitment to be otherwise.
Don Briggs, *Pressure Cooker: The Story of the Men and Women who Control Air Traffic* (1979), p. 12.

History . . . the nail on which the picture hangs.
                                        Alexandre Dumas, père.

Much of the provocation for the August 1981 strike can be traced back over a half century to the very origin of the modern controller's role. Undervalued and overlooked at the outset, the nation's air traffic controllers were obscure airline company minions in the early 1930s, poorly supported CAA employees in the postwar 1950s, and increasingly frustrated FAA professionals thereafter.[1]

Across the years the controller's role changed from that of an unskilled, part-time rural aide to the most selective, skilled, and highest paid technician in federal employ. Unfortunately, the position consistently failed to earn congressional, FAA, or public support when it counted, and the toll taken on controllers by an inadequate environment and inferior tools was considerable.

If the August 1981 strike is to be adequately understood, then it is necessary first to review briefly its antecedents in 50 years of neglect and disappointment, 50 years of the evolution of a profession whose practitioners grew increasingly worried about its prospects—and about the safety of everyone involved.

When air passenger traffic first began in the early 1930s it became clear that continued growth of payloads meant schedule reliability, and this meant instrument flying. Everyone worried about the specter of an unprecedented number of aircraft moving about without knowledge of one another's whereabouts. Accordingly, by 1933, one of the largest airlines initiated a ground-to-air radio system of exchanging pilots' position reports, altitudes, and estimates among airlines having aircraft in the same vicinity at the same time. By 1934 the federal government felt obliged to issue its first rudimentary regulations, and with its initiation of directional altitude separation the government began the modern ATC regulatory system.

Containing "Big Brother."   Eager to remain in command and hold the government's power to a bare minimum, some of the airlines in 1935 entered into a joint agreement to operate three experimental airway traffic control stations, the better to curb the peak and hazardous congestion their instrument flight schedules were now causing. Offices were opened at Newark, and, in 1936, in Chicago and Cleveland, the direct antecedents of modern federal air route traffic control centers. Later in 1936, however, the federal government had its Bureau of Air Commerce (Department of Commerce) acquire the three company-run offices, and this brief experiment at privatization ended before it had really begun.

With the addition of new federal centers at Detroit, Los Angeles, Oakland, Pittsburgh, and Washington, D.C., the air traffic control (ATC) responsibility in the late 1930s became an integral part of the government's various services—and the original eight controllers in the 1936 takeover were soon joined by scores of new hirees (controller ranks reached 13,000 by 1959, and topped off at 17,000 before the 1981 strike).

World War II and the "Fruitless Fifties."   A massive reordering of the nation's economy during the 1939-1946 period, along with major breakthroughs in radar uses, helped the federal government commit itself to boosting further the fledging air travel and transport system. Years of miserly neglect ended in the late 1940s with the allocation of overdue federal funds to the Civilian Aeronautics Authority (then in the Department of Commerce), and the modern era of the air traffic control (ATC) system finally got underway.

However, the ATC equipment still being utilized in the 1950s (ex-military radar systems stripped from naval aircraft carriers and terminated air force radar facilities) drove controllers wild with its unreliability and inadequacies. With the jet age clearly dawning in commercial aviation, over 99 percent of America's entire civil aviation system nevertheless remained on a *non*radar basis, though neither Congress nor the flying public seemed especially concerned.

Not, that is, until June of 1956, when two avoidable air tragedies in a 12-day period claimed 202 lives. An investigation team concluded that air travel was unsafe because we had let the air traffic control system become "outmoded and overloaded," much as individual controllers, lacking any other forum, had complained to one another. Public pressure forced Congress to authorize substantial funds to modernize the system's hardware and expand the ATC rolls, a task it turned over in 1958 to a new bureaucracy, the Federal Aviation Administration, which replaced the discredited Civil Aeronautics Authority.[2]

Gaining Clout.   Technically responsible only to Congress, the FAA was charged with providing the necessary facilities and personnel for regulation and protection of air traffic—among scores of other functions. By 1961 the FAA had 13,000 air traffic controllers in its employ (along with 28,000 other staffers), and was the second largest independent agency of government (only the VA was larger).

Parting of the Ways.   Unfortunately, it took still another avoidable air tragedy, a major midair collision in 1963, to awaken the interest of Congress and the flying public in the doings of the FAA—and what was uncovered dismayed all. This time an investigation team concluded that air travel remained unsafe because the FAA, the very body established to beef up the system, was operating instead to block overdue reforms and cover up its record of pennypinching neglect. The team condemned the FAA's failure to have hired any new controllers since 1961, and criticized the agency's continued reliance on increasingly archaic hardware (used and obsolete military castoffs).[3] Congress responded by authorizing more funds than ever, and urged the FAA to satisfy the team's reform recommendations.

By this time, however, the nation's air traffic controllers had grown increasingly disillusioned with the FAA. The ranks seethed with horror stories of an evolving workplace culture the controllers judged both an affront to their professionalism and a serious threat to their ability to do the job as it should be done:

Military-like discipline was standard, and if a controller challenged an order he could be hassled and threatened with dismissal. No grievance procedure existed, and, until 1962, unions were not welcomed in the federal sector.

Controllers with a medical disqualification were left to handle a position until overwhelmed by stress, and then were dismissed as no longer meeting FAA's qualifications: No effort was made to link them up with medical retirement or Federal Employment Compensation (FEC) claims.

While knowledgeable parties recognized that accidents were the result of system errors, and that the air control system depended on a mix of weather, pilot reaction, aircraft performance, the controller, and luck, among its other components, the FAA invariably tried to place the primary responsibility or blame for mishaps on the controller involved.

Controllers were expected to work 8 to 10 hours a day, 6 days a week (because of a lack of backups), and overtime in the mid-1960s became mandatory (with the hours prorated, so that a controller could actually receive less money than on straight time).

No controller need receive advance notice of compulsory overtime, and if the FAA called someone in on Saturday, the threat of reprisals assured compliance.

As this (incomplete) list makes clear, the FAA and its workforce grew ever farther apart, and the situation became increasingly untenable.[4]

Controllers who tried to change conditions for the better found their professional associations reliant on very meek, mild, and precatory aproaches (including pleas for reforms at congressional hearings, and timid and tentative exploration of legal remedies). The FAA, in turn, singled out persistent "troublemakers" and whistle-blowers for special treatment that led many to resign in disgust or defeat.

Slowly, however, a small number of particularly aggrieved and proud controllers, especially incensed about the unsafe and frustrating nature of FAA hardware, began to organize in defense of their professionalism and their notion that public safety required better ATC staffing, superior system equipment, and a responsible FAA regard for controller needs.

Chapter 2

A DAY IN THE LIFE*

Excerpts from the O'Keefe Survey: 1984

. . . the job was so intolerable I suspect if we were to have to do it again, we would. I know I would walk again!

We are only a small group of people that face, on a daily basis, a government that is less than concerned with people. This strike could have been avoided, even the union could have been eliminated, if the FAA/government had moved to correct management problems. I doubt this will ever happen. I know the same problem exists in the "outside world," but that does not justify what I saw in the inside.

If 12,000 controllers had gone crawling back in when Reagan threatened us, everyone would have been convinced that we were just money-hungry crybabies with no real cause. We proved that his was more than just an economic strike, and that the problems in the FAA were serious enough to force 12,000 people (give or take a few weak-kneed jack offs) to make a tremendous sacrifice.

There has to be some way that the side of the controller can be brought out in a manner that people would understand why we did what we did . . . Also, I would like to get the true comments from the controllers that stayed. What's going on in the inside?

---

*by David Skocik

I will not accept re-employment with the FAA. As a controller with 15 years time my mental health was about shot. The strike was right, and knowing that I would be dismissed or fired I would do it again. Our day will come . . . I believe that the reason our family has survived so well is because we prepared so well. My wife and children backed me and believed in me and I in them. Even if we had lost everything we still would have our pride.

A Typical Day.   To attempt to explain any occupation or profession is very difficult, since one must actually do a job *truly* to know what it's like. But, to help give the uninitiated a glimpse into a controller's world, I have created "Bill Benson," a composite of several real-life people I've known over my own career as a controller:

It was 6:30 a.m. on a weekday when Bill wheeled into the parking lot of the New York TRACON (Terminal Radar Approach Control), formerly the New York Common IFR Room. His car pool discussion with three fellow controllers had covered the usual topics: family problems, vacation plans, and finally, as they approached the facility, what traffic would be like and what would probably be malfunctioning today. A weather report coming over the car radio from WNBC had soured things a little, as the forecast had called for thunderstorms throughout the eastern Long Island area. Although Bill and his colleagues worked indoors in a controlled climate, his "clientele" would be directly affected by the bad weather—and in consequence, so would they.

(Thunderstorms and their associated turbulence occurring anywhere in Benson's complex maze of airspace would cause problems and increased work load. The reason was simple. Corridors, or thin extensions of airspace extending outward perhaps 50 miles, could be completely blocked by small, but turbulent storm cells. The effect was the same as if arterial roadways leading into or out of a city were blocked. This problem became even more critical during rush hour or peak traffic periods. Obviously, aircraft could not stop or pull over to the side of the airway when delayed. As anyone even vaguely familiar with aviation knows, aircraft are put into that bane of all modern travelers, the holding pattern, and the thought of ensuing extensive delays was enough to make even experienced controllers shudder.)

As Bill untangled his headset cord, he glanced over notices from the "read and initial" file. Although the R & I was updated daily and contained general information on facility operations, Bill specifically looked for equipment status. If some piece of radio, radar, or mechanical support equipment had gone out since he last worked, he wanted to be aware of it. Bill noticed that a radio frequency had been acting up and logged out. Generally, a backup transmitter took the place of published channels, but in this case the backup was also out of commission. He made a mental note not to inadvertently change anyone over to that frequency today.

Because he was roughly 10 minutes ahead of the rest of the day shift crew, Bill got his choice of positions to relieve. It was a position he would probably stay at for the first 30 minutes of the morning rush. After each position was transferred to relief, the crew chief sent his overflow to first breakfast (or coffee break, depending upon individual constitutions), in the cafeteria downstairs. They would return in 30 minutes, charged up with caffeine (no de-caf mud for these heroes!), ready to do their part to get the 7–8:30 a.m. "push" out safely.

The "high" of successfully working heavy traffic was akin to that known by early morning joggers. But it was also the greatest source of apprehension for a controller. The system was set up to run on adrenalin—the faster the better! Bill had been trained and was expected to run his traffic as though nothing could go wrong. Unfortunately, much often did go awry, and with little, if any, useful warning.

It was called "betting on the come." It referred to such things as vectoring a fast-climbing corporate jet to follow a lumbering airliner, knowing from experience that the smaller aircraft would easily outclimb the other before catching up to it. Or aiming two aircraft toward the same point, knowing one would keep his speed up longer and arrive first. Any controller worth his salt could run several such operations at once.

In busy facilities, such savvy was required. Of course, the test of real talent was the ability to change tracks quickly if the anticipated didn't happen: "Bet all you want, just never lose!" Never far from a controller's consciousness was that the objects he was juggling were full of people. It was a complicating detail which had to be "forgotten" at the risk of becoming gun-shy.

Within the space of 5 minutes, Bill had seven departures airborne. All were being vectored toward their respective routes. Their number presented no particular problem. But it was becoming increasingly obvious to Bill, as he glanced nervously at his handoff man that he might have to "eat" this batch. The aircraft were rapidly approaching the boundaries of his airspace, and the center, usually quick to take handoffs, was not responding, either electronically through the computer or on the voice-activated phone lines. That usually meant the controller on the other end was "going down the tubes."

A decision would soon have to be made whether or not to break the chain of events by turning them back. Options included "delaying" vectors or setting up impromptu holding patterns. Both would take full attention and wreak a major disruption in the smooth flow of traffic. Through the foresight of Bill's handoff man, a not-to-exceed 250 knot speed restriction had earlier been issued to the control tower and relayed to all departures. Federal air regulations restricted all commercial aircraft operating below 10,000 feet to no more than 250 knots. This was due to the numerous small private aircraft which operated below that altitude; many never bothered to call controllers for traffic advisories and this rule simply gave pilots more time to see and avoid one another.

However, once a pilot reached that altitude, unless restricted by ATC, he was allowed to increase to whatever speed he chose. A Boeing 727 might increase to 400 knots. The restriction was paying off by giving Bill more time to think out alternate moves. It could, of course, be lifted by Bill at any time, but he saw fit to keep it in effect. Aircraft with their speed up to around 400 knots took several miles to complete a turn, which required that much more lead time. The judgment when to spin aircraft was a subjective one, and would vary according to the experience of the controller. The only rule was that if the handoff was not taken, any and all departures had to be contained within the controller's own airspace.

To cross the electronically displayed line on the scope was to stray into the unknown and invite trouble. Just as Bill's saturation point was being reached, a message from center activated the speaker above the departure position. The cryptic message iced it: "Spin 'em!"

By the time Bill called the control tower to stop any more from becoming airborne, he had his hands full. He was beyond the point of optimum efficiency because he had gotten more traffic than he wanted and maybe more than he could safely handle. The tower always seemed to have a good excuse for launching one or two more after they were told to stop. This time was no exception. It seemed they had one in position, ready to go. That happened to be a legitimate reason; because of a strong headwind, both arrivals and departures were using the same runway. To block it would mean stopping all inbound aircraft and compounding the departure sector's problem. Complaining about it wouldn't do any good now. Bill would just have to make room for another customer.

He was already pulling the quick reference book off its perch on his scope, and refreshing himself on the various holding instructions he needed to issue. He had them memorized, but he couldn't afford to take any chances. As always in this field, there was a certain prescribed way of doing things to avoid misunderstandings, and Bill wanted to do it right: "TWA two eighty-nine, hold southeast on the Solberg zero six one radial, three zero DME. Make left turns, one minute legs. Maintain one zero thousand. Expect further clearance at one six four zero, time now one six two five."

Bill had given the pilot a point in space to set up his holding pattern (made up of published electronic radials from ground navigational aids), direction of turns, altitude, and finally a time he could expect to continue on with his filed route. Now all Bill had to do was issue similar instructions to each of his other aircraft, depending on which direction they were headed. Ten minutes later, the trick of stacking his traffic in holding accomplished, Bill's main function had become one of caretaker. The crisis of having to rapidly adjust his operation had passed.

On the far side of the facility, another man was facing a different weather-related challenge. His position, handling arrival traffic from the west, would be the first directly hit by the encroaching storm. He would likely be affected in one of two ways: his traffic would spend a lot of time in holding, or the weather would remain clear of his immediate area and he'd only feel its indirect effects through restrictions from other controllers. He was mentally prepared for either option, but had also been through the unexpected tricks weather can play.

Everyone looks for certainty, especially an air traffic controller. Whether he geared up mentally for spinning aircraft in a holding pattern or just ran them through his area made little difference to him. He just didn't want his traffic veering arbitrarily out of his airspace in order to avoid pockets of turbulence he couldn't see on radar.

Such a prospect was not unusual. Pilots cared little about who owned the airspace, they needed to dodge turbulence and avoid discomfort for their passengers. It didn't take much of a deviation to leave the narrow confines of arrival corridors. When it happened, immediate coordination was required.

The arrival controller wasn't in position 10 minutes when New York Center called with his first customer. In fact, they had gotten two, with three more inbound. He was expecting them; the computer printer had spit out their data strips 20 minutes earlier. The center controller advised that the storm had already passed through his area and was reported to contain moderate to severe turbulence. These first two aircraft, a DC-10 and Boeing 727, made it through, but each reported encountering light to moderate turbulence. So far, so good.

Although radar could not pick up turbulence, it did usually see storm cells. Those cells which showed up best generally had pretty nasty conditions associated with them. The arrival controller didn't like the look of one which was ominously moving north to south, and would soon be blocking the narrowest part of his corridor, creating a bottleneck. Just what his stomach needed.

Several minutes later, the center controller was attempting another hand-off, but saw what was happening and called for instructions. In fact, the pilot had already seen the mess on his weather radar and was asking for vectors off the airway around it. That meant coordination with other in-house controllers who owned the airspace the pilot was coveting. Borrowing someone's airspace at the last minute like this was something one might get away with once, maybe twice—but one shouldn't push his luck. A quick call, and permission was granted for a southbound deviation, along with a half-serious admonition not to let it happen again. A half-hour later, it looked as though our man was home free. Then, in the middle of a little rush of traffic, a plaintive call for assistance came over the frequency. Things might get worse yet.

The occupants of a small, single-engine Navajo had become disoriented because of instrument failure. The pilot was only certified for flight in visual conditions, meaning he had to keep the ground in sight at all times. He had been using his aircraft's automatic direction finder to practice homing in on ground radio beacons when it suddenly stopped working. He maintained he still had the ground in sight, but was unsure where he was. He also noted somewhat emphatically that he was being knocked around by up and down-drafts that were the remnant of the turbulence reported earlier. While the disoriented pilot had been in the vicinity for some time, he was afraid to call earlier because he thought he could work it out himself.

It seemed he got really concerned when, as he put it, "a 727 came out of nowhere and almost knocked us out of the box."

Even though his perceived close call might have been the catalyst which forced him to call, the pilot was also concerned about the turbulence he was encountering. Rightly so. Moderate turbulence to a B727 could be severe to a light aircraft. It had been known literally to rip the wings from small aircraft. The first step in responding was to determine the aircraft's position and alti-tude. Even if he was in the arrival controller's geographical area, he might not be in his altitude stratum, again meaning coordination with the controller who "owned" it.

As it turned out, coordination was in order because the pilot was re-questing vectors and descent to the nearest airport. The necessary calls were made and the airspace was "blocked" (protected from other usage) for the small aircraft.

Some tense moments followed as the Navajo pilot several times lost sight of the ground during descent. (That could prove deadly for someone not in-strument trained, because without visual reference to the horizon, vertigo could result—the normal sense of balance, controlled by the inner ear, thrown out of kilter. Everyone has experienced it at one time or another, and the senses quickly recover when visual contact with the world about is reestab-lished, or when a steady object is grasped. However, when no visual reference to the horizon is available, as when a pilot becomes lost in a cloud, sense of up and down quickly become confused. And when a pilot doesn't know whether he's in a dive, his life span may be gauged in seconds.)

The coordinator behind was carefully monitoring the situation, and had contacted the tower at the small airport to which the Navajo would be taken. He had received landing clearance and passed it on for relay to the pilot. He had also called the center to temporarily retain any more inbounds for this position until this minidrama had played out. Fifteen minutes later the Na-vajo had the runway in sight and was issued the local altimeter, wind direc-tion, and landing clearance without even having to speak to the tower. What service!

Stress (or Excedrin Headache #943).   The air traffic review board's state-ment was curt and to the point: "This is to notify you that you are officially reprimanded for . . . Improper Performance of Duty."

The incident which prompted the letter of reprimand (and put the controller in jeopardy of suspension or firing for future offenses), involved a near miss between a B727 and a Lear business jet.

The incident in question occurred during the final days of August, 1979, at the New York Common IFR Room, at that time located at JFK airport. August in New York is always hot, which has special meaning to a controller. Airplanes ride on air, of course, but when air heats up it becomes less dense. This means that on hot days, airplanes take more runway to get airborne and climb much more slowly than on cool days. The impact on the controller is that he must plan to hold onto his charges longer until they make the altitude restrictions necessary to leave his airspace.

That could, in a restricted area like the Manhattan-Newark area, mean vectoring aircraft in daisy chain fashion while they climb. And that meant extra work for the controller and departure delays. To further complicate matters, not all type aircraft are affected the same way on hot days—not, at least, to the same extent. Small business-type jets, such as the Lear, will easily outclimb larger, struggling passenger jets, adding to the complexity of the operation. It was best to get as many of the fast climbing aircraft off and running before the larger ones.

The controller, though sitting at his radar scope at JFK airport, was, thanks to the age of microwave communication, controlling departures off LaGuardia and Westchester airports. His primary responsibility was LaGuardia, but chunks of his airspace extended as far as 40 miles in other directions.

He didn't hear his assistant, or handoff man, issue control instructions to a Westchester controller to climb his departure above his 5,000 foot ceiling. The Lear jet was told to climb to 8,000 and proceed southwestbound to intercept the airway and contact LaGuardia departure control. Unfortunately, a United B727, having departed LaGuardia several minutes earlier, and on a northwestbound heading, was also climbing to 8,000.

LaGuardia is about 30 miles southwest of Westchester County airport, and the flight paths conflicted. Before the controller realized what was happening (he had nine other aircraft under his control), the targets merged. The transcript, as it appeared on the review board's record, is below. DR is departure controller; punctuation is omitted because there is no natural pause between words in actual transmissions. The rhythm of air traffic control is almost like a singsong language at a busy facility:

> 1204:10 (DR): United nine forty three LaGuardia departure radar contact turn right heading three six zero intercept Deer Park three zero eight on course climb maintain one four thousand.

> 1204:20 (UA943): Okay three sixty on the heading three oh eight and up to one four thousand.

1204:25 (DR): And United nine forty three strike that maintain eight thousand. (The controller realizes he already has possibly conflicting crossing traffic from Newark already level at 9,000.)

1204:30 (UA): Maintain eight United nine forty three.

1206:15 (N163A): LaGuardia departure Lear one six three alpha passing five point eight for eight thousand. (Thinking this is a LaGuardia departure, but not seeing a radar target, the controller becomes momentarily confused and hesitates. As previously stated, he is working eight or nine other aircraft which aren't on the transcript. Five seconds later . . .)

1206:20 (DR to control tower): Stop departures stop departures.

(Tower): Check.

1206:25 (DR): Lear one sixty three alpha, roger. (Controller acknowledges N163A's call, but still isn't sure where he is.)

1206:55 (DR): United nine forty three turn right zero four zero. (The light has come on. The controller has had N163A pointed out to him by his handoff man and is trying to turn UA943 away from his southwestbound target. The adrenalin is flowing freely in his system.)

1206:59 (UA): Zero four zero United nine forty three.

1207:00 (DR): One sixty three alpha turn right to two seventy. (Trying now to turn the Lear away from UA)

1207:05 (N163A): Six three alpha right to two seven zero.

1207:10 (DR): Maintain your present altitude. (He realizes the aircraft are not going to turn in time and is hoping to level the Lear jet below the UA jet.)

1207:15 (N163A): Six three alpha seven point four six three alpha. (Now the errors are mounting. The pilot thinks the controller has asked him for an altitude check and continues climbing to eight.)

1207:15 (DR): United nine forty three turn left now to two seven zero to intercept the two seventy to ah intercept Deer Park three zero eight on course.

(The controller assumes that UA will now pass behind the Lear jet and is attempting to turn UA back toward the airway. It will turn out to be a bad call because of crosswinds in the area.)

1207:20 (UA943): Okay two seventy three oh eight on course.

1207:25 (DR): And United nine forty three continue climb to one four thousand.

1207:30 (UA943): Okay United nine forty three to one four thousand.

1207:35 (UA943): Oh we got ah close one here right on our nose.

1207:35 (DR): Ah he's a thousand feet below you sir.

(N163A): Negative sir, we're at eight thousand feet, that's where we were cleared.

The transcript continued, but that was the essence of the incident. Over a period of just 3½ minutes, the controller had gone from a heavy but smooth operation to a near miss.

Beyond the initial shock of such an incident comes the pervasive sense of fear: fear of losing one's touch, and then fear of possible punishment, which could be anything from a letter of reprimand to a suspension. But the greatest fear is kept purposely locked in the back of the controller's mind—the consequences of what could have happened—the instantaneous death of hundreds of people. Near misses don't often happen to experienced controllers, but the gnawing feeling they evoke deep in the psyche is manifested in the pit of the stomach.

Externally, a controller quickly learns that it really doesn't matter what goes wrong with the equipment or procedures which may have contributed to the incident. What really counts is that the FAA and its managers *must never appear to be wrong*. And, since the FAA has final say on official reports defining causes of incidents, there never was much chance of that. Move the traffic and bend the rules to do it. But if something goes wrong there's only one person who will be left twisting slowly in the breeze—the controller.

Part II

ON THE MAKING OF A UNION

Excerpts from the O'Keefe Survey: 1984

There is another world out there. I loved my job, but hated the crap that went along with it. My biggest problem was management. Until someone realizes a great need for quality people who can communicate with the controller, there will always be problems.

The FAA must be brought down for what they did, and for what they are now doing. I am of firm belief that ALL of FAA management, from the very top to very bottom team supervisors are mental midgets . . . For what they did to 11,541 hard-working, dedicated people, one can only conclude they must have sick minds and are basically evil people. However, there is one thing they do very well, and that is lie . . .

I was one of the few that knew, in 1978, what was going to happen in 1981. I had 15 years of ATC, and both me and my family were fed up with it. If there was to be no strike, I had already planned to make my exit one way or another. But I don't care. . . . We're still "kicking their ass."

It's only a matter of time before the real truths are known—we were forced to strike—too many problems inherent in the job—money is only a small portion of the problem.

We should have stressed the safety *issue (hours, overwork, stress, etc.) to arbitration. Put the* safety *issue in some arbitrator's lap and let him stress up!*

I feel that our primary goals prior to the strike were good and correct. Management attitudes in the FAA must be changed so we can work together to make this an honorable and survivable profession . . . We were right, and I'm not, by God, going to say or imply that we were wrong!

Chapter 3

GETTING OFF THE GROUND

1962-1970

A "West Point" of Labor is in order to study not just the PATCO strike as the military has dissected the U.S. Civil War, but also to study the growth of PATCO, which in many aspects could serve as a model of labor movement growth. PATCO did achieve many of the goals the AFL-CIO still has not secured . . .
Jack Maher, PATCO cofounder (with Mike Rock), letter to Art Shostak, Spring 1985.

. . . We are cleared for takeoff and we're going to maintain runway heading in our climb out, and will not level off until we have topped all the clouds on the horizon.
Arthur Godfrey, honorary Chairman of PATCO, 1968.

Ironically, many controllers got their first taste of collective action from an anti-union, pro-management, FAA-dominated group, the Air Traffic Controllers Association (ATCA).[1] Endorsed by the instructors at the FAA's training school (Oklahoma City), ATCA enrolled most eager trainees who suspected that signing up was "the right thing to do." Only later at the annual national convention would they learn that 90 percent of the delegates were FAA managers, and only 10 percent represented actual controllers, a ratio that helped make ATCA's priorities and philosophy very clear.

Until 1962 ATC was the only "professional association" accepted by the FAA. Not surprisingly, its officers were either top FAA officials or controllers being groomed for management careers, and it accepted financial contributions from major airlines who valued their corporate membership. While many controllers signed up ("the only game in town"), ATCA's "company union" culture had many dues-payers curious about alternatives much less beholden to the boss.

Camelot and Controllers.   Exciting new possibilities opened up in 1962 when President John F. Kennedy kept a vital campaign pledge to his labor union backers. Kennedy's Executive Order 10988 permitted unions to vigorously organize in the public sector, and for the first time, obliged federal agencies to deal responsibly with them. To be sure, the scope of bargaining remained *much* narrower than was standard in the private sector: No union of federal employees could bargain over wages, hours, insurance, retirement, or other such relevant matters. Those were determined by the U.S. Civil Service Commission, and often required the passage of new congressional acts. Even with this severe limitation the Kennedy Executive Order was hailed for giving a green light to the unionization of hundreds of thousands of employees previously unavailable to the labor movement.

Almost immediately, the National Association of Government Employees (NAGE) invited controllers to form their own facility-based locals. And in Minneapolis, New York City, Palmdale, (CA), and Washington, D.C., restless controllers took this historic step. On the west coast, the Los Angeles Controllers Association was formed, and a John F. Kennedy Controllers Association appeared next at the airport of the same name. All of these groups, however, whether ATCA, NAGE, or independent facility-based associations, were isolated from one another, though many wanted to remedy this obvious weakness.

O'Hare Fires the First Shot.   In 1967, an immediate upgrade in pay was demanded by O'Hare Tower controllers who had argued for months with the FAA that understaffing and compulsory overtime at their facility warranted extra compensation. When the FAA perfunctorily denied their last request, even though its Regional Director had allegedly approved it, the O'Hare controllers resorted to an unprecedented "rule book" job action that slowed and snarled air traffic from coast to coast. An astonished FAA quickly agreed to grant O'Hare controllers three step-increases at one time, and the elated controllers thereby won an immediate $1,100 raise. To help save face the Agency linked its concession to Chicago's high cost of living, its staff shortages, and its failure to attract transfers. As well, the FAA sharply warned that it would not authorize the new O'Hare raises elsewhere.

Controllers at certain other major air traffic sites—Atlanta, Kennedy (New York), and Los Angeles—refused, however, to accept the FAA's rationale. They insisted that the O'Hare's situation was nearly identical with their own, and they urged the FAA to implement an entirely new method of compensation—one that would reward on the basis of responsibility and intricacy of operations, rather than simply on the number of operations per year.

Controllers at the Los Angeles Tower quickly formed a nonaffiliated association, and it filed a salary-increase petition with the FAA Regional Director, but to no avail. Next, the L.A. association hired a lawyer/public relations expert, and, with his help, began to explain its case to the airline companies, the pilots' union, and the Congress. Taking care at the same time to work only "by the book," the L.A. association stirred airline outrage over ensuing delays, and the angry companies helped exert more and more pressure on the FAA. In short order the Agency found merit in the L.A. case, and raises were ordered for the "rule book" strikers over the next 2 years.

Invigorated and inspired by the O'Hare and Los Angeles victories, two more groups of controllers, one in Atlanta and the other in Chicago, devised a new non-slowdown strategy they dubbed "Operation Snowman." They met and worked out an elaborate plan and formula for reclassifying every controller everywhere in the country. If nearly all ATCs signed their petition, they expected such an unprecedented joint action to force the FAA to grant a salary upgrade to all.

In the fall of 1967 the first-ever meeting of far-flung representatives of controllers was held to weigh the pros and cons of "Operation Snowman." At the Newark, N.J., gathering, an often-heated discussion finally resulted in the elevation of New York to the wage levels sought by Atlanta and Chicago—and a deal was struck that promised Eastern seaboard signatures for the petition. While nothing ultimately came of this first-ever petition drive, the ATC attendees were never again satisfied with merely local actions—for the dream of a single national organization had been stirred and clarified by the Newark get-together.

"Take Me to Your Leader."   Shortly after the Newark meeting brought controllers together from Atlanta, Chicago, Kennedy, Newark, and Philadelphia, the four worksites in the New York area joined in the first-ever regional organization, one they called the Metropolitan Controllers Association. Formed in 1967 by Jack Maher (NAGE local president, New York Center) and Mike Rock (NAGE local president, LaGuardia), the MCA turned its attention quickly to the need Newark had highlighted for a coast-to-coast ATC organization.

Once MCA concluded NAGE would not measure up, a search began for a well-known charismatic personality around whom controllers might rally, a "dynamite" leader whose energy and ideas could help a fledging organization get off to a solid start—and who, not incidentally, might advance or even make a gift of some of the necessary start-up funds.

Enter the "F-Lee".   At the December 1967 monthly meeting of MCA, its acting chair, Mike Rock, put the name of criminal defense attorney F. Lee Bailey before the group. One of the most popular and well-publicized lawyers in the nation, he was also a private pilot, a very wealthy individual, and a legendary speaker. But as his fees were assumed to be astronomical, no one gave the idea a chance of ever succeeding.[2]

Mike Rock persisted, however, and on January 4, 1968, the MCA delegation of about six New York area controllers met with Bailey to discuss their dream of a national ATC organization. Impressed by their story, Bailey offered to devote 6 months to their cause for a fee of only $100 plus expenses. Wary of unions and very skeptical about the role of collective bargaining, the criminal lawyer was pleased no wish was expressed by the MCA group to form a labor union. Instead, attention went to their need for a professional association that could serve as the voice of controllers nationwide, one that could force the FAA to update and reform working conditions and its operation.

At Bailey's urging, the founding fathers tackled the question of a name for the proposed organization, and the ensuing debate cast a long shadow over the operation: Jack Maher wanted to emphasize air safety over working conditions and salary, and therefore opposed any name with the connotation of unionism. Mike Rock, in turn, wanted to emphasize working conditions and salary increases; he therefore favored a name and a move toward creating a traditional labor union. Others urged that any name or form that resembled ATCA or NAGE be avoided, and they generally lined up with Maher in worrying that the connotation of unionism would turn off many prospective members. "Professional Air Traffic Controllers Organization"—PATCO —was the compromise choice, with Rock an insistent advocate of the flattering qualifier "Professional."

This critical matter settled, the (penniless) PATCO was led by Bailey to rent a hotel ballroom (using his credit card), and its nervous founders scheduled a January 11 general meeting. Hoping to draw perhaps 100 off-duty controllers attracted by Bailey's celebrity status, they also followed his advice and invited ATCA locals to send representatives (in the hope of eventually drawing them into one united organization). Everyone was astonished when over 600 controllers and about 100 wives crowded into a standing-room-only ballroom. Controllers from 22 states, including Alaska, were present, and all agreed it was the largest and most geographically diverse such gathering in the history of their profession.

Bailey did not let his backers down, and in a spellbinding, 2-hour, noteless address, outlined both the needs and remedies of greatest concern to the audience. (An attendee, Stanley Gordon, recalls that the speech brought the listeners to their feet 11 times cheering, and some of the most enthusiastic backers were 50 to 60 local FAA supervisors and the FAA's Eastern Regional Director.)[3] Bailey hailed the overdue formation of PATCO, and promised that it would "make noise" in the media and Congress on behalf of the controller's side of the story—a pledge PATCO immediately helped promote by circulating tape recordings of Bailey's speech to controllers in all 50 states (it was also often played surreptitiously on the FAA's nationwide phone hookup late at night).

Within 30 days over 4,000 controllers had signed up (though some hedged by keeping their membership in both NAGE and ATCA). Bailey's flying team continued a concerted recruitment campaign, and increasingly successful rallies were held in Miami, Washington, D.C., Boston, Los Angeles, and Kansas City. Everyone who distinguished himself in recruiting members was considered a candidate for the PATCO Board, and Maher and Rock hand-picked 35 such members—an unwieldy group dedicated enough to use their annual leaves and sick leaves to work for PATCO at their own expense.

Constitutional Convention.   Between June 30 and July 5, 1968, about 350 controllers came together in Chicago to formalize PATCO's 6-month-old existence by drafting and adopting its first constitution. Bailey, the dominant force, used his training as a trial and corporate attorney, rather than as a labor lawyer, to design PATCO much like an incorporated business organization.

Convinced that controllers were best suited to "move traffic," and were not prepared to run their own professional association, Bailey recommended that PATCO's executive director be someone other than a working controller. Similarly, while he agreed controllers could serve as regional directors, Bailey's constitution established a role for an attorney as chief executive in each of PATCO's eleven regions: All of these attorneys were to be chosen by, and to report to the general counselor, F. Lee Bailey, (who, incidentally, was rehired at a fee of $50,000 plus expenses, payable only if PATCO had a successful second year).

With the enthusiastic passage of his constitution, Bailey nominated an acquaintance of his, a noncontroller, to fill the $50,000 post of PATCO executive director, and Maher and Rock (both of whom still worried about long-threatened FAA dismissal) were also put on the new PATCO payroll.

Before the 1968 constitutional convention could adjourn, however, two other far-reaching issues had to be resolved. A delegation of FAA supervisors lobbied to be allowed to remain as PATCO members, and they secured support from the Minneapolis PATCO local and from Bailey himself. Nevertheless, opposition led by Maher and based in the New York delegation won a floor vote, though only by a 3 percent margin. (It is fascinating to speculate how differently the 1981 strike might have turned out but for this vote, as it indicated to FAA as far back as 1968 that PATCO saw an "us versus them" conflict steadily building.) And a PATCO Safety Committee convinced delegates to approve an unprecedented plan for a nationwide "work-by-the-book" slowdown, dubbed "Operation Air Safety." With the help of a last-minute guest appearance by an enthusiastic Arthur Godfrey, PATCO's honorary chairman, the constitutional convention ended with high excitement over PATCO's impending nationwide job action, another first in its fast-growing list of milestones.

"Go Ahead, Make My Day!"   Delegates left the 1968 constitutional convention in Chicago abuzz with excitement over the prospects of PATCO's impending foray against FAA complacency. As a July 3 PATCO press release explained, its 6-month-study of current air traffic conditions proved that FAA separation distances of 3 miles and 1,000 feet were not always safe enough. Accordingly, any public inconvenience caused by increased separation standards was a small price to pay for substantial gains in air traffic safety. More honestly put, "Operation Air Safety," as implemented by PATCO, would slow down and clog up the air industry from coast to coast, dealing an impact by which PATCO expected to get the FAA's full attention.

From about July 4 through late August when PATCO officially called the action off, certain controllers across the country "worked by the books." And, within the first 3 days, New York alone was running 12-hour delays, and holding planes as far away as the U.K. and Western Europe. The FAA, of course, was not without its supporters among controllers who thought the job action unprofessional and unsafe (50 percent of New York Center controllers, for example, refused to join the slowdown, as did most of the South and the Southwest). But the ensuing confusion and public complaints were enough to force an outraged FAA to call for negotiations—something that had never happened before, and that signalled PATCO's first real victory.

Ten days after the start of the job action a delegation of 40 controllers and legal counselors flew at FAA expense for a joint meeting at the agency's Washington headquarters. Much of the opening time was taken up by an outpouring of controllers' grievances: A delegation of 40 FAA leaders, including the agency's top administrator, listened without response to complaints that had festered for years.

PATCO next presented three demands as the price for calling off its national "rule-book" job action:

1. Facility wage levels were to be reclassified, and upgraded where warranted.

2. FAA's Oklahoma City Academy, closed for the *past 7 years*, was to reopen, and a new supply of trainees recruited to help relieve serious understaffing in the system.

3. Controllers were to be exempted from civil service regulations that kept them from earning time-and-a-half for overtime.

As each of these reforms required congressional legislation the FAA requested time to evaluate them, and the unprecedented meeting adjourned with both sides seeing the other in a new light, and as if for the first time.

By November 1968, 4 months later, the FAA had completed the salary-shaping upgrading of several key facilities (Atlanta, Chicago, Cleveland, New York, Los Angeles, and Washington), along with certain major towers. Congress, at the request of the FAA, appropriated about $14,000,000 in new funds to permit the reopening of the FAA's Oklahoma City Academy and the hiring of 1,000 additional controllers. Finally, Congress passed a law exempting the ATCs from civil service overtime regulations, consummating PATCO's triumph.

The "Johnny Carson" Caper.   Bailey was invited by a personal friend, TV personality Johnny Carson, to appear on his popular show and "alert the public to the air control problem." When PATCO learned of the June 17, 1969 show date, a decision was made to use this rare media opportunity to signal the start of a nationwide sick-out, the second-ever PATCO effort to wring new concessions from Congress and the FAA.

Remarkable ineptitude swamped this entire ill-fated, amateurish, and embarrassing venture. Maher failed to clarify with members the exact words Bailey was to use on TV as a correct signal for the job action. And, as fate would have it, the East Coast was blacked out that night for gubernatorial election coverage.

Whether or not Bailey ever used the words Maher is supposed to have chosen—"It's going to be a long hot summer"—remains a matter of enduring controversy. Bailey told Rock immediately afterwards he had not, and insisted later in his 1977 book on his PATCO involvement that he had no knowledge of any sick-out signal role for himself. Moreover, Bailey argued in 1977 that he would have strenuously opposed such an illegal action.[4] But TV-glued controllers in Denver and Kansas City swear they heard the Maher signal from Bailey's mouth. Large numbers then went out on an illegal sick-out they believed PATCO was coordinating.

PATCO was thrown into turmoil. Hurried phone calls from headquarters to locals around the country soon had everyone aware the FAA had told PATCO it intended to fire the luckless, isolated Denver and Kansas City strikers. Support came quickly from concerned locals in Houston, Los Angeles, New York, Oakland, and Washington, D.C. Of PATCO's 7,100 members, 477 joined the Denver and Kansas City controllers in calling in sick over a 3-day, 30-hour crisis period (June 18-20). That number was enough to bring the entire air traffic system almost to a standstill.[5]

Officially (on the advice of its counsel), PATCO waffled on whether or not it had actually called a job action. But some PATCO leaders were quoted in the press as claiming the "illnesses" were caused by intolerable working conditions. Backers continued to hope it would dramatize the urgent need for the FAA to hire additional controller personnel. Even many PATCO members, however, remained confused about the sick-out's real origin and objectives. The entire incident entered the association's annals as a prime example of how *not* to "control" a job action.

FAA Crackdown.   PATCO was summoned to an emergency meeting with a frantic Secretary of Transportation. Guided, however, by Bailey's continued insistence that they stick to ATC work, Maher and Rock did not attend, and this encounter was undertaken by Bailey and his legal associates.

On his return Bailey assured PATCO a sound deal had been cut by honorable and trustworthy men. All "sick" controllers would receive immunity from prosecution. GS-15 grades would be granted to all radar controllers. GS-14 grades would be awarded to all nonradar controllers.

These attractive concessions were contingent, of course, on the immediate termination of PATCO's sick-out. None of the concessions had been committed to writing (an unnecessary detail when the word of gentlemen had been given). Maher and Rock were deeply troubled by the absence of a signed-and-sealed agreement, but reluctantly went along in phoning their locals to end the job action.

Three days later the misgivings of Maher and Rock were borne out when the FAA reneged on everything allegedly promised to Bailey. Explaining that it had no intention of going to GS14 and 15 upgrading, the agency suspended the 477 PATCO stalwarts who had called in sick, informing them that the Secretary of Transportation had never agreed to immunity or any other such shield from punishment.

Instead, two moves by the FAA were aimed at pulling the rug from under PATCO. Controllers were denied 2 days work for each day they called in sick, a deterrent to joining any further such job actions (80 controllers received up to 15 days' suspension). PATCO's new dues check-off privilege was revoked by the agency on the grounds that it had changed from a "professional association" to a militant labor union. As PATCO was not yet recognized by the Department of Labor as a bona fide union, the FAA felt no obligation to go along with its dues check-off service. Perhaps the sharpest loss, however, was a significant erosion in confidence by certain controllers in Maher and Rock, and their increasing doubts, in turn, about the current value of Bailey's continued stewardship.

An especially harsh blow followed in October 1969, when the FAA denied PATCO exclusive national recognition. PATCO insisted that it met all the criteria of President Kennedy's 1962 Executive Order 10988, and reminded the FAA that over 60 percent of all controllers had joined the organization. The FAA countered that PATCO had already had more than enough solicitous attention from lower management levels. Still smarting from "Operation Air Safety," the FAA wanted no further national level contacts with PATCO, except possibly to hear it express the opinions of its members, an option the FAA extended to any concerned organization. This insult brought relations between PATCO and FAA to a new low, and bitterness festered for many years to come.

"Who Asked You?"   The incident that sparked PATCO's next job action was FAA's attempt to force the involuntary transfer of four activists from their Baton Rouge tower. An earlier grievance, in PATCO's interpretation, involved the hounding of its officers, Mike Rock and Jimmy Hays (PATCO's first elected president) out of FAA careers. The agency forced Rock and Hays to choose between returning immediately to their ATC duties or going full-time with PATCO. Nothing, however, triggered such outrage as the unprecedented FAA move to force controllers to accept new assignments they had not sought. PATCO viewed this as a raw union-busting attack. One PATCO regional vice-president threatened to take his entire Southwest region out of the union unless the FAA move was blocked. PATCO acknowledged the seriousness of the situation, fearing that management intended to discipline other association leaders in this way, thereby destroying their organization.

An Executive Board meeting of 300 debated options. After a violent course of action was emphatically rejected, the vote was cast for another major sick-out, though one hopefully free of all the "Johnny Carson" foul-ups. Warnings were officially sent to the FAA, and PATCO urged mediation. But the FAA's response was a pledge to punish the concerted withholding of services exactly as it would an illegal strike.

Seeing It Our Way.   In the midst of this steadily building donnybrook the morale of the controllers got a much needed boost from an unexpected corner. The Task Force that the Secretary of Transportation had commissioned in April 1968 to explore ATC grievances released its official findings in January 1970.

The blue-ribbon panel known as the Corson Committee backed many of PATCO's major points. Controllers were a "unique professional group" whose jobs required more of them than those of most federal employees. Controller work schedules were thought unnecessarily cruel in their impact on an individual's personal and family life. Controller morale was undermined by a fear of burnout between ages 40 to 50, and resulted in inability to work at the one job many really wanted.

Reforms urged on the FAA included a sharp reduction in work hours; the upgrading of equipment and facilities; the reduction of required overtime; the expansion of intervals between shift rotations; and the revision of pay criteria. Most significant, the Corson Committee recommended the FAA undertake these overdue changes through calm and conciliatory negotiations with appropriate employee organizations.[6]

The report was not without criticism of PATCO for "ill-considered and intemperate attacks on FAA management." But it came down hardest on the "failure on the part of FAA management to understand and accept the role of employee organizations," and on the agency's costly tolerance of "ineffective internal communications." PATCO hailed the 1969 document as a "rallying cry" that "legitimatized most controller grievances against the FAA." Three innovative Corson proposals particularly gratified the association. A career development plan might be formulated to provide a systematic national program for controller advances. New incentives might be tried to help draw the most able controllers to the most difficult ATC posts in the country. Congress might be asked to pass "early retirement" legislation for controllers who had given their all, and who could not profit from either retraining or reassignment to less stressful tasks.

The Corson Report warned that employee-management relations with the FAA were in a "state of extensive disarray"; and PATCO soon perceived that the FAA would implement only a few of its pro-management recommendations. Nevertheless, some PATCO leaders forever after cited the document as the source of whatever union-management hopes they ever entertained.

Another "Gentleman's Agreement" . . . Broken.   In February the FAA was warned by PATCO that if the "Baton Rouge 4" were not relieved of the transfer order, controllers would make "an impact on the system" Sunday, February 15. As before in these situations, the FAA requested a meeting to forestall the job action. This time, however, it invited the Federal Mediation and Conciliation Service (FMCS) to attend, because legally the FAA could not negotiate with an organization it had declined to recognize. PATCO was pleased that circumstances had forced the FAA to seat a third party in PATCO-FAA talks for the first time ever, and hopes rose somewhat for a peaceful resolution.

PATCO's Executive Board met the night before the meeting, and voted not to let it adjourn until they had a satisfactory agreement in writing. They had learned this lesson the hard way through the union's previous betrayal by FAA "gentlemen."

On Sunday, February 15, the delegates from PATCO, the FAA, and the FMCS began 2 days of negotiations that produced a 4-point understanding:

> The four Baton Rouge controllers would remain at their posts until the FCMS could work out a reasonable solution with lawyers chosen by PATCO and the FAA;[7]
>
> the FAA administrator would notify all management personnel to immediately stop discouraging controllers from belonging to or participating in PATCO; and vio-

lators would be prosecuted by the FAA for unfair labor practices;

the Department of Transportation and the FAA would remain impartial throughout PATCO's ongoing campaign for national recognition (under Executive Order 11491); and

the FMCS would urge the Dept. of Labor to speed PATCO's recognition on the grounds that such status would facilitate the resolution of FAA-PATCO disagreements.

An elated PATCO delegation asked that these highly acceptable terms be committed to writing. At this, a chill descended over the procedures.[8]

Once again, as he had done months before, PATCO's General Counsel, F. Lee Bailey, rose to disagree publicly with his clients. It was unnecessary to put it on paper, he admonished them, since the FAA and DOT representatives were Cabinet-level gentlemen, and the FCMS delegation had witnessed the entire negotiations. Maher and Rock tried to stand their ground, renewing the union's sick-out threat. Bailey was not to be gainsaid, however, and he soon persuaded 14 union representatives in attendance that the verbal agreement was ironclad. Despite the orders of PATCO's executive board, the PATCO negotiators voted to go along with a verbal, rather than written settlement.

Little more than a month later, the silence was broken by the sound of the FAA trashing the "ironclad" verbal agreement. The FAA scheduled the involuntary transfer of the Baton Rouge 4 for March 25. The agency's explanation was that PATCO was still not an officially recognized union. Therefore the FAA was not bound by any "unofficial" discussions it might have held with the employee association.[9]

FCMS officials immediately complained to the Department of Transportation that the February agreement had been solemnly concluded, and its implementation was incumbent. DOT's reply was that since its Secretary had not remained for the second day's marathon negotiating session, the agreement then reached was not binding on *him* (this notwithstanding that the FAA negotiators worked for DOT). Under the pall of this déjà vu, PATCO eyed Bailey's role with mounting restiveness.

"Sick and Tired of Being Sick and Tired."   Convinced it had no choice, the PATCO Executive Board met and voted to conduct a national sick-out on March 25. A press release was circulated on the 24th warning the air traveling public and the FAA that "swift, severe dissipation of air traffic services" would occur in 24 hours.[10] On the 25th, despite FAA telegrams to all facilities on the possibility of firings and criminal sanctions, the usual absenteeism

rate of 4 percent rose to 20 percent as nearly 3,300 PATCO members—about one out of four controllers—called in sick.[11]

Almost from the start, PATCO's efforts appeared doomed. Vastly inflated reports of cooperation were phoned in by overly enthusiastic and poorly disciplined local site representatives, and PATCO headquarters was seriously misled about its actual strength and the strike's real impact.[12] PATCO wired assurance to the Department of Defense that the labor organization's patriotic members were never too sick to rush back to work to meet a defense emergency; and this ill-advised document was used effectively against PATCO in many ensuing court actions. The FAA jolted many strikers by withholding the paychecks of all too sick to report to work. National ATC support remained very uneven, with controllers in Boston, Newark, and much of the South and Southwest deserting PATCO at the outset. Bailey attempted to use a nationally covered TV press conference to get the media to call the sick-out a "walkout." But the more damaging label, "strike," was ineradicable.[13]

On the fifth day, the FAA struck with a move PATCO had not anticipated. Subpoenas were simultaneously served in every major city on every PATCO backer of the sick-out. Lawyers retained by PATCO ranged far and wide to assume their legal defense, but being pulled into 50 federal courts at one time was a predicament for which PATCO was never set up. Almost overnight, it was bankrupted by the fees of its 50 attorneys, and that was possibly the least of its problems.

The Air Transport Association instituted a major lawsuit against PATCO for $100 million; the ATA cited airline losses, allegedly $7,000 a minute, because of inadequate ATC services. Nearly 500 "sick" controllers were subpoenaed to appear in a Brooklyn Federal Court entirely at their own expense, even while the FAA froze previously earned paychecks. A federal judge in Cleveland asked a panel of three leading psychiatrists to examine presumably mentally distressed controllers; and it was cold comfort to PATCO and to the strikers that nine out of ten were found mentally unable to return to work.

Then a federal judge in Washington, D.C., demanded that Bailey, Rock, and Hays go on national TV and call off the sick-out. Otherwise, he would send Rock, the PATCO chairman, and Hays, the president, to jail; strip Bailey of his license to practice law in the District of Columbia; and also charge Bailey with conspiracy against the United States.

This last convergence of pressures was more than PATCO's General Counselor could withstand. Bailey went on TV alone on the fifth day of the job action (one that lasted nearly 3 weeks) to advise all controllers not legitimately sick to return immediately to work. Soon thereafter the Brooklyn Federal Court finally ordered the striking controllers back to work—which Rock and Hays had agreed they would not do until all the conditions were finalized in writing and were acceptable to PATCO.

While few realized it at the time, the greatest blow was the Fall 1970, stipulation-order of a Federal Judge in the Brooklyn court that warned PATCO would pay the ATA $25,000 *or more* if it ever struck again (". . . in any manner, calling, causing, authorizing, encouraging, inducing, continuing or engaging in any strike . . .").[14] With this order the ATA secured an open-ended weapon of critical importance later in '81.

Paying the Bill.   In a brilliant stroke, PATCO moved swiftly to convert the disaster to a triumph. Strikers across the country were encouraged to return in a blaze of glory. At McArthur Terminal, the 350 strikers, carrying an American flag and another with a rattlesnake and the motto "Don't tread on me" marched behind costumed bagpipers, with an escort of six police cars and local fire crews.[15] Similarly defiant and colorful returns were arranged elsewhere, and the unity of the PATCO stalwarts briefly reached a new high.

Once back inside the strikers moved with unrelenting hostility against former workmates ("scabs") who had undermined the 1970 job action. Ostracism was almost total at work sites where returnees made up a sizeable bloc. Sensitive line supervisors moved quickly to reassign the most vindictive returnees to 30-day detail tours away from nonstrikers, hoping in this way to let tempers cool down. And, much to its credit, the FAA cautioned its managers not to unnecessarily antagonize returnees, though it did permit their being reassigned for as long as 6 weeks to wasteful or menial tasks.

Rumors swept the ranks that the FAA was weighing the pros and cons of firing everyone who had called in sick, or over 3,300 PATCO members. While the bankrupt labor organization watched powerless from the sidelines, the FAA began to suspend the "foot soldiers" and fire the sick-out leaders. Worse yet, the FAA began to solicit from cowed nonstrikers written statements that strikers on the FAA hit list had "bad-mouthed" the agency or had been feigning illness when they claimed to be on medical leave. Between this, and the ostracism tactics of the returnees, the typical ATC workstation was turned into a "snake pit" of thoroughly demoralized personnel.

Ironically, then, PATCO left its own sick-out almost fatally ill. The Department of Labor disqualified it as a bargaining agent for its members for 126 days. Nearly $1 million in bills had accumulated, with over half owed for unsuccessful legal services. PATCO was increasingly divided over the worth of the advice it was getting from F. Lee Bailey. Membership was falling monthly, and many who remained were unreliable about sending in the $52 a year dues PATCO deperately needed. Hostilities between regions, and among facilities within the regions undermined already uncertain bonds of solidarity. Clearly, the FAA would soon be entirely free of this nettlesome bunch, unless this dark phase in PATCO's history gave way soon to a new day.*

---

*See the appendix interviews with Stanley A. Gordon, PATCO's first secretary-treasurer, and Jimmy Hays, PATCO's first president.

Chapter 4

PATCO COMES OF AGE

The Leyden Presidency
(1970-1980)

> *Under John Leyden's leaderships, PATCO assumed an important position in the vanguard of the trade union movement—the organization of professional workers. The high regard John enjoys throughout the labor movement for his integrity and courage has brought new respect to PATCO as a dynamic union fighting for its members.*
>
> Lane Kirkland, President, AFL-CIO, *PATCO*, January 1980, p. 4.

> *I sense an unconquerable resolve growing within our union. That same relentless spirit which held a young, battered group of American controllers together during the hard times of the past, will lead us through the even tougher times of the future.*
>
> Robert E. Poli, President of PATCO, *PATCO*, March 1980, p. 4.

When about 200 PATCO delegates (112 from New York alone) gathered in mid-April 1970 for their third national convention, nearly all of the delegates carried the unwelcome distinction of FAA dismissal notices (the Alaskan representatives were still on sick leave, as no PATCO officer had remembered to phone them that the sick-out was over).[1]

The mood, understandably, was grim, despite the Las Vegas glitter that surrounded the bedraggled group. Heavy questions dominated the agenda: Who would be in charge when the convention ended—Rock, Bailey, or someone else? Would Bailey's corporatelike constitution be retained, or substantially revised? Would PATCO remain independent, or affiliate with an AFL-CIO union?

Changing of the Guard

Answers to the last three questions became more predictable after the delegates had resolved the first, and arch-dilemma: Who was next to lead PATCO?

From the beginning it was clear that either Mike Rock or Jimmy Hays could have the presidency for the asking, but both felt a new face was imperative. The two men whom delegates placed in nomination, Bob Greene from the Western Region, and John F. Leyden from the New York Center, met privately and agreed that Leyden fill the top slot. Despite heavy opposition from Bailey, who knew of Leyden's avowed intent to clip his wings, the New Yorker was elected on a "two-coast conciliation" platform.

PATCO then really began anew. John F. Leyden, former president of the local at the New York Center, was a man with over 10 years' ATC service, and an FAA designation of "outstanding employee." He had been rueful that only 50 percent of his coworkers supported the 1968 rule book job action at the system's busiest en route center. But nearly 100 percent backed the 1970 sickout, thanks to Leyden's crisp and sensitive direction of local events (24-hour command posts were manned at two hotels, beneath large signs that read "PATCO Headquarters," and three update and rumor-control meetings were held daily with strikers and their wives).

Leyden fully intended to bring a comparable orderliness and caring ethos to a reoriented PATCO, even if that meant first shaking things up. He began by persuading the Las Vegas delegates that PATCO had to be "returned to the controllers," and the organization's attorneys and noncontroller staffers shorn of power. Backed by Maher and Rock, he got the constitution revised to confine policy-making authority exclusively to controllers. A union-oriented structure was adopted to replace Bailey's corporatelike form, and the delegates were "psyched up" by this for the next historic decision Leyden wanted them to make.

Professional Association or Labor Union?

From the very outset, indeed in late 1967, before PATCO was created, Maher and Rock had wrestled with the question of which way to steer a yet-to-be-formed controllers' organization: toward the prim-and-proper posturing of an association of professionals? Or toward the rough-and-tumble world of modern trade unionism?

Both men had been approached by a UAW organizer in 1967 and offered $500,000 plus expenses to lead their NAGE local and others into the Auto Workers Union. Overtures had also since come to PATCO from the American Federation of Government Employees, the Machinists Union, the Teamsters Union, the Transit Workers Union, and others.

One possibility, however, stood out far above all others. Maher and Rock had been steered by a Capitol Hill transportation expert toward the Washington-based Marine Engineers Beneficial Association (MEBA).[2] This powerful, wealthy AFL-CIO union of 10,000 professionals (who averaged $50,000 a year) had some of the most impressive political connections of any union in the country—and a charismatic, cigar-chomping, straight-talking, longtime leader whose personality appealed to controllers.[3]

Jesse Calhoun, MEBA's colorful and unflappable president, made a strong impression months before the Vegas Convention when he had deliberately put in an appearance at a Denver meeting of PATCO's board. Barred from the room as an outsider by a suspicious F. Lee Bailey, and disinclined to speak in any other room (for fear it might be bugged), Calhoun held court on a hotel balcony, and won plaudits for his "savvy." Calhoun warned that PATCO would be soundly defeated if it struck the FAA, and his urging of nonstrike approaches to grievance resolution sat especially well with conflict-weary PATCO members.

Maher and Rock met several times thereafter with Calhoun to get his advice on how to approach the Baton Rouge 4 challenge. His unqualified insistence that PATCO could not take on the President and Congress with a national strike and hope to win, made a deep and lasting impression on the two PATCO founders.

John F. Leyden was introduced to Calhoun at the 1970 Las Vegas Convention, and it was arranged that the two would discuss affiliation on their return flight to New York City. The delegates dutifully passed a resolution in favor of putting the MEBA matter to a general membership mail ballot (which later earned 92 percent support), and the upshot was a June 15 formal alliance of the two organizations. Thus PATCO relinquished its independent status, and in the eyes of its pro-union members, finally came home to the labor movement.[4]

(Throughout the 11-year association that followed, MEBA gave PATCO complete autonomy. While PATCO officers often asked advice from Calhoun, he gave it only on request, and the recipients characterized it years later as invaluable. Exactly what the 95-year old MEBA got out of the alliance, outside of a paltry per capita flow it never really seemed to need, still bewilders PATCO insiders. Some suggest that Calhoun once dreamed of a single giant union of various types of transportation-related workers.)

Exit Bailey

Along with moving to set his financial house in order, Leyden acted to consolidate power in his presidency. He was finding many of his orders countermanded by Bailey, and he resented being perceived by the FAA and the Secretary of Transportation as a messenger boy for the union's flamboyant General Counsel.

A showdown occurred by design at a June 1970 meeting of the Board. Feelings ran high, for all sensed that PATCO was at a crossroads. Many felt ties of gratitude, respect, and loyalty to a man they had worked intensely with throughout PATCO's tumultuous 2-year existence, one without whom PATCO would never had gotten started. Some believed Bailey to be the genius who kept PATCO going, and feared the controllers would deep-six their union if they alienated him. Nevertheless, after 8 hours of bitter wrangling, the Board upheld Leyden, Bailey tendered his resignation, and a reign ended.

Winning Recognition. As a new affiliate of a long-established AFL-CIO union, PATCO filed with the Department of Labor for official recognition. The FAA petitioned to bar this, charging that PATCO's sick-out strike justified its denial. To PATCO's chagrin, the FAA petition was backed by both ATCA and NAGE, its predecessors and jealous rivals.

As was anticipated, the Hearing Examiner found foursquare against the PATCO contention that the 1970 sick-out strike had been none of its doing. More importantly, however, and to the outrage of the FAA, he set only three conditions on his authorization of PATCO's recognition:

1)   PATCO was to cease and desist from asserting that it had the right to strike—a right clearly denied by statute to all federal employees.

2)   PATCO was to post notice at ATC work sites for 60 days that it was guilty of an unfair labor practice, and would *not* strike again.

3)   PATCO's application for recognition was to be held up for a 60-day period.

A jubilant PATCO celebrated at what one of the attendees (Stan Gordon) recalls as "perhaps the first full-blown party we've had in many, many months."[5]

Winning Resolution. Next to win favorable, though constraining, closure was the perilous matter of the $100 million damage suit filed by the Airline Transportation Association. In return for agreeing in September 1970 to a token financial settlement (a fine of only $100,000), PATCO was placed under a permanent injunction never again to violate the ban against work stoppages by federal employees—or feel the full wrath of the federal courts, the Justice Department, and the Law!

Seeking to put the best face possible on this ruling, PATCO represented the court-ordered settlement—with ATA's willingness to take $100,000 on its $100 million suit—as evidence of the industry's newfound trust in the union's conciliatory stance. PATCO then adroitly went on to urge the FAA to follow suit and meet PATCO halfway.[6]

Union Recognition.   In June 1971 PATCO applied to the Department of Labor for official designation as the sole bargaining agent for all of the FAA's air traffic controllers, rather than only its own members, as until that time. PATCO had previously sought the benefits of a dual identity. As a "professional society" it met an FAA qualification for earning the "right to discuss" equipment, procedures, techniques, etc. As a "labor union" it met an FAA qualification for the right to process grievances, and discuss the work load, general working conditions, and so on.

With its new request of the DOL, the union sought to force the FAA to deal *evenly* with PATCO on all of these matters, though the FAA warned that it would henceforth downgrade any discussion of "professional association" topics when meeting with PATCO representatives. (This tactic dismayed those in PATCO who had always opposed the decision to "go 'union'," and helped drive still another wedge between members.)

When the Labor Department sent out a mail ballot to the controllers (the first time this tool had ever been used in the public sector), 87 percent voted in favor of the union—the highest level of endorsement won up to that time by *any* union in the public sector. Delighted with the tally (much of the credit for which Leyden attributed to MEBA advice, $250,000 in outlays, and manpower), PATCO became officially recognized on September 20, 1972.[7]

Reinstatement.   This was finally won for PATCO by MEBA, thanks to a stroke of luck. The White House wanted the maritime unions to rescind their 20-year-old refusal to handle Russian ships and cargo. Jesse Calhoun agreed to go along, and to persuade the Longshoreman's Union to join him, provided that U.S.-manned ships were used exclusively *and* that the 114 controllers fired in 1970 were reemployed as controllers by the FAA. To the fury of that agency, the Calhoun-White House deal was struck, and PATCO again took on a golden aura at ATC work sites across America.

A Balm for Excessive Stress.   Guided by shrewd MEBA lobbyists, the union of air traffic controllers endorsed Richard Nixon in 1972 for the presidency (even as MEBA gave a $50,000 contribution to the Nixon Campaign).[8] Against this backdrop PATCO focused in the first-half of 1972 on securing congressional passage of its Second Career Retirement Bill. As drafted by PATCO's lawyers the bill had one major premise and two major provisions:

> A controller experienced more debilitating stress than any other type of federal employee, and therefore deserved special consideration where retirement and vocational retraining were concerned.

> A controller should be able to retire early at 50 percent of his base salary at age fifty with 20 years of service, or at any age after 25 years of service.

> A controller should be eligible for vocational retraining for
> 2 years within a 3-year period, at full salary and bene-
> fits, if for psychological or physical reasons he could no
> longer keep up with rapid technological changes in
> ATC work.

In contrast, other federal employees could only retire at fifty-five after 30 years of service, or at sixty after 20 years . . . much less generous terms.

While PATCO's Air Traffic Controllers Career Program Bill passed without controversy in the House, it was about to die of neglect in a critical Senate committee. On learning that only one more vote was needed, PATCO offered and delivered a legal political donation to a key senator (who flew back from campaigning to cast the decisive vote). President Nixon soon thereafter signed the PATCO-written bill into law, and when it was read to PATCO's 1972 Convention by Clark McGregor, a personal representative of the White House, delegates were applauding and cheering long before the reading ended. (Years later, however, PATCO leaders were still waiting for Congress to authorize funds to actually implement the program in any signifi-cant way.)

On a Roll!   Membership soon began to top 8,500, and with new loans of funds from MEBA, the controllers' union began the all-round recovery Leyden had held up as attainable—provided members reduced internal dis-sension, the perpetual bane of PATCO's brief existence.

Early in 1973 PATCO initiated its first negotiations with a wary FAA. To its gratified surprise, the talks yielded a first-ever contract more generous than the union had dared hope.[3] PATCO sought and won

1) a dues checkoff;
2) an improved FAM trip program;
3) guaranteed prime vacations;
4) a new grievance procedure; and
5) contract language that allowed for on site investigations of accidents by PATCO's specially trained representatives.

Above all, the union was pleased to have an FAA pledge to enter with it in a joint study of ATC reclassification, a mutual research project that could help promote a more positive relationship between the adversaries.

FAM Trip Flap.   This newfound self-confidence was almost immediately put to the test when, in 1974, two traditional adversaries, the airline industry and the FAA, moved jointly and separately to clip PATCO's wings. In appar-ent concert, the pair announced a plan to discontinue the FAM, or familiarization flights certain controllers had come to value as a coveted "perk" of the job. While ostensibly implemented to help them familiarize themselves with new cockpit equipment and procedures, FAM was widely suspected of serving controllers more for joyrides, PATCO-linked missions, and the controversial like. On the expiration of PATCO's first contract, the FAA began to stall at the bargaining table over terms of a new agreement.

PATCO met both threats head on with its first job action since 1970, a series of scattered rule book slowdowns throughout 5 days in September. By October, the FAM privilege was again secure, and PATCO had won a highly acceptable second contract.

Through the Back Door.   Among the toughest puzzles PATCO confronted in 1975 was the fact that Civil Service Law forbade federal workers negotiating salaries, which was precisely what PATCO intended to do.

An unanticipated breakthrough, much like the lucky stroke of the MEBA leverage on the Soviet wheat deal, had occurred earlier in 1974 when the FAA finally agreed to honor its contract pledge, and joined PATCO in a reclassification study. PATCO hired a union-related expert in such matters to guide it, and stealthily set about using the joint committee findings to alter classifications only one way—*up*. The final report in 1975 of the PATCO-FAA committee, a report soon known as the "Blue Book," was hailed by the union as well worth immediate implementation by the Department of Transportation.

Civil Service Showdown.   Unfortunately for PATCO, while it was busy manipulating the Blue Book findings, the U.S. Civil Service Commission (CSC) decided to do its own study of controllers' pay scales, their actual tasks and responsibilities and how these all complemented one another. To the indignation of controllers everywhere, the CSC wound up recommending the downgrading of the Boston, Kansas City, and Oakland facilities, along with 46 of the smaller rural area towers. No more massive and high-level a threat had been dealt controller earnings since PATCO's 1968 founding.[9]

PATCO dug in its heels, and advised its members that a job action might soon be necessary to prevent the CSC downgrading, to force the FAA to agree to its first GS-14 rating for at least four GS-13 facilities, and to win implementation by the FAA of major Blue Book reclassifications, as had been bargained through in the Joint Committee.

The 1975 PATCO convention was utilized to announce that members would be polled for the first time in the union's history to determine their willingness to act in a militant way (no one was surprised when the final tally announced weeks later was emphatically in favor). An ensuing 6-day slowdown in June 1975 brought chaos overnight to the nation's air traffic industry, especially in Chicago, New York, and Washington, D.C.—another victory for a jubilant PATCO.

While the work-by-the-rule-book slowdown was still in effect, both the Department of Transportation and the Civil Service Commission rushed to open negotiations PATCO demanded, and DOT agreed to an unconditional amnesty for all the "strikers." With this assurance in writing, a signal from PATCO had the entire 50-state air traffic control system functioning normally within 2 hours.

The Civil Service Commission in turn agreed to table its downgrading proposal for the time being, and finally capitulated entirely in January 1976. Using what Maher now calls a "masterful, pokerlike bluff," Leyden warned that still another slowdown might be called to complicate the elaborate planning then underway for the inauguration of a new President (Jimmy Carter), and he urged a nervous CSC not to force PATCO to take that very undesirable move.

Blue Book Blues.   While many in PATCO cheered the results of its June 1975 6-day slowdown, others were quite disappointed with the Blue Book impact on their particular facility. Despite the best effort of Robert E. Poli, PATCO's chief representative on the joint committee, and the union's executive vice president since 1972, some PATCO members who took risks by participating in the illegal slowdown got nothing in return.

Leyden had repeatedly explained before the job action that PATCO was unable to push the FAA-PATCO committee into recommending something for everyone. Instead, the union's realistic motto had been "as much as possible for as many as possible."[10] Unfortunately, no one on the West Coast received anything, and as their backing of the slowdown had been commendable, some controllers out there felt misled or even betrayed by PATCO—a reaction that fed unhealed bitterness among regions and facilities.

Blue Book Boasts.   By and large, however, PATCO exulted in what it believed it had won. Despite the threat earlier posed by the U.S. Civil Service Commission, no controller in America had been downgraded. By 1978, almost 10,000 controllers had been upgraded. PATCO had made a strong case for moving some GS-13 facilities up to GS-14, and that unprecedented advance seemed closer than ever.

Above all, PATCO believed it had uncovered a technique for circumventing the Civil Service ban on negotiating wages, and in the reclassification of facilities now had a vehicle for bargaining in the way unions outside the federal sector took for granted.

Alone among all federal employees, the nation's air traffic controllers, thanks to PATCO, had achieved something that resembled genuine collective bargaining. While other federal employees remained subject to the rates set by the Civil Service Commission, the controllers were significantly influencing their own salary levels—and their self-esteem.

Consolidating Gains.   Much that the Leyden Administration had achieved was bolstered in a relatively quiet year, 1977, through two major union innovations. A National Controllers Subsistence Fund, sometimes known as a strike fund, was established by increasing PATCO dues from 1 percent to 1.50 percent of a controller's gross salary, a move that earned the Fund 15 percent of all annual dues. A training program for PATCO facility representatives was established at the AFL-CIO's George Meany Center for Labor Studies (Silver Spring, MD). Led by Jack Maher, the school helped controllers learn labor history, labor law, grievance processing, industrial psychology, and political action techniques. With 600 students a year, enrollees gained an appreciation of what all controllers were up against, and many forged bonds of personal friendship that stood PATCO in good stead in the 4 stormy years that remained to the union.

Eager and increasingly ready to take on ever tougher challenges, PATCO closed out the year—the last before an all-out FAA counterattack in 1978 helped change everything—with a promise to seek the complete separation of controller pay scales from the control of the Civil Service grade structure. An increasingly cautious John Leyden urged his rank and file to remain patient, and to trust to his unrelenting lobbying efforts. In this way, rather than through the appealing macho fantasy of going "one-on-one" with the FAA, the union could realistically expect many more gains such as those Leyden had already won.

PATCO's Third Contract.   Pleased with gains earned in its first two agreements with the FAA, the union sent Leyden, Poli, and Rock around the country to discuss forthcoming contract negotiations with over 400 facility representatives. To their dismay, grassroots spokesmen delivered the message "Get what you can, but don't count on us this time for any militant gesture."

Convinced by this that they could not pull off a successful nationwide rule book strike or sick-out, PATCO opted to try to bluff the FAA—a desperation move doomed from the start. The agency had many "pipelines" into PATCO—controllers bucking for promotion into FAA ranks served as informers throughout PATCO's existence, even as PATCO claimed to have "insiders" among FAA top echelons.

PATCO tried to throw a smokescreen over its ("No strike!") impotence by summoning nearly 425 facility reps to an emergency meeting. The union notified the FAA that its dissatisfaction with ongoing contract negotiations was so great it was considering breaking off the talks—and then held its breath. The FAA, however, was not bluffed. When the dust had settled and the third contract for 17,000 controllers had been signed, the parties had ceded almost nothing of value to one another, and PATCO denounced the indignity and unfairness of the current system of "collective begging." Co-founder Mike Rock boasted that with this contract PATCO had "achieved all of our 1970 goals," but few in the membership were impressed—especially since their sights were set on 1979, not 1970 goals.[11]

FAM as Leyden's Folly.   PATCO's sole gain in the hapless 1978 negotiations concerned the FAA's agreement to allow *overseas* FAM trips, a concession relevant to only 50 to 100 controllers a year, and one that ironically helped set Leyden's downfall in motion, as he told members this gain somehow justified signing the new contract.

Shortly after the lackluster 3-year contract had been ratified certain airlines like National, Northwest Orient, Pan Am, and TWA voted "no" on FAM trips. To PATCO's anger, these companies explained that the FAA had not spoken for them, and they were disinclined to provide free passage for controllers on overseas "familiarization" flights. Despite many tense meetings among the parties, the airlines stood firm, and PATCO effectively lost even this one 1978 contract advantage.

Leyden was not so easily denied, however, and he began to phone key local leaders to line up support for a fight over the FAM cancellation. When delegates gathered in Las Vegas for PATCO's tenth annual convention, Leyden announced a May 25 date for the start of a nationwide slowdown—and immediately ran into opposition from the floor.

Jack Seddon, a leader of New York area controllers, argued that the issue did not warrant the penalties in large court fines and insulting FAA retribution that a job action would bring down on the union. Traditionally militant locals, like those in Chicago and Cleveland, agreed their members did not feel strongly about the FAM setback. Seddon and his allies warned it would be difficult to generate enthusiasm for a slowdown that only seemed to have FAM at its heart.

Leyden vigorously countered that the opposition completely missed the point. He urged the delegates to understand that far more was at stake than the FAM privileges: the issue was one of *contract integrity*. Leyden warned the delegates that if the airline industry could strike down this one provision of the contract without resistance by PATCO, a dangerous precedent would be set. PATCO would stand revealed as a paper tiger, unable to oppose the chipping away of contract components more valued than FAM, and the contract would survive only at the mercy and discretion of the airlines.

With Executive Vice President Robert E. Poli acting as a mediator, Seddon and Leyden reached an understanding in Las Vegas that allowed the May 25 slowdown to go off as scheduled, but cast it as a trial of Leyden's mode of operation. Before the scheduled date, Seddon called an unauthorized, unofficial meeting of facility reps, and went over with them many of the anti-slowdown arguments he had earlier presented in Las Vegas. Known ever since in PATCO lore as the gathering of the "Big 9, Crazy 8, and Little 7" (referring to the size and reputation of the facilities represented), the unprecedented meeting sent a strongly worded resolution to Leyden (who knew, as did Poli, of the session, but was barred from attending).

The signers demanded that PATCO devise a method to protect controllers who always backed a union job action, and suffered thereafter from FAA punishment. These controllers were increasingly bitter that many others ignored the union's mandate, and escaped any consequences from both the FAA and PATCO alike. With their sentiment now on record, the "Big 9, Crazy 8, and Little 7" met once more (perhaps 600 strong), and went on to back the May 25 slowdown, as Seddon had promised Leyden.[12]

While the two unauthorized meetings were being held at the Dutch Inn on Long Island, Leyden was earnestly negotiating with the Air Transport Association for restoring the overseas FAM provision. Despite his Las Vegas authorization to call a job action over the issue, the ATA would still not budge.[13] On May 25–26 and June 6–7, a very spotty and irregular rule book slowdown was conducted in certain major cities: a job action that showed members' ambivalence about taking on the FAA and running personal and system-safety risks for an isolated provision of the contract.

Leyden's Last Stand.   Speaking to the 1978 convention, Leyden had warned that PATCO would not accept any meddling by the airline industry in the contract it had hammered out with the FAA.[14] But as Seddon and others had sought to explain, a "sanctity-of-the-contract" argument was hard to get across to the rank and file, and the job action therefore mobilized meager support. Seddon and the "Big 9, Crazy 8, and Little 7" controllers tried not to convey an attitude of I-told-you-so, but their calls to PATCO headquarters made it plain that they had their fill of ill-conceived and poorly supported slowdowns. If and when a job action was again deemed necessary, the Seddon cadre of militants wanted to feel trained, disciplined, and thoroughly prepared.

One member, writing later in the *PATCO Newsletter* (August 1979), tried to find a silver lining in the fiasco:

> In the summer months of 1978, because of our ineptness both in the field and at the national level, we suffered what has been called our most serious loss of all the battles we have ever fought. Serious because we not only lost a sum of money in fines ($100,000) levied against us, but more importantly because we lost some members over the FAM issue, and yet other members started losing confidence in the leaders of PATCO at all levels, local, regional, and national. But that defeat can be as revealing as victory and seen for what it is—a learning experience.[15]

At the time, however, the major lesson seemed to be that winning a job action against the FAA was getting harder and harder, especially when factionalism split the ranks.

Cracks in the Dam Wall.   As if the FAM fiasco was not enough, 1978 brought more related setbacks. An FAA undertaking that had initial PATCO support, "Project Professionalism," proved a major disappointment. Certain facility chiefs allegedly used it to disregard the contract and/or harass the controller workforce. After 6 months of monitoring the project's implementation, PATCO announced unequivocal opposition to its continuance: a setback for Leyden's preference for collaboration, rather than conflict with the FAA.

A 1976 agreement with the FAA to liberalize the dress code for controllers ran into more and more management resistance, and it became necessary to arbitrate the wearing of blue denim, khaki slacks, and other departures from the "IBM"-style dress preferred by the FAA. While PATCO won many grievances using the "neat-and-clean" provision of Article 61, the friction on this score in 1978 was considerable.

Representatives of the National Black Coalition of Federal Aviation Employees, the majority of whose members were controllers, met with PATCO's Executive Board and aired many long-ignored grievances. The NBCFAE outlined a number of cases where minorities and women were dissatisfied with FAA or PATCO policy, and sought PATCO's aid in making more EEO and Affirmative Action progress—a prospect that lacked enthusiastic support from PATCO's overwhelmingly white male membership.

Congress cut off funding for PATCO's second career program, and the FAA attributed this to anger over the union's FAM slowdown fiasco. Leyden vigorously denied any connection, and urged the FAA to join PATCO in solving this problem—an idea the FAA ignored and Leyden's detractors ridiculed.

Given this only partial record, it is little wonder that Leyden's end-of-year Christmas message to the membership noted that "candidly, this will not go down as one of PATCO's proudest years. . . ."[16]

The FAA—as "The Greatest Organizer PATCO Ever Had."   Relations with the FAA, despite an early "honeymoon" period with Administrator Langhorne Bond, rapidly soured as hopes faded that Leyden's direct (and behind-the-scenes) appeal for PATCO-FAA cooperation would produce significant gains. Instead, the FAA used a 1978 air disaster, the largest ever in this country (144 deaths), to initiate what it characterized as the "most sweeping and comprehensive changes in the air use system in U.S. history."[17]

Within a very few months PATCO was highly critical of many new FAA initiatives. A 3-year-old program that assured controllers and pilots of immunity from reprisals for reporting "incidents" and unsafe conditions was targeted by the FAA for termination. PATCO joined with ALPA, and, for the first time, with the Air Transport Association, in urging the FAA to reverse its opposition to immunity provision—though without success. After months of equivocation the FAA came out against the resumption of the Second Career Program. In testimony to Congress the FAA "impugned the reputation of the controller work force by characterizing them as thieves or conmen. . ."[18]

The FAA also used the new 750-page Rose Report, its 5-year $2.8 million study of controllers, to insist that the job was no more stressful than that of a bus driver, and therefore warranted no special remedial legislation.[19] FAA's 1980 budget request asked for more than a doubling in the number of Terminal Radar Service Areas, and an expansion of control in the en route portion of flight, but only proposed a token increase in the number of air traffic controllers. PATCO, already distressed by "critical staff shortages," urged Congress unsuccessfully to force a change in the FAA request, as the changes meant a "vast increase in controller responsibility."[20]

What seemed to hurt the most was the union's inability to convince anyone that the abuses congressional investigators had found in the Second Career Program were not its fault, but were the result of such blatant FAA mismanagement that "an objective observer would be hard pressed to deny a deliberate attempt at sabotage."[21]

When given an opportunity in Congressional testimony to sum up the 1979 situation, Leyden reminded the lawmakers that the Corson Committee report in 1971 had noted an "unprecedented degree of mutual resentment and antagonism between management and employees. We do not believe the relationship now to be appreciably different from that described by the Corson Committee."[22]

Exit Leyden.   For all the reasons mentioned, dissension built steadily throughout 1978 and 1979, and more and more members of the Executive Board began to doubt whether Leyden's continued leadership was still in PATCO's best interests.

At the time, and ever since, PATCO members have puzzled over causes for the sharp and total break of Leyden and Poli, a pair once so close Jack Maher used to call them "Batman and Robin." As late as December 31, 1979, Leyden expected to run unopposed in April for another term as PATCO's president (though friends were struck by the absence of Poli from Leyden's New Year's Eve party). When Poli came to Leyden's office a day before the scheduled January 3, 1980, Board of Directors meeting, and announced his intention to run in April against his boss of 10 years, Leyden was shocked and angered to a degree that helped lead the next day to the unexpected offer of his resignation.

Why the rift? In part because each man had come to represent a different approach to the unrelenting anti-union stance of the FAA. Each assessed
the performance of the union's General Counsel quite differently, with
Leyden content to give his friend in that slot two opportunities to improve after he concluded that unfair tactics were being used against the lawyer. Each
enjoyed the personal support of different members of the Board, and friction
there continually worsened.

After 10 fruitful years of collaboration, Leyden and Poli had reached a
point where at least Poli was convinced—perhaps a year or more before the
actual January coup d'etat—that the "Dynamic Duo" had outlived its usefulness. As he explained later to *Time* magazine, "We could see there might be
cause to strike. I knew I would be ready for it, and John might not be."[23] Encouraged in this viewpoint by some PATCO officers, Poli worked discreetly in
1979 to line up support, a campaign that required him to co-opt a secret
PATCO committee placed in his charge by his longtime colleague, John F.
Leyden.

The "'81 Committee."   To understand how and why Poli backers could
unseat the 10-year head of the union, it helps to return to a prophetic incident at PATCO's 1976 San Diego convention.

As recalled affectionately years later by participants, one of PATCO's co-
founders, Jack Maher, had his daughter bring back from a shopping trip to
Tijuana a large number (perhaps 100) slouchy-style cowboy hats (of the type
Gabby Hays used to wear in the movies). He gave these to the most devoted
and militant of the convention delegates, and with his very popular gift,
stirred the notion in 1976 of bonding together a cadre of ardent PATCO
types within the body of the general membership—a cadre whose morale
seemed to grow greater and greater all the time.

In 1978, Maher, distressed by the failure of that year's work-to-rule slowdown, phoned activists around the country and talked up an old Auto Union
idea, the notion of a "committee of responsible militants." This group would
review the plans for all PATCO job actions *prior* to any involvement of the
general membership, and this "cowboy hat" cadre would keep both Leyden
and Poli alert to activist ideas. Based among the alumni of PATCO's Meany
Center training program (devised and overseen by Maher since 1977)
the new cadre soon became, in Leyden's eyes an unelected, unconstitutional
elite leadership tier. Poli, however, lined up firmly with the new group,
known then as a "strike force," and its members soon returned the compli-
ment.

When the FAM fiasco seemed to warrant some militant type of response
from PATCO's president, Leyden created a secret "Choirboy Committee"
and charged it with responsibility for toughening up the union before the

1981 contract negotiations got underway. Jack Maher, a charter member, called an activist friend, Jack Seddon, and asked him to design a formal training program to help "unionize" controller trainees by indoctrinating them in PATCO ideas and values. On completion of their special schooling these graduates would be recruited into a "choirboy" stratum of PATCO membership, a select cadre which the leadership could expect to exert that extra effort that might make all the difference in ensuing job actions. Not surprisingly, seven activists tapped by the regional vice presidents to run the "Choirboy Committee" were all "cowboy hat" militants, controllers who had demonstrated their individual self-discipline, loyalty to PATCO, and proven leadership ability.

As the months went by, Poli and the Committee, staffed by Jack Maher, grew closer and closer. The Committee gave Poli a stage, some props, an audience, and high visibility, all critical elements in helping him decide later to challenge Leyden: a decision he kept secret until a week before the Chicago showdown. While pledged to remain "neutral," nearly 100 activists, many of them choirboys, forced a 4 a.m. confrontation between the two men before the January 1980 Executive Board meeting in Chicago. After hearing a blistering attack from PATCO staffer Dennis Reardon against Leyden's alleged failure to meet the responsibilities of office, many of the activists made early morning phone calls around the country to rally support for either one of the adversaries.

Leyden's Walkout.   At a highly dramatic meeting of the Board in January 1980, both a confounded Leyden, and the leader of his opposition, Executive Vice-President Robert E. Poli, wound up submitting their resignations, leaving PATCO bereft of its top two officers. After summoning cofounder Mike Rock and Poli-backer Dennis Reardon for consultation, the Board voted 6 to 1 to accept Leyden's resignation, and to ask Poli to withdraw his. At this verdict, a stunned Leyden stormed out, thereby ending his PATCO career. (Years later, in a 1984 interview with me, Leyden recalled that he had simply "had enough at the time, enough damage had been done . . . I projected everything that was going to happen next, a form of anarchy . . . a leader must be responsible for his actions, and Poli wasn't: other people were calling the shots.")[24]

Characterized in his last appearance in a *PATCO Newsletter* as a "worthy, respected adversary" by FAA Administrator Bond, he was termed "one of the most forward-looking union officials I've seen in my lifetime" by MEBA president Jesse Calhoun.[25] As outgoing president, one for whom PATCO had "been in my blood for more than 10 years," Leyden wished the organization "every success in the days ahead," and proceeded to cut off significant ties with it.[26] (Indeed, his refusal to vigorously back a candidate against Poli in the

April 1980 election helped assure Poli's victory in a tough and mean-spirited election.)[27]

Summary. From a most inauspicious start in 1970, with the union penniless, and the FAA firing 114 PATCO leaders and suspending over 3,000 other sick-out collaborators, PATCO rose to scarcely envisioned heights by the end of 1980. Among other lessons PATCO had learned, the union now placed six foremost:

1. Confident professionals like air traffic controllers wanted to be fully in charge of their own employee organization— almost regardless of their initial dependence on an outside leader of great distinction, even an F. Lee Bailey.

2. Such professionals could be led to explore conciliatory alternatives to unrelenting guerrilla war, provided that a PATCO leader like John F. Leyden undertook this change of course as a personal crusade.

3. PATCO victories were attainable and meaningful (union status, a negotiated contract, reinstatement, "Blue Book" reclassification, etc.). But they required patience, persistence, expensive lobbying, and an artful mixture of "prim and proper" conduct with occasional resort to (illegal) "rulebook" slowdowns or sickouts.

4. The Federal Courts would *not* be trifled with, and while the DOT/FAA and the Justice Department did not yet seem to know exactly how to respond to PATCO strikes, the federal courts could impose very severe penalties if PATCO ever again dared defy a strike ban.

5. Imaginative "backdoor" solutions could be found to even the most formidable obstacles, as in the union's use of an FAA-PATCO Joint Committee to circumvent the Civil Service Commission's grip on ATC earnings.

6. Preparing for a better future meant helping nearly 600 rank and filers get a pro-labor education every year, the better to build a cadre of well-versed PATCO activists equal to whatever lay ahead.

Guided by these hard-earned insights, and inspired by its securement of one of the best retirement systems in America *and* the best collective bargaining position of any union in the public sector, PATCO looked forward confidently to many more such distinctions.*

> *There was a lot of confusion when Leyden got booted. We heard all kinds of stories and rumors, and nobody knew what to believe. When the dust settled it looked like he was doubted because he wanted to settle things through talk while the supermilitants felt it was time to take action! With Leyden off the scene the big buildup started, and everything speeded up.*
>
> PATCO activist interview West Coast, August 1985.

---

*See appendix interviews with John F. Leyden, PATCO's second president, and also with a Boston activist.

Chapter 5

CHANGING DIRECTION

The Poli Presidency (1980-1981)

Jealous of the pilots, fearful of being slowly worn down by the stresses and responsibilities of their own task—yet proud of their skills and fascinated by the space-age gadgetry they have mastered—the controllers gradually came to the conclusion that they had been taken for granted too long. The Government would have to be taught a lesson.
William A. Henry, III, "Turbulence in the Tower," *Time*, August 17, 1981, p. 17.

"We are a union. We have proven to our adversaries a number of times that the controller resolve is unequalled. We have learned our lessons well. Together, there is nothing we cannot accomplish . . . We shall execute the will of the membership."
Robert E. Poli, *PATCO Newsletter*, March 25, 1980, p. 4.

"Like life itself, a trade union is creative in character and largely unpredictable in outcome."
Frank Tannenbaum, *A Philosophy for Labor* (1946), p. 106.

Robert E. Poli's stewardship of PATCO lasted barely 2 years (January, 1980– December 31, 1982), but what extraordinary years they were! Morale soared, and the members came together as never before. PATCO seldom left the front pages, and an almost undeniable yearning grew to have it out, once and for all, with "Goliath." Proud and feisty, fairly itching to prove that Leyden's reliance on moderation and haggling could be outdone by the clearcut use of superior power, the Poli-"Choirboy" combination led PATCO rapidly to a point of no return, a point crossed sometime in a turbulent and troubled 1980—though few activists seemed to notice or to flinch.

Physician, Heal Thyself! The union's new chief executive officer assumed charge of about 21 long-term employees, all of whom he assured had nothing to fear from the "changing of the guard." (Indeed, in a private discussion of the situation in that time with me, in my role as a survey researcher for PATCO, Poli expressed puzzlement over fear of himself he sensed among lower-echelon office employees. As he felt he had been "father confessor" to many over his 8 years as office director, Poli ranked himself a low 1.5 on a hypothetical 10-point scale of authoritarianism. He was angered, however, by the mysterious appearance of a derogatory cartoon on the office bulletin board, and also suspected that someone among his office employees had deliberately scratched and marred his auto the previous night. After I urged no witch-hunt, Poli assured me he intended to remain open and friendly to all; and Maher complimented him for serving as a "crying towel," in contrast to Leyden's aloof demeanor with PATCO office workers.)

In short order, however, the office force decided to form an independent union, with coworker Jack Maher's advice and encouragement, and this new entity requested recognition and job security contract terms from PATCO.

Although Poli was initially receptive, and had assured his friend Maher there would be no problem, he suddenly changed his mind, and withdrew the staff union recognition (he said the unit should not have included four office supervisors in membership). Freed by this denial of recognition to pursue his own course, Poli fired three or four of the office employees, and accepted the immediate resignations in protest of another three or four, including PATCO cofounder Jack Maher, who felt betrayed by an inexplicable act he condemned as "union busting."

Before the dust settled the ill-fated staff union had written on August 4 to PATCO's 450 facility representatives explaining their charge of unfair labor practices against Poli, and urging support for their position. Poli, in turn, wrote on July 30 and August 14 to the same representatives, and, on August 28, to all PATCO members, denouncing the staff union: an increasingly bitter exchange that seemed to rally the rank and file to the side of Poli (in whose fiery rhetoric PATCO, now under attack from all quarters, was justified, and would overcome!).

On August 7 the NLRB held in favor of PATCO, much to Poli's relief. To be sure, his losses involved the services of 15 of 21 seasoned employees, and the support of one-time backer and adviser, Jack Maher. But his authority was left firmer than ever, and by the time, in May of 1982, that the 1981 pro-Poli decision was reversed on appeal, and PATCO and Poli were found guilty of unfair labor practices against the staff union, there was no union left to order to reinstate the ex-employees.

As the media chose to neglect this entire matter, and as Poli appeared to hold the support in it of most PATCO members, its major significance appears to involve the unease this alleged union busting caused among certain PATCO activists: men who, like Maher, first began with this fracas to worry that "something was definitely *wrong*, some kind of mean-spirited feeling had settled over the union . . . something had changed, and definitely for the worse."[1]

FAA Response: The Bad and the Bad of It. Two months after the ouster of Leyden the FAA threw down the gauntlet—or so the "choirboys" interpreted the act—by creating a Management Strike Contingency Force. Although the FAA-PATCO contract still had another 12 months to run, the FAA seemed determined to be better prepared for *any* contingency than ever before in its stormy 12-year relationship with the union.

Before the year was out the FAA had signalled in every way possible its readiness to do battle, even though the law and norms guiding federal labor-management relations required the parties, then and now, to bargain in "good faith" and to strive to avoid unnecessary conflict.

As if to drive home its intention to play hard ball in 1981, and never again to have a federal judge upbraid it for being indecisive and soft on an illegal job action (as had happened in court after the 1979 FAM fiasco), the FAA welcomed Poli with a seeming crackdown on his union members:

> Minor, unintentional violations of work rules by PATCO members drew punishments, while similar infractions by nonmembers were ignored . . . Management also began criticizing the union publicly. In June 1980, the chief of the Oakland, California traffic control center declared on a radio talk show that PATCO did not care about air traffic safety. Soon after, the chief of the Spokane, Washington, tower refused to allow controllers to wear PATCO T-shirts to work. In both instances, unfair labor practice complaints filed by the union were upheld by the Federal Labor Relations Authority.[2]

In these controversies, and, to hear the "choirboys" tell it, in many more such clashes, the guilty FAA supervisors were let off with inconsequential warnings by the agency.

FAA administrators explained that their 1980 crackdown was to expose PATCO's advocacy of an illegal strike in the months ahead. They urged media attention to a long list of alleged unfair labor practices they charged against the union:

> Kansas City controllers who had worked overtime after their PATCO local urged them not to later found the tires of their cars deflated.

A Philadelphia member who had accepted an overtime call-in assignment in violation of PATCO's policies had later been "discriminated against" by the union.

PATCO members had refused to handle Aeroflot (Russian) jet aircraft, and, in Florida, a PATCO militant had allegedly directed a Braniff jet aircraft toward a thunderstorm—both of which incidents the FAA condemned as an indication of strong militant sentiment on the part of PATCO members (albeit the Braniff allegation came to nothing). The FAA especially resented the Aeroflot incident since it suggested the agency was not in complete charge of its own employees.

PATCO had mailed an educational package to its locals that explained how to establish networks, security committees, welfare committees, effective communications, and picket committees in the event of a strike. The package warned that arrest and imprisonment might follow, and explained how bail bondsmen and other legal services might aid jailed controllers. (When asked about this "how-to" package, PATCO insisted the advice had never been meant to be used until strikes by public employees were legalized.)[3]

PATCO had been mailing questionnaires to members that inflamed pro-strike sentiments by asking, among other things, "After you have reviewed PATCO's 1981 contract proposals, would you vote to strike in order to obtain the contract benefits you consider important?" When asked about this research, PATCO insisted "the questionnaire is just that, a questionnaire. It's about something that may or may not ever come about."[4]

Thoroughly unconvinced by PATCO's insistence that it was not steadily preparing for "the big one," the FAA filed charge after charge against the union. While conceding by June 1980, that they hadn't made their case yet, the agency insisted it was only a matter of time "as we keep marshalling evidence. This puts the charges before the public, the FLRA, and everybody."[5]

PATCO, in turn, pointed to about 50 nationwide complaints against the FAA it had pending with the Federal Labor Relations Authority, and the union insisted most were settled eventually by an FAA admission of wrongdoing. Poli and his top officers enjoyed warning that the FAA's efforts to publicize the likelihood of an illegal strike by controllers could backfire: Such talk might anger PATCO members so much Poli would find it very difficult to get them to accept a contract settlement negotiated without any job action! (FAA Administrator Langhorne Bond conceded that "arguably, this could make a strike more likely because people become angry. But," he insisted, "the idea is to make it public. We don't think this [strike preparation] should be done in secret.").[6]

Even with all of this bitter jousting, Poli in 1980 was still willing to make little publicized olive-branch gestures that Leyden loyalists would have appreciated, but that finally availed him nothing. He sought a personal meeting for off-the-record dialogue with FAA Administrator Langhorne Bond. But though he reached the vestibule, lawyers for the FAA hurried to the scene to bar the session as ill-advised and inappropriate, given that 1981 negotiations were soon to get underway.

Little wonder, accordingly, that in October 1980 congressional testimony, his first as PATCO president, Poli dwelled on the overdue need for deep-reaching changes in the FAA's approach to its employees in general, and to PATCO, in particular. Quick to assure the anxious congressmen PATCO hoped to avoid a strike in 1981, and that he had no desire to engage in an illegal job action, Poli urged policymakers on the Hill to recognize that without a rapid change in FAA's style of management the union might have no choice but to go one-on-one with the agency.[7]

Counting on Politicians.   Casting about for ways to reduce the risks it anticipated running in 1981, PATCO sought to take advantage of the oldest game played in the District of Columbia—trading current election support for a favor owed from a campaigning politician.

Impressed by the way MEBA and its canny president, Jessie Calhoun, used ties with both the Republican and Democratic parties, PATCO followed its lead in taking an independent line with political endorsements. In 1972 the controllers' union backed the G.O.P. candidate Richard Nixon for president, a move related to PATCO's campaign to win reinstatement of fired PATCO activists. In 1976 the controllers' union remained neutral, though it did not share the AFL-CIO's enthusiasm for candidate Jimmy Carter. In 1980 the controllers' union backed the G.O.P. candidate Ronald Reagan for president, a move related to campaign promises PATCO believed it had secured from the Republican standard-bearer.

The Reagan endorsement was a popular one with upwardly mobile, middle-class air traffic controllers. And it remained important long after the 1981 strike, as many ex-controllers initially hoped this election support might somehow now earn them a White House reprieve—and job reinstatement.

During the 1980 campaign Poli talked with candidate Reagan during a Florida whistle-stop tour. That encounter left the PATCO president "favorably impressed by his concern, his feeling for air traffic controllers . . . he felt the problems that air traffic controllers have must be addressed immediately."[8]

Members of the Reagan-Bush election team soon forwarded a letter to Poli from Reagan that PATCO rank and filers have never stopped citing as the source of their 1980–1981 faith in the Republican standard-bearer:

> Dear Mr. Poli:
>
> I have been thoroughly briefed by members of my staff as to the deplorable state of our nation's air traffic control system. They have told me that too few people working unreasonable hours with obsolete equipment has placed the nation's air travelers in unwarranted danger. In an area so clearly related to public safety, the Carter Administration has failed to act reasonably.
>
> You can rest assured that if I am elected President, I will take whatever steps are necessary to provide our air traffic controllers with the most modern equipment available, and to adjust staff levels and workdays so they are commensurate with achieving the maximum degree of public safety.
>
> As in all other areas of the federal government where the president has the power of appointment, I fully intend to appoint highly qualified individuals who can work harmoniously with Congress and the employees of government agencies they oversee.
>
> I pledge to you that my administration will work very closely with you to bring about a spirit of cooperation between the President and the air traffic controllers. Such harmony can and must exist if we are to restore the people's confidence in the government.
>
> Sincerely,
>
> Ronald Reagan.[9]

Three days later PATCO endorsed Reagan for President (as did MEBA and the Airline Pilots Union, among the very few other labor organizations that broke ranks in this way).

Ten months later, when asked after the August 1981 strike about the Reagan endorsement, Poli insisted no mistake had been made. A private breakfast with Reagan in October 1980, just before a press conference to announce PATCO's preference, had left Poli impressed with Reagan's warmth and fairness, and, "knowing his reputation for sincerity and straight talk, we pledged our support to him."[10] (Poli has never turned on Reagan, and insists to this day the President was "tragically ill-advised and fed false information that gave him few alternatives.")[11]

Chicago Strikes—Again!   Another choice PATCO was obliged to make in 1980 concerned the challenge posed by a wildcat strike of O'Hare activists, an ill-timed and embarrassing job action that forced PATCO to choose between "benign neglect" or strong backing of the Chicago militants. Poli's critical decision to stand by this "withdrawal of enthusiasm" earned him much credit with feisty controllers across the country, although some moderates in PATCO leadership circles resented Poli's failure to censure and punish "anarchy" in the ranks.

As had been the case only 8 years earlier, the O'Hare controllers in 1980 concluded that their work load was going seriously under-rewarded. On July 30, the PATCO local wrote and asked the FAA both to provide a tax-free bonus of $7,500 for every O'Hare controller and to upgrade the Tower to a Level 5 facility (all other towers were categorized 1 to 4 based on the quantity and complexity of traffic handled). On being told their demands were non-negotiable, and were viewed by the FAA as a "threat of an illegal job action," the O'Hare controllers retaliated by working "by the rules" between August 6 and 15: During those days, more than 600 flights experienced delays of 30 minutes or more, and traffic was bollixed and slowed from coast to coast.

A temporary restraining order was awarded the FAA on August 18, and the O'Hare controllers picked up the pace—without having won a thing, and worried now about FAA punishment. To their surprise and relief, however, PATCO's lawyers earned a rare courtroom victory on December 15, 1980, when they convinced a district trial court to dismiss the FAA's case.

PATCO had argued that the recent enactment of the Civil Service Reform Act—a measure vigorously opposed by PATCO—had the effect of depriving all such district courts of jurisdiction in these matters. The Court advised the FAA to seek relief by applying to the new Federal Labor Relations Authority for an FLRA complaint, and a decision thereafter from the FLRA's general counsel. With this fresh interpretation of applicable legislation the district court went on to dismiss the FAA request for a permanent court order—and PATCO cheered. (Poli enjoyed reminding critics forever after that his union had never been found guilty of conducting the Chicago slowdown.)[12]

What had been feared at first as likely to produce another major legal setback had unexpectedly and dramatically turned into a major legal victory, or so it seemed to PATCO pro-strike activists who had dreaded a federal court crackdown on the O'Hare jump-the-gun militants. It looked now, however, that a way out from under the dreaded 1970 antistrike injunction of a federal court might have finally been found. And while the FLRA also forbade strikes by federal employees, the FLRA appeared far more available to political pressure than did the increasingly testy federal court system.

Although the O'Hare controllers had won nothing, the 1980 pro-PATCO court ruling—later reversed in 1981, and never concurred in by any other district or appellate courts—gave PATCO morale a momentary boost.

"Counting the House."   Determining just what the members wanted, how much they wanted it, and what they were willing to do to achieve their goals

was another major 1980 project, and one in which the principal author of this book played a part.

Hired by Jack Maher to help PATCO conduct a series of five surveys of rank and file views, I wrote five lengthy reports on the survey findings for the union. I also flew to the 1980 Chicago board meeting to brief the field reps on early survey findings—a task made all the more difficult at that time by the Leyden-Poli showdown. Months afterwards I flew to Boston to brief key PATCO leaders on later survey findings. Naturally, I also went often to PATCO headquarters to help discuss what members seemed to want Poli and others to understand.

While the five reports encompassed over 125 pages and scores of data-rich, computer-driven tables, only five major findings need be cited here to help make the point that PATCO's leadership was in close and informed touch with its 14,500 members:

1. Rank order preferences in contract issues remained unchanged from the first survey in 1979 through the last in 1981: PATCO members were concerned first, about winning an acceptable *pay increase*; second, winning a *shorter work week*; and third, winning improvements in their *early retirement plan*. Close behind was a desire to win independence from the Civil Service system, and thereby the right to strike.

2. As many as 84 percent of 11,400 respondents (or 78 percent of PATCO's membership) indicated their *willingness to back a PATCO strike* (5 months before the August 1981 walkout).

3. *Prostrike members* on the average were younger, felt they had heard the issues discussed, were firm in their point of view, and felt strongly about placing the highest priority in contract negotiations on winning salary gains.

PATCO leaders were cheered by this affirmation of the assertive stance the union was taking, a stance that earned increasing endorsement from each succeeding survey (the five were taken at roughly 3-month intervals).

To be sure, the findings over the 18-month study period (July 1979 March 1981) were not without an antistrike component:

4. Between 25 percent and 31 percent of the respondents remained *uncertain* about whether or not they would support a properly sanctioned strike.

5. PATCO members with many years of FAA service and union membership were *far less supportive* of the strike option than were other dues-payers.

Overall, however, as the percent of respondents increased over the 18-month study period (from 51 percent in 1979 up to 78 percent in March 1981), PATCO leaders gained increasing confidence in their grasp of rank and file sentiment, and welcomed the militant views of at least the younger plurality of their membership.

Going First to Congress.   Ever since winning passage in 1972 of its Second Career Program Bill, the union had dreamed of pulling off a comparable coup, and 1981 appeared a strategic time to press the matter. Since the FAA could only provide controllers with contract gains that Congress had approved in special legislation, PATCO determined to put the cart before the horse this time, and win congressional passage of PATCO's contract demands (in the form of a new bill) even while negotiations were still proceeding with the FAA. In this way, or so PATCO reasoned, its supporters in Congress would send a compelling message to otherwise intransigent FAA negotiators: "Do *right* by PATCO, even as *we* have, in our new pro-PATCO legislation!"

On February 3 Congressman William Clay (D-Mo.), a fiery orator who had electrified the 1980 PATCO convention with his "politics of survival" speech, introduced a bill drafted by PATCO, the "Air Traffic Controllers Act of 1981" (H.R. 1576). Under its provisions PATCO members would have won

a higher wage scale than the one that applied to government workers generally;

a cost-of-living provision;

compensation for "unusual or strenuous hours or work";

reduction of 40 hours to a 32-hour level "assuring optimum performance, efficiency, and safety";

a retirement plan that "objectively recognizes the unusual occupational hazards of such employment";

a substantial increase in the number of controllers; and

the clarification of FAA obligations in the bargaining process.[13]

PATCO lobbied strenuously thereafter on behalf of its handiwork. On April 1, for example, over 730 members and spouses visited 350 Senators and Representatives to urge support (nine new cosponsors signed on before the day ended).

Nevertheless, the ill-fated bill (and its Senate counterpart, S. 808) caused unexpected problems for PATCO from the start. When the Congressional Budget Office concluded that the Clay bill would cost $13,000,000,000 over a

5-year period, the media hit PATCO hard with this astronomic figure; and Poli was put on the defensive even before the FAA-PATCO negotiations had actually begun. Later amendments that PATCO had Rep. Clay introduce significantly modified the bill's "outlandish demands," and included a ban against strikes by controllers. But by that time substantial PR damage had been done, and few friends of PATCO were paying attention any longer to a controversial bill with zero prospect of passage, one which only showed up the union's lack of congressional support.

"Gentlemen, Come Out Fighting!"   Negotiations started in mid-February, and Poli opened the bargaining by presenting a prioritized list of 96 demands. It was made deliberately long to drive home the point that there was much that frustrated and angered his members, and much that had to be corrected. The FAA, in turn, dismissed the union's "wish list" as excessive, and a slow process got stiffly underway.

Over the $2\frac{1}{2}$ months of fruitless bargaining that followed, Poli made it clear that three of PATCO's 96 demands were the *major* concerns of his 14,500 members (as revealed privately to him by questionnaires completed by those controllers):

1) *Salary Gains*—Poli asked for a $10,000 across-the-board annual increase for all controllers, along with a twice-a-year cost-of-living increase that would be $1\frac{1}{2}$ times the rate of inflation and a new maximum of $73,420, up from $49,229.

   The FAA countered with an offer of a $4,000 increase (though $1,800 of this amount was a raise being given to all federal employees in 1981); PATCO considered the $2,200 offer (exclusively for controllers) completely inadequate.

2) *Reduced Work Hours.* Poli asked for a reduction in the 5-day, 40-hour week to a 4-day, 32-hour schedule. The union cited the length of work week asked of controllers elsewhere in support of this demand: Switzerland, 38; Australia, 35; Canada, 34; West Germany, 33; France, 32; and Eurocontrol, 29.

   The FAA countered that concessions here would open the floodgate for similar demands from other federal workers, and this would threaten a budget-busting trend when the new President wanted general spending cuts.

3) *Retirement Aid.* Poli asked for the liberalization of provisions for retirement, claiming that his members gave more, and burned out sooner than any other federal employees.

   Under the old contract a controller could retire with

half pay at age fifty if he had worked for 20 years, and at
any age if he had served 25 years. PATCO wanted retirement permitted after 20 years at 75 percent of base salary.

The FAA countered that *any* liberalization would violate the White House desire to hold the line against future
government expenses.

PATCO also asked that the FAA join it in urging Congress to pass the Clay
bill ("We want the FAA to acknowledge that air traffic control is a difficult job
and to support the legislation").[14]

While the media seized on the dollar issues (and the $10,000 figure, a
legitimate opening gambit in the "poker game" of negotiations, haunted
PATCO ever after), the union also promoted nonmonetary issues, or so-
called social contract demands that meant a lot to its membership, such as:

> *Voluntary Reassignment*: When a controller felt he or she
> could no longer do their best at a high-density facility,
> they should have a right to reassignment to a less
> stressful facility. And this pro-safety move should come
> at no cost to their earnings or career prospects.

> *Equipment Utilization Input*: When the FAA was considering
> changes in the hardware, software, or character of the
> equipment controllers relied on, the FAA should wel-
> come the informed input of the professionals who
> knew the most about it, the nation's air traffic control-
> lers.

> *PATCO Office Space*: When the FAA was reallocating scarce
> space in its facilities, it should respect the right of the
> union to an office conducive to the conduct of PATCO/
> FAA business. (PATCO worried that it could now be
> evicted or bounced around at the whim of the local fa-
> cility chief.)

These, and related nonmonetary matters, spoke as directly as did better-
publicized "megabuck" demands to the central question of *respect*. The refusal
of FAA negotiators to make concessions here came to grate more on some
PATCO leaders than even the stalemate over headline-grabbing financial
items.

Fish, or Cut Bait.   PATCO members began to lose patience when the contract expired on March 15, and negotiations had not borne fruit. Led by the
"choirboys," a large number of controllers manned "informational" picket

lines in 20 cities on March 15 and 16. Their carefully-drafted placards urged air travellers to recognize that controllers were working under the terms of an expired contract, one that must earn significant improvements in a new ratified version, soon.

To help contain short-fuse emotions in the ranks PATCO reminded everyone that the negotiation process was

> . . . complex, time-consuming, and restrictive . . . We were fully aware of our vulnerability to delaying tactics and false promises from government officials. Such concerns were among the ingredients comprising our plans. However, two other significant elements were factored into our formula for success: PATIENCE and ORGANIZATIONAL DISCIPLINE . . . Now, we—the entire PATCO membership—must continue to practice these attributes. Otherwise, we fail; and failure has no role in PATCO's plan.[15]

Despite such counsel, the word from the field—as anxiously conveyed to headquarters by facility reps, regional vice presidents, and the tireless "choirboys"—seemed to be "Produce results—and soon—or there's no saying what we'll do!" Sensitive throughout to the orchestration of militancy, Poli took the occasion of PATCO's 1981 convention in May (in New Orleans) to announce a June 22 strike deadline . . . and the attendees gave him a 10-minute standing ovation.

Down to the Wire!   Just before the June 22 deadline, the Reagan Administration made two moves that heartened Poli, and stirred PATCO hopes that it really had secured a friend in the Oval Office. FAA Administrator J. Lynn Helms, who had stayed away from the negotiations, was replaced by Drew Lewis, his boss as Secretary of Transportation. Lewis and Poli hit it off very well, and the two resolved in hours items unsettled over previous weeks of bitter sessions with FAA representatives.

Lewis offered a final FAA package of $40,000,000 in improvements, complete with a 10 percent pay hike for controllers who also acted as instructors (or, $4,200); an increase in the pay differential for night work to 15 percent (from the present 10 percent); and a guaranteed 30-minute lunch period (to replace the option FAA supervisors had of requiring that lunch be eaten at one's scope if traffic was heavy), all stretched out over a 3-year period.

Poli insisted the first version of the package did not go far enough, and in bargaining that lasted until 5 a.m. on June 22, just 3 hours before the strike deadline, he won two additional gains. Controllers would be paid a "responsibility differential" of time-and-a-half pay after 36 hours (though the work week would remain at 40 hours); and medically disqualified controllers eligible for the Second Career Program would gain extra retraining benefits (if and when Congress ever re-funded the defunct program).

Sweetened in this way, the final offer of the FAA was characterized as a "generous offer" by a White House spokesman, a "more than reasonable offer" by a strike-leery *New York Times*,[16] and by Poli as "the best possible deal I could get . . . with the present economic conditions it is a good package for us."[17] Poli asked Leyden to help him sell the offer in the New York region, and began to campaign on behalf of his deal with Lewis.

"Protect Me from My Friends."   Shortly before Poli gave PATCO's tentative approval at 5 a.m., the union's membership declined at 4 a.m. to give its president a strike vote. This embarrassing refusal left Poli with no choice but to go along with the FAA's last proposal. In keeping with hesitation stirred by any mention of an illegal job action, a very small minority among the rank and file voted against striking and checkmated the desire of PATCO militants to show the world the union was ready to "go the distance."

PATCO's strike plan provided that 80 percent of the controller work force, and 93 percent of the union's membership, had to authorize a strike before the Executive Board could call one (a safeguard insisted on by members still angry over "high-handed" and costly Board acts in the 1970s). The prostrike element *almost* rallied enough votes to give Poli the green light he needed to force additional concessions from Lewis. But they fell short by barely 5 percent, denying the PATCO president the symbolic tool every top union negotiator regards as indispensable. Lewis was left gloating over his advantage (PATCO stalwarts believe he learned of the vote defeat from a tap on the union's phones, and, between 4 and 5 a.m., took off the negotiating table certain concessions he had earlier offered, and declined to improve the "final offer," even though he might have).

Half a Loaf or None?   Although most knowledgeable parties agreed the FAA's last offer was very far from PATCO's "wish list," its few supporters emphasized four points:

> PATCO had achieved a milestone by actually getting the FAA to negotiate about wages, something that it had previously refused to do.
>
> PATCO had set a precedent here that could eventually help separate controllers from the civil service system, long a goal of those who felt stifled by system wage ceilings.
>
> PATCO had earned funds for retraining, and other desirable gains high on the 96-item "wish list," *albeit not among the "top 5."*
>
> PATCO had earned an immediate pledge from Congressman Ford and others to win speedy congressional pas-

> sage of the necessary enabling legislation, and these legislators were confident their colleagues would approve the June 22 Poli-Lewis terms.

Hailing the accord as significant and substantial, its few PATCO supporters (with Leyden in the lead) noted finally that both Poli's and PATCO's credibility were at stake, and warned that the union would no longer be taken seriously if Poli was unable to make good on his June 22 concurrence.

Opponents of the June 22 contract were quick to absolve Poli of blame, and he himself kept insisting the eleventh-hour failure of the strike authorization vote had left him no choice but to agree to it. Not surprisingly, therefore, the Board was uncertain how to recommend the members vote in the union's mail ballot on the agreement.

At a stormy meeting on July 2 in Chicago, the Board initially split over the wisest course to take at this juncture, all recognizing they might be voting a strike into PATCO's future. Given the revealing failure of members to authorize a strike on June 22, a few board members thought it best to accept the Poli-Lewis terms. In this way the union could focus its energy on building a stronger and more united membership, one more responsive to any future call for a strike authorization.

The more numerous opposition insisted the level of militancy would never be higher, and the June 22 vote had failed by an insignificant and easily rectified amount. They warned that acceptance of the insulting FAA offer would demoralize PATCO's stalwarts, hold the union up for ridicule both within and outside the air control system, and invite harsh anti-PATCO moves by gloating FAA supervisors. Still a third bloc argued that the Poli-Lewis $3\frac{1}{2}$ year contract failed to address PATCO's second and third top-ranked demands, and that without reduced work hours and a more liberal retirement plan the union could not face the membership—regardless of the risk of forcing a strike. When the discussion closed, the PATCO board voted to recommend a "no" vote, and reassured one another Poli could wring still more concessions from an affable Drew Lewis, who, after all, took his cues from PATCO's sympathetic friend in the Oval Office.

Shortly thereafter Poli called a July meeting of selected "choirboys" to review the June 22 terms. Much like the board, they also flatly rejected the FAA offer, and dispersed to campaign against it back at their facilities. To no one's great surprise, 95 percent of an increasingly combative rank and file voted by July 30 to reject the terms of the Poli-Lewis agreement.

Try, Try, Again!   While PATCO was wrestling with its response, Transportation Secretary Drew Lewis was emphatic in warning that the FAA would make no further concessions. After the rejection vote by 20-to-1, Lewis petulantly withdrew from the reopened negotiations, and the man PATCO had gotten nowhere with the first time around, the sorely disliked FAA Administrator, J. Lynn Helms, was returned to head the FAA negotiations team.

As if this were not bad enough, evidence grew of increasing displeasure with PATCO's persistent talk of a possible strike. Fifty-five senators distributed a letter on July 30 accusing the controllers of trying to hold the public "hostage" with threats of an illegal strike. The senators urged President Reagan to use "the full force of the law to protect the public interest" in the event of a PATCO walkout, and it warned the union a strike would be viewed by Congress with "extreme disfavor."[18]

The *Washington Post* joined the *New York Times* and other influential organs of opinion in urging PATCO to focus on a redistribution of the $40 million offered by Lewis, and to "give up its more ambitious ideas." The *Post* warned that Congress would oppose any further concession to the controllers, regardless of the position Reagan took on such a development: "In a year of belt-tightening throughout government, it is a little difficult to make a sound case for even the pay increases the controllers have already been offered."[19]

Impatient with labor-management dramas that went beyond one act, and decidedly unsympathetic to PATCO's insistence that controllers deserved more, a number of concerned outsiders increased pressure on both the union and the FAA to rapidly resolve the contract impasse, or, face their wrath.

Eager to appear responsive to this advice, PATCO made much of its decision to scale down its bargaining demands by $285 million below its initial February proposal (the July pricetag was $490 million, down from $775 million—as against an FAA "firm" offer, however, of only $40 million). In July, PATCO also had Rep. Clay introduce a substantially scaled down version of his Air Traffic Controllers Bill, designed this time to meet unexpectedly sharp criticism encountered from the Reagan administration. In place of a top salary for controllers of $79,000, the new draft called only for $59,000 (as against the current $50,000). The new draft further stipulated that controllers could not legally strike: a far cry from PATCO's original hopes for this bold (and throughly bottlenecked) legislation.[20]

Striking Out on Stress.   Along with its problems on nearly every other front, PATCO also had to mitigate what history may judge its single greatest pre-strike loss—its inability to make an effective case for the alleviation of excessive job-related stress. No single issue set PATCO's contract demands apart from those of other unions as did this. No other issue was as vital to PATCO's success.

Ever since its 1968 founding the union had sought to convince the public, the media, and policymakers of two critical contentions. Far too few workers were receiving direct help alleviating the causes or symptoms of unnecessary negative stress at work. The air traffic controller, however, had a union-designed set of reform recommendations ranging from shorter hours to increased say-so in the choice of workplace hardware, and these reforms promised significant relief from burnout components. But until PATCO's stress-relief reforms won implementation, the FAA would exacerbate ATC stress with its indifference to acute staff shortages, dangerously out-of-date equipment, poor training methods, limited opportunities for transfer or retraining, and harsh authoritarian leadership (no input into decision making; lack of sensitive response; nonacceptance of PATCO; etc.).

Emphasized at every opportunity by the union, this thesis argued "Our stress is unique! Toxic! Preventable! And caused by the FAA *system*, rather than by our jobs per se!" PATCO's entire case for deserving benefits given no other federal employees hinged on winning agreement with this stress-relief thesis. Here the union could not afford to fail, and here it did.

Pundits in the media, critics on the Hill, and FAA spokesmen urged rejection of PATCO's stress-relief thesis for four telling reasons:

1. The most comprehensive study of the occupation, the Rose Study in 1978, found no direct link of hypertension to the job. Moreover, controllers who were required to pass yearly physical exams were found to be generally healthier than same-age people. Medical proof of the job's hazards remained "conspicuously elusive."[21]

2. PATCO's oft-repeated point that 89 percent of its members never survived until normal retirement was labelled a sham: Widespread abuse of the medical leave program that encouraged disability claims had led Congress to clamp down, and the FAA boasted that fewer than 25 controllers were retiring each year with a stress-related disability.[22]

3. If the job was the killer that PATCO claimed, how could it explain the love its members professed for it? And, the long waiting list of applicants to the FAA's academy for controllers?

4. If stress was unique to the controllers' job, then why, as satirist Mike Royko asked, did "almost as many people head for bars at 5 p.m. each workday as get on commuter trains or expressways. . . . A lot of people would like to give the striking controllers a pat on the back. But their own hands are shaking too much."[23]

Since PATCO was unable to convince outsiders it was not the task, as much as it was the autocratic rule of the FAA that produced murderous stress, the average American was inclined to find PATCO's demands not only unreasonable, but even offensive.

The nod went instead to the FAA, which succeeded in either clouding the matter enough to defuse PATCO's case for stress relief, or convinced outsiders that workplace reactions to stress were simply a matter of individual coping styles—a personal reaction. As such, stressors did not merit labor contract concessions, and certainly did not call for organizational changes or reforms in the context of the job—a beguiling rebuttal that sent stress levels soaring among frustrated PATCO activists.

Counting on the Cavalry.   Over and over again, anxious heads at PATCO headquarters turned in the direction of the White House, and speculation focused on Reagan's reliability. As late as April of 1981 certain PATCO officials had met with top White House staff members, and confidence still held high that Reagan would come through. Since PATCO had been one of only three major unions to endorse the G.O.P. candidate, Poli would probably have agreed with the government official who bluntly explained to *Business Week*, "The crux of this thing is what the Administration is going to do in light of the endorsement."[24]

Two labor relations factors soon complicated the picture, however, both to PATCO's dismay. The White House fended off a March 1981 strike threat by the Airline Pilots' Union, and key people around Reagan were quick to conclude that this sort of antistrike success could and should be repeated. (When the pilots threatened to shut the system down, the President forced them to accept his appointment of a study commission. After the commission recommended against the union's position, the union acquiesced and successfully defused the issue among its well disciplined members.) The White House grew increasingly concerned about negotiations scheduled after PATCO's in 1981 with the union of two hundred thousand postal workers, and even later, with many other federal employees. A determination grew to draw the line with the 14,500-member controllers union and send a clear message on behalf of "restraint!" to all the others.

White House aides took considerable satisfaction in their early success with the Pilots' Union (many of whose leaders were G.O.P. backers), and linked this to their desire to hold the lid on federal contract gains. Reagan spokesmen promised to take an especially hard line concerning *all* ensuing federal negotiations, though PATCO seemed to believe this warning somehow did not apply to it.

The Clock Runs Out.   When the last round of talks began on July 31 Drew Lewis's mix of candor and evasiveness convinced the PATCO team that the FAA intended only to tough it out; *nothing* was likely to be achieved! Accordingly, Poli announced a strike would occur at 7 a.m., Monday, August 3, only 67 hours away, unless the negotiations soon took a far more positive turn.

All that stood between PATCO and the 80 percent vote needed for a strike authorization was a three-tier voting scheme carefully written into the 1981 Strike Plan by union co-founder Jack Maher. When the FAM slowdown failed in 1980, it was agreed that the new 1981 Strike Plan would bar any job action that did not have adequate support from key locals, or those whose co-operation was indispensable if PATCO was to pressure the FAA into a desirable settlement. Maher divided the FAA's 400 towers and 20 centers into three categories, and assigned different weights to each, a balloting device that assured that PATCO's 80 percent authorization could only be reached if the key locals led the parade.

To this day controversy persists over whether the original three-tier plan was finally used, altered, or scrapped to assure an affirmative tally. Poli critics believe certain major locals fell so far short of the 80 percent "yes" vote that their numbers should have kept the national tally below 80 percent, thereby denying Poli the strike authorization he had failed to get once before on June 22. Poli backers maintain in rebuttal that validation agents, drawn from the ranks of the "choirboys," double-checked all the vote counts at the local level. All that is certain is that when Poli and Lewis met for the last round of negotiations on the night of August 2, both men knew that PATCO believed it *had* gotten the numbers, even if only by an incredible razor-thin margin of 80.5 percent.

But neither Poli's new power to make good on the union's threat to strike, nor the word Lewis shared of the firings promised by anti-PATCO hard-liners among White House aides, could alter the foregone conclusion of the hapless late-hour sessions. After a final flurry of charges and counter-charges, with neither side willing to budge, the strike that had been threatening for over a decade finally hit. This was the "definitive strike" *both* sides had been explicitly gearing up for since the 1978 overseas FAM fiasco, and *sotto voce* welcome was audible from both sides of the "Let's get on with it!" trench lines.*

---

*See the appendix interview with Jack Maher, PATCO co-founder.

Part III

ON "BRINGING TWO TOGETHER": THE 1981 STRIKE

I have consistently found that the FAA has either dragged its feet or ignored recommendations from various responsible bodies on how to improve the system . . . It's no wonder you find them dragging their feet on the matter of negotiating responsibly with the members of PATCO.

Congressman Buddy Roemer, *Hearings*, June 1981.

. . . every air traffic controller in ths country knows of the possibility of their being jailed . . . But with the state of the FAA right now, the conditions that exist, the possibility of it getting much worse, they don't have an alternative. They must take a stand at this particular time.

Robert E. Poli, *Hearings*, June 19, 1981, p. 86.

. . . we're committed to looking back for only one reason: to be reminded of what not *to do. If we don't, we'll just continue to cause ourselves even more pain. . .*

Editorial, *USATCO Newsletter*, November 1983.

Chapter 6

WHY WE HAD TO STRIKE*

Excerpts from the O'Keefe Survey (1984):

I feel that the strike was not only necessary, but long overdue. The government conspired to punish us and left all *the reasons for the strike not only unanswered, but reinforced.*

. . . the strike, our dismissal, and no reinstatement was the best thing that could have happened to me personally. I know a lot of brothers don't have that attitude and are still bitter about the events. But I still believe the strike was right, and if the vote were held again tonight, I would again vote "yes!"

Strike was inevitable, the FAA wanted it to happen whether we did or not, There were mistakes on our part, but weighing the principles alone, I would do it again tomorrow, and my family backs me.

I am not sure that the word "strike" is appropriate. I believe this was the only reasonable and rational action that a group of conscientious concerned professionals could take to secure their own rights, as well as the rights and safety of others.

Strike was necessary, as all other efforts to resolve problems were not taken seriously.

---

*by David Skocik

Should have been averted, but the FAA gave us no choice. I feel the FAA wanted the strike to happen, for obvious reasons.

It was probably the best thing that ever happened to me. Reagan, the FAA, and the rest still stink!

Given the same set of circumstances at any given time, I would do it again. There is no doubt history will prove PATCO was right in their actions. Maybe legally wrong, but surely morally right.

July 1981 was a time of optimism and rhetoric. As at any time of heightened emotions, there was also denial of another feeling—fear.

Controllers and management alike knew a confrontation was just around the corner, but the forces impelling it were inexorable. The air was charged not just with the usual job tension, but with an animosity on both sides that seemed to feed on itself. PATCO members wanted to be good employees and good union members. But both goals seemed increasingly to conflict. Not that people weren't performing their jobs properly—professional pride took care of that—but it was becoming difficult to function without stepping over the battle lines which had been drawn.

Contrary to the Administration's line, union members did not create animosity among controllers; the vast majority of controllers were already PATCO members. The union was, however, more than happy to point out inequities that had existed all along which management had no intention of changing. It had become easier to take a stand and get membership support against poor equipment and practices such as forced overtime and intentional contract violations.

Management's position was simple: good controllers were not rebellious. They did what they were told and questioned later (when they could be ignored at leisure). If "moving traffic" called for ignoring terms of the contract, like spending more than 2 hours on a single heavy-traffic position or using unreliable equipment, so be it. Such things were safety considerations the union had worked years to achieve and were considered sacrosanct. Safety was the first consideration, but protection ranked a close second. If controllers were going to be held totally accountable for their errors, then they wanted some say in their working conditions.

The FAA, however, was not as concerned with the long-term picture as with the day-to-day numbers game. As long as traffic moved, things went relatively well in the facilities. Any issue which threatened to slow traffic, however, became of paramount importance. The problem was that rather than resolving the issue, it seemed that management's position was to react against those who brought it up. (It reminds me of the 1937 Soviet census board who, in the midst of Stalin's Great Purge, reported a population deficit of some 23 million. For their trouble, they were accused of trying to discredit the revolution and were shot.)

Because traffic delays were generally perceived by the FAA as reflecting discreditably upon it, the logic followed was that they were somehow caused by the union. And nowhere was the conflict more evident than at the high density facilities like New York.

PATCO had to be one of the most democratic unions ever founded. Its sole existence was to reflect the unified concerns of controllers. Its members saw it not as a bureaucracy, but as an organization truly made up of the sum of its parts. With few exceptions, the issues that concerned the work force in any one facility were of equal concern in all facilities.

That is the reason that when a local of the union was challenged through, for instance, an intentional violation of the contract, the membership perceived it as a challenge to all locals. The responsibility for making the system work with unreliable equipment (if the computer fails only once each day when you've got maybe 10 aircraft, that's unreliable) and unresponsive, yet never responsible management, seemed to be more unfairly balanced every day.

It should be noted here that this is the misleading side of technology. No matter how sophisticated computer systems become, they instantly die when electricity, their life force, is cut off. I strongly suspect that designers of traffic flow capacity (actually requirements) have never taken that key point into account or been in the position of having to "eat" a dozen airplanes when the almighty computer fails.

Immunity Conflict. It would be hard to document a stronger example of barely suppressed rage in a "captive" work force than when then FAA Administrator, Langhorne Bond, refused to honor the Immunity Provision of the 1978 3-year FAA/PATCO contract. Pilots and controllers are human and make mistakes. In an industry in which even minor errors can take a heavy toll, the only things worse than committing a foolish mistake is repeating it. That is why in the early 1970s a unique three-way gentlemen's agreement among controllers, pilots, and the FAA was consummated.

It was a simple yet novel idea. Research had shown that many of the operational errors committed by pilots and controllers were of a simple but repetitive nature. In other words, certain common mistakes were being repeated over and over, but by different people each time. The quandary was how to encourage people to exchange information on, and thereby learn from, each other's mistakes without fear of ridicule or retribution. The innovative solution was to set up an outside, disinterested party which could act as a buffer between the FAA and system users.

Because such an agency could guarantee anonymity to those filing reports, it would also serve as a screening device against possible disciplinary action from the FAA. The agency chosen was NASA, the National Aeronautics and Space Administration. It would set up a special committee which would carefully analyze reports from around the country and look for trends, or common mistakes, which could lead to accidents. Regularly published reports would then be circulated throughout the aviation industry, making system users aware of common pitfalls.

The plan went one step further. It guaranteed the right to report one's own error; so long as a controller or pilot reported an incident within 72 hours, he was immune from disciplinary action. The reporting process was simplified to a form requesting all the particulars. The portion with the return address of the filer was detachable and used only to stamp a control number on and mail back. Once the receipt was returned, no other identification remained to tie an incident to a pilot or controller. In fact, the only way the FAA could find out that anything at all had occurred was if one of the parties filed a formal incident report.

For instance, if a pilot decided to file an official report with the FAA, all the controller had to do was produce for the review board the little nameless receipt bearing a control number assigned by NASA. Should a board be called, one could bank on the fact that he would be asked to show his receipt. The only potential weakness in the program was that constant violators could theoretically use the program to shield themselves.

That is exactly the reasoning Mr. Bond claimed when he arbitrarily terminated the program in 1979. Arguments against his action were twofold: (1) Anyone making enough mistakes to need a shield that big wasn't likely to be around long in such a critical field; (2) It was an outrageous violation of a hard-won contract provision. It was as if Bond purposely set out to further erode already poor employee relations. Bond's stated intention was to reduce the ever-increasing number of reported incidents. Amazingly, pilots and controllers were asked to continue reporting their mistakes despite the fact they would be at the mercy of the FAA, which would make the determination of any disciplinary action. In one sense, the plan worked. Incidents continued, but they weren't reported as often. Controllers and pilots just kept their fingers crossed that neither would write the other up.

It should be noted that this was at a time when the FAA was asking its controllers to handle increasing traffic loads with staffing already less than met the agency's own standards. Of course, that was easy enough to remedy. When the union pointed out that staffing was stagnant while the number of aircraft operations was growing steadily (along with the number of managers), the FAA simply revised its facility staffing standards to legitimize the situation. The problem was that when it came to an FAA-supervised review board when something went wrong, somehow the system was always absolved, while the controller bit the bullet.

On the other hand, if the union asked its members to protect themselves by abiding by the FAA's rules, it was accused of slowdown tactics and vilified in the press as irresponsible. The term "slowdown" is well known to the public and has negative connotations for almost everyone. But it is a truly inappropriate term in relation to air traffic control because separation standards are based on safety, not convenience. Accidents are always the result of an absence of safety rather than convenience. The FAA mission, according to the Aviation Act of 1958, is the safe, orderly, and expeditious flow of air traffic—in that order.

Personality Conflict.   As study after taxpayer-funded study has revealed, one does not deal with self-motivated, highly competent people through threats—not, at least, if one is truly interested in efficiency. But this, FAA managers, by and large, never learned, or refused to believe. Various studies, such as the Corson Committee report in 1970, placed much of the blame for poor employee relations on the employer's autocratic management style, which demanded unquestioned obedience.

Perhaps one thing which most people on the outside never understood about the makeup of air traffic controllers was that they were essentially conservative people who did not favor rapid or arbitrary changes in the workplace. That might come as a shock to the average person introduced to the controller by the Reagan administration as a radical seeking to bring the nation to its knees.

On the contrary, the majority of the PATCO controllers were Vietnam-era veterans who had gained their experience in the armed forces. Ironically, the very people who would later be portrayed as disloyal were in many cases those who had obediently gone to Vietnam while others scoffed and burned their draft cards. Stranger still, some of those who had scorned the government's authority to endanger them were in a position of power over the veteran. Then Budget Director, David Stockman, who had been a conscientious objector, recommended cutting funding for veteran counseling centers (as a budget-trimming measure).

Most controllers had just transferred directly from the military into the FAA. In retrospect, it would seem that agency planners could not have acquired a more malleable work force if this had been their criterion. Much of the military-oriented terminology and mind-set also followed the new employee. One "took leave," rather than vacation; was "AWOL" if he didn't return on time; was sent to "chow"; went "to the head"; and if difficult, was given a "direct order" to straighten up or ship out. There never was any sense of belonging to an organization that constantly let one know he was expendable.

Prior to the origin of their union in 1968, and even for some time afterward, controllers were expected to wear white shirts, ties, and close-cropped hair—this at time when society saw nothing wrong with protesting in the streets. From a management standpoint, the exploitation of previous behavioral training provided tremendous leverage. Of course, such tactics were inevitably perceived more as an attempt at crowd control than honest employee relations. Highly paid psychologists predicted time and again that such attitudes must change or rebellion ensue. Their reports were discredited and shelved.

Supervisory Conflict.   Despite the gains that had been made over the years, by mid-May 1981, conditions between management and labor had deteriorated to perhaps an all-time low. Day-to-day contact with first line supervisors remained stable; they were former controllers all, and for the most part identified with the problems of the working controller. Most had been members of the union prior to their acceptance of a management position; some had been part of the 1968–1970 slowdowns and sick-outs which brought the union before the public eye. Those were dangerous days; the FAA considered the fledgling union to be nothing more than a meddling bunch of troublemakers who needed to be taught a lesson.

Those heady days and the worthwhile changes they wrought were a mutual heritage to the average controller and first line supervisor. Many of the lower level supervisors openly supported PATCO's goals. Some still had the fire; each saw it as a safe route to improve his own lot. After all, what labor got, management got too. Of those who sympathized with the union, many had battle scars from 1968 job actions. As union founders, they had been suspended and seen some of their cohorts fired for daring to stand up the FAA. Those types of supervisors got the support they deserved; they also gave it. They realized that when things went wrong and traffic slowed, it wasn't likely that the union was being uncooperative. It was because equipment and human beings have limits.

Many first line sups would put a headset on and work traffic with their crews. But the assistant chiefs, people acting as direct liaisons to the facility chief, sometimes made life miserable for everyone. In the case of the New York Common IFR Room, three assistant chiefs, each representing a sector (Newark, LaGuardia, JFK), sat at a separate console at one end of the facility.

From there each could selectively monitor all communications in his sector, both inter- and intrafacility, including conversations with pilots. They also had the authority to write up controllers for anything from nonstandard phraseology to rule breaking. This Orwellian option of selectively and discreetly listening in was exercised depending upon who was at the desk and who was working a given position. Union activists were generally monitored more closely than their colleagues. That made it easy to selectively log mistakes and build a case for future leverage.

Compensation Conflict.   A misconception which most nongovernment workers hold is that civil service employees have it *made*. They are imagined to have paid health plans, excellent working conditions, and outstanding retirement benefits. *Some* government jobs *are* superior to those available in the private sector. However, most jobs cited as a basis for comparison are not meant to be career-long propositions. The fact of the matter is that in this age of "streamlined" government, workers can take nothing for granted.

Most workers pay for their own health insurance and must fight for benefits and working conditions like anyone else. Nothing is exempt any longer to the budgetary knife, especially during election years. And because most civil servants are barred by law from striking, administrators are often viewed as under little pressure to negotiate in good faith. Such feelings of helplessness can lead to alienation and frustration with a system seen as unfair.

The originally agreed-upon no-strike clause might have been acceptable in light of so-called "guaranteed" benefits accrued from government service. But as rules concerning rights and benefits are altered, (sometimes unilaterally), so too is the original compact in the employee's mind. The loyalty once felt might be replaced by anger and feelings of betrayal by an employer who thinks nothing of changing the game rules to his benefit.

Work Conditions Conflict.   U.S. controllers, even at 40 hours (to say nothing of the required 48-hour work week in some facilities), had the longest controller work week in the world. It was based on safety, pure and simple. In the larger facilities, controllers who refused to work a 6-day week were threatened with disciplinary action.

The long work week was productive for the FAA in the short run, but took a heavy toll in careers. Even more absurdly, because the income of federal employees was capped to the salaries of Congress, senior controllers who earned more than a congressman's base pay (because of 6-day weeks, differential, and overtime) couldn't be paid for the overage (beyond $50,000 reportedly). In other words, some were being ordered to report for work even though they couldn't be compensated for their services. (The average pay for controllers, it should be noted, was $31,000 in 1981.)

PATCO's mistake was in allowing the government to focus on economic demands, and to characterize PATCO as greedy in a time of economic retrenchment. Despite rhetoric to the contrary, PATCO's primary concern was job survivability. The $10,000 demand killed us in the media. It was always negotiable; anyone who believed it would come to pass was dreaming. Of primary importance to most was a *reduced work week* and an *achievable retirement* —which meant hiring more controllers.

Survival Conflict.   An unusual event took place in early 1981 at a restaurant on Long Island. Controllers from the New York TRACON got together and threw a going-away party for one of their own. A senior controller in the LaGuardia sector had made it all the way to retirement as a working controller. Air traffic retirees are generally former controllers who years earlier had

bid into a desk job or were able to transfer to a small tower somewhere in Po-
dunk. For someone to retire normally from a high-density facility was almost
unheard of. Put another way, the TRACON was a facility with a contingent of
almost 200 controllers, yet no one could recall having attended such a party
before!

Possibly the greatest incentive to band together existed in the busiest facilities. Controllers didn't have to look far to see what was becoming of their
cohorts. The vast majority were being medically retired because of physical
problems related to the job. Of course, the government's position was that
heart attacks, ulcers, hypertension, and alcoholism had nothing to do with the
job, but would probably have occurred anyway. It seemed that the official
public policy was to make people feel as though the government was doing
controllers a favor through medical retirement. It seemed to controllers that
their employer was asking, "Where else can a forty-year-old collect disability?"

The question should have been, "Where else can someone who should be
on his way up, find himself put on the street, like garbage, with 40 percent of
his salary and a damning medical record?" An FAA spokesman in 1980 went
so far as to imply that people prone to the ailments which forced controllers
from the work force tend to be those who seek out "exciting" jobs like air traffic control. This was analogous to the tobacco industry's suggestion that people prone to contract lung cancer tend to smoke. Controllers who had buried
colleagues were enraged by such rationales.*

---

*See the appendix interview with a Columbus activist.

Chapter 7

GOING DOWN FOR THE COUNT

For those of you who think it is revolutionary for government workers to strike, I tell you that this is the only country in the free world that does not allow government workers to strike. I know a strike causes inconveniences. It is supposed to. . . .
   Terry Duffy, USATCO member, *USATCO Newsletter*, July 1983, p. 23.

We do need these people. They're very highly qualified. They perform a difficult task, and we'd like to have them back. And it's not any cakewalk to operate this system the way we're going to have to operate it. It takes a lot of our supervision that could be doing other things that could be constructive for aviation, and they're tied up. It's going to cost us a lot of money to train new people. But nonetheless, the President feels very strongly, and I support him.
   Drew Lewis, August 5, 1981, *The MacNeil-Lehrer Report*, TV transcript, p. 4.

For many years now, you and I have been shushed like children and told there are no simple answers to the complex problems which are beyond our comprehension. Well, the truth is, there are simple answers.
                                        President Ronald Reagan

At 7 a.m. on Monday, August 3, about 85 percent of PATCO's membership, nearly 13,000 controllers, honored the call for a strike. Over 6,000 flights of a daily load of 14,200 were immediately cancelled.[1] With almost 3 years of preparation behind it, the union put its 1981 Strike Plan into crisp and impressive operation. When the White House declared negotiations suspended until PATCO ordered its members back to work, the union maintained that this mandated prior completion of rewarding negotiations. By the week's end this stalemate saw some 11,345 strikers fired, and PATCO's expectations veering sharply off course.

Reagan Roars!   Whatever lingering hopes Poli might have held of help coming from his presidential nominee should have been doused on August 3 when, in quick succession, the President took to television to warn only 4 hours into the strike that any controllers who did not report for work within 48 hours will "have forfeited their jobs and will be terminated." In a Rose Garden appearance he ad libbed a request that reporters emphasize "the possibility of termination, because I believe that there are a great many of those people, and they're fine people, who have been swept up in this and probably have not really considered the result."[2] The President had the Justice Department file federal court actions to impound PATCO's $3,500,000 strike fund, and then had his aides ask the Federal Labor Relations Board to decertify the union as the representative of the nation's air traffic controllers.

To help drive the point home, the White House circulated word that a furious Reagan had wanted a stringent 24-hour, rather than a more lenient 48-hour "window" within which returning (ex-)strikers might rescue their jobs. In the Rose Garden, Reagan praised to reporters an unidentified striker who, according to a radio news report, had resigned from PATCO saying, "How can I ask my kids to obey the law if I don't?"[3] Then, in his Rose Garden text, the President went out of his way to highlight an issue that sorely hurt PATCO. Millions heard him intone an oath Congress required all Federal employees to take:

> I am not participating in any strike against the Government of the United States or any agency thereof, and I will not so participate while an employee of the Government of the United States or any agency thereof.

Reagan's emphasis on the union's lawlessness in repudiating this no-strike oath put PATCO behind the eight ball in the struggle for public sympathy.

The AFL-CIO and the American Civil Liberties Union rushed to protest that the oath was clearly unfair in denying public employees a fundamental civil liberty (the right to strike), but Reagan had drawn blood, and PATCO never effectively recouped from this body blow, one which took a heavy toll on many of its members.

The greatest loss Reagan inflicted was on PATCO's sense of being in control, for he departed dramatically from any script for which PATCO had prepared. Instead of moving to jail Poli and his top leadership, or relying on antistrike injunctions and stiff fines, the White House targeted all 13,000 of PATCO's (initial) supporters. The White House also declared that any controllers fired for striking would never be eligible to work for the government again, and Lewis maintained that the Reagan Administration intended to hold to that unprecedented lifelong blacklisting.

FAA Takes Charge!   Freed by the walkout for the first time in 13 years to do it *their* way, with no interference or hassling from those they considered snivelers and whiners, the FAA jumped into the fray with a spirit resembling exuberance. The agency was confident that within 10 or 12 working days the vanquished strikers would come crawling back, and the dishonored union would be on its way to bankruptcy and possibly decertification.

Not surprisingly, therefore, the FAA response to the PATCO strike took several clever and well-prepared tacks: Helms moved immediately to discredit PATCO's claim of strike effectiveness. Figures released showed a steady improvement in percent of airline flights operating as scheduled: Monday, 65 percent; Tuesday, 67 percent; Wednesday, 72 percent; Thursday, 83 percent; and so on.[4] Helms further contended that 22 percent of the nation's 17,000 controllers had come to work at 7 a.m., with the number up to 29 percent by early afternoon and climbing steadily (PATCO pointed out that 12 percent, or about 2,000 controllers, had not been members, nor ever expected to strike. Poli also noted that court papers filed by the Government asserted only 10 percent had reported for duty).[5]

Helms challenged PATCO's point that the system was no longer safe because its 3,000 supervisors and 500 military controllers were unqualified and raised a "safety hazard." Helms argued that the supervisors had been preparing to man the boards for months leading up to the strike, and with the help of 2,000 nonstrikers would keep the system up to appropriate safety standards. Moreover, the FAA would substantially increase its aircraft separation regulations, prohibit the stacking of circling aircraft, and sharply limit the number of rush hour flights. (By the week's end the FAA had ordered the 22 largest airports to cut scheduled flights back 50 percent for at least a month.)[6] Consistent with the closing of the return-to-work, 48-hour "window" on Wednesday, August 6, the FAA announced plans to triple the number of new controllers (currently 1,800 a year), and 125,508 applications flooded the agency in the first 10-day posting period.[7] FAA spokesmen boasted that "law and order" had been restored, and this claim earned it much approval from spit-and-polish Reagan supporters and many anxious air travellers.

But one anti-PATCO move stood out beyond all others, for much like Reagan's surprise assault on every striker ("Work, or be fired!"), this move was not adequately anticipated, was never effectively countered, and cost PATCO dearly. In 1980 the FAA published a strike contingency plan that set extremely low targets for post-strike flight traffic, and threatened the most severe disruptions in passenger, mail, and freight service.

After the June 22 down-to-the-wire drama of the near-strike, the FAA had certain staff specialists completely redo the 1980 plan, and this time the airlines were invited to participate fully in the process. The new plan, completed only hours before the August 3 strike got under way, was a substantial improvement in that the FAA spread out dramatic "peaks and valleys" it had previously tolerated in daily operations.

PATCO had expected the FAA to falter in implementing its second-rate 1980 plan; the agency took PATCO unaware with its 1981 update, and this "flow control" version enabled it to handle 83 percent of the former volume with less than 50 percent of its prestrike controller work force—with the number of errors reduced by an alleged 30 percent.[8]

PATCO was on record before the strike as urging the very "flow control" the strike had now forced the FAA to implement. But the agency had long resisted this because the major airlines resented any interference with scheduling as they chose. Now, in early August, the FAA used the PATCO flow control idea effectively against the union's strike, and many pickets at the nation's airfields bitterly noted the irony.

One student of the strike has since concluded flow control was the single most promising issue PATCO possessed going into the strike—and wasted:

> . . . it truly would have benefited its members while helping to win the public to their side . . . The FAA was clearly vulnerable: its refusal to consider flow control exemplified the agency's lack of concern for controllers as well as its history of catering to the airline industry.[9]

Exactly why Poli and the PATCO negotiators failed to make this a major bargaining issue mystifies commentators to this day. PATCO insiders boast it was high on their list of 96 contract demands, but go on to explain that it was not an issue over which most members would "go the distance."

Labor Takes a Position.   Aware that PATCO might have the airlines grounded on Monday morning, August 3, the members of the AFL-CIO's Executive Council hastened to Chicago over the preceding weekend for their regularly scheduled Summer Meeting, and, early Monday morning, all hell broke loose.

Tabling their preannounced meeting agenda, the union presidents turned immediately to the PATCO-FAA showdown. They agreed they had no special love for PATCO, and many bitterly recalled the union's haughtiness, its sublime indifference since 1968 to their picket lines at various airports, and its previous coziness with Reagan White House aides. Complaints were voiced over Poli's failure to keep the AFL-CIO Public Employees Department abreast of strike-related developments (a responsibility Poli has since insisted he did meet).

William Winpisinger, president of the Machinists Union, offered to shut down the nation's airports by calling his aircraft-serving members out—a move that could have won the strike for PATCO, or at least have forced a major reassessment by the White House. But he would only take that step, which was illegal, if the other unions in the room agreed to pull their own people out.

By the end of the session the delegates agreed to hold off on action pending direct discussion with Poli, though it was becoming clear that few labor leaders believed their rank and file felt strongly for the controllers or their strike. Determined, nevertheless, to promote union solidarity, and fully cognizant of the seriousness of the Reagan onslaught, the AFL-CIO's president Lane Kirkland called a press conference on the afternoon of August 3 to express the will of the Executive Council.

Kirkland explained to reporters that he "respects the law," but "when working people feel a deep sense of grievance, they will exercise what I think is a basic human right, the right to withdraw their services, not to work under conditions they no longer find tolerable. I think that is a right that is inherent, and one that's not adequately addressed by legislative remedies simply saying that it's against the law." Kirkland concluded by condemning the 48-hour return-to-work pressure on the strikers as an invitation to an unsafe system. "The one thing I want in that control tower is people who are reasonably happy in their work, whose morale is good, and who are satisfied with their working conditions."[10] As if to underline its earnestness, the entire Executive Council suspended its Tuesday morning session and bussed out to O'Hare airport to march with cheering PATCO pickets.

On Wednesday Kirkland offered still another contribution by detailing to reporters how the appointment by the White House of a special mediator could offer both Reagan and PATCO a face-saving way out of a no-win impasse. The AFL-CIO went so far as to have the president of the Air Line Pilots Association meet with White House aides to weigh labor's nomination of W.J. Usery (Secretary of Labor in the Ford Administration) for the mediation role.

Rhetoric and gestures notwithstanding, many labor leaders remained "highly critical of Poli for calling an unpopular strike with so little warning and without seeking the help or advice of other veteran union strategists."[11] Auto Union President Douglas Fraser probably spoke for many in worrying aloud that the PATCO strike "could do massive damage to the labor movement."[12]

Nevertheless, over the weeks and months ahead, the AFL-CIO created a relief fund headed by Msgr. George Higgins that distributed over $840,000 in aid to 1,264 needy controllers across the country; certain unions, notably the Independent Federation of Flight Attendants, the Teachers Union, the Machinists Union, and MEBA, took out newspaper ads defending PATCO, and even provided free meeting space and supplies to PATCO locals across the country. PATCO spokespersons were invited to every imaginable kind of labor function to explain the strike, solicit contributions, gather leads on temporary jobs, get related aid, and rebut anti-PATCO misinformation and allegations. Most significant was the covert role certain union leaders, especially Kirkland, Blaylock, and Shanker played in an effort to "unfreeze" White House opposition to a compromise settlement and avoid PATCO's decertification (of which more in the following chapter).

The salient fact, however, is that PATCO was denied decisive all-out labor support that might have forced Reagan to seek a face-saving settlement. For instance, the Machinists Union could have kept planes grounded by directing 90,000 maintenance personnel to respect PATCO picket lines (they were skirting any direct confrontation with the pickets by using alternative routes to work). The Airline Pilots Association could have kept planes grounded by declaring the system unsafe to use. Instead, they turned on PATCO with a vengeance, and rushed to parrot every FAA insistence that the strike had not diminished safety one whit. And mass picketing at airfields across the country, manned by the 100 unions PATCO had wired on August 7 asking them to honor its picket line, could have discouraged air travel, and led the airlines to clamor for a speedy settlement.

Instead, understandably reluctant to take on a new U.S. President by going all out in support of an illegal and instantly unpopular strike, the labor movement fussed and fumed, finally to stand exposed as a paper tiger, beleaguered and relatively impotent. Criticized by Poli and the militants for aid that always seemed "a day late and a dollar short," the AFL-CIO and its key unions took far less action than PATCO's increasingly desperate situation called for—if the unthinkable was not to occur.

Overseas Controllers (Almost) Come Through!   In dramatic contrast to the grumbling and hesitation of the American labor movement, certain unions of controllers in Canada and Western Europe responded just as PATCO had hoped and planned. For 2 highly charged days in mid-August, it looked as if PATCO might still pull out of its nosedive. Canadian controllers called work stoppages on August 10 and 11 that stranded thousands of travellers on two continents. The Canadians refused to handle flights bound for or originating in the U.S. Pro-PATCO commentators in Canada and here hoped the disruptions might force the White House to moderate its tough, no-talks stance—as the Canadians provided "the most effective support the American strikers has received since beginning their illegal nationwide strike."[13]

PATCO's bad luck took over, however, and the situation reversed dramatically on August 12. Taking a leaf from the Reagan Administration the Canadian government suspended more than 25 controllers and threatened to levy $5,000 fines against each controller persisting in the job action. Ottawa promised to conduct an inquiry into whether the American situation created hazards, and the Canadian controllers reluctantly returned to work in full force.

While a flurry of similar shows of support developed elsewhere (controllers in France, New Zealand, Portugal, and Spain, in particular, sent funds and messages of solidarity), the Canadian gesture was the one that initially lifted PATCO spirits highest, only later to dash them. With the collapse of the Canadian effort the dream dimmed of soon achieving concerted and effective action by air control unions across national boundaries.

Judicial Clout. From the very first day, and thereafter, seemingly almost without end, PATCO took a beating in court.

On August 3, a federal judge in Washington, D.C. found PATCO in contempt of court, and imposed fines that could total $4,750,000 in a week. (Indeed, by 4:35 a.m., $2\frac{1}{2}$ hours *before* the scheduled strike, the Justice Department had a temporary restraining order.) On August 4, Federal Judge Thomas C. Platt in New York slapped fines of $100,000 an hour, or $2,400,000 a day on PATCO for defying a 1970 injunction against striking. He also ruled that PATCO was liable for millions of dollars in daily losses suffered by the carriers.

On August 5, five union officials (including a vice president, Gary Eads) were jailed for violating back-to-work orders, as part of Justice Department action against union locals in 57 federal courts across the country. The government had criminal complaints issued against 39 PATCO leaders: if convicted they faced a fine of up to $1,000 a year and a day in jail, or both. (One such activist, Bill Taylor, has since carried "the dubious distinction of being the first American convicted of a felony for striking against the federal government."[14] Another, Steven L. Wallaert, who was marched away in handcuffs and shackled from waist to feet in chains, became "the first PATCO official to feel the full power of the courts, and thus, was a potential martyr."[15]

And by August 5, only 2 days into the strike, Poli was forced to concede that PATCO did not have the funds to pay its fines, had lost access to its impounded $3 million strike fund, and might be facing its destruction. Nevertheless, he avowed the court actions would "not end the strike. I just wish they would act as strongly against organized crime as they are against our union."[16]

Media and Public Opposition. Consistent with the treatment meted out by the courts, and the actions of Justice Department, the media and the public seemed of one mind throughout, and PATCO was uniformly vilified.

N.Y. Daily News: . . . they deserve all that is coming to them.

Except for a handful of labor leaders and professional civil-rights pleaders, public support for the President appears overwhelming. To the public, as to Reagan, the dispute ceased to be a controversy over pay and working conditions when the controllers walked out. At that moment, it became a test of whether public employees can flout the law with impunity.

It was a challenge from which Reagan dared not flinch. Concessions or compromises would only have emboldened other federal unions to hold essential government services hostage to the demands.

. . . the inconveniences will be a small price to pay for upholding a principle that is the very heart and soul of a democratic society based on law." (Editorial, August 6, 1981).[17]

Editorials from other major papers, including the *Boston Globe*, the *Washington Post*, the *Chicago Tribune*, the *L.A. Times*, and the *San Francisco Examiner* took much the same tone.

Public opinion was even less friendly, if that was possible. An early Gallup poll, released on August 8, found 60 percent of the public approved of the President's decision to fire the strikers, and 67 percent felt the PATCO backers had been wrong to walk off their jobs. While 42 percent thought the strikers should be rehired at the strike's end, 44 percent felt they should not be eligible to resume their FAA careers.[18] On August 16, only 22 percent of the public favored the Reagan Administration's taking a softer line than the one it was pursuing.[19] Irate letters to the editor reflected public rejection of almost every PATCO argument and a backlash of withering proportions.

PATCO—Talking to Itself.   Very little of this surprised the union or the strikers. Every job action going back to 1970 had evoked similar cries of outrage—though later, over a year later in the case of the 1970 sick-out, PATCO was vindicated. The FAA was forced to give a little. Congress conceded overdue job gains. And PATCO began to dream of a still better victory the next time out.

Accordingly, confidence ran high in early August that everything would work out. Even if the victory wasn't what the 3-year-old strike-preparation dream had envisaged, the strikers could not be too badly let down nor PATCO seriously hurt. As any concerned party could grasp, the system *required* the talent, experience, and expertise of the missing 11,345 controllers; and *they* required PATCO. (Poli, of course, promoted this line of reasoning with every media appearance, as when he declared on TV's *Face the Nation* on August 16 that strike-caused economic and safety strains meant PATCO "will prevail.")[20] Underlying all this was the conviction that Reagan, Helms, the FAA, and Congress could not move aircraft without PATCO controllers. Therefore, nothing that they could do would have any real effect on whether the union had the power to win in 1981.

"Dirty tricks" and picket line violence were officially *and* unofficially discouraged, as the union's Strike Plan urged the projection of an image of law-respecting adults victimized by a lawbreaking FAA that refused to bargain in good faith. Although the agency found instances of alleged mayhem to spot-light as tempers rose and picket line discipline eroded, PATCO repudiated such incidents and strove to win "clean and fair"—a strategy with which some hotheads disagreed at the time, and even more strongly afterwards.

PATCO locals remained committed to putting their part of the Strike Plan into operation. Their spirited activities, the rallying of many of the cause and to "the family," lent credence to Poli's avowal that "PATCO is not a union; it is a religion".[21] Locals set up strike-related committees, including one to help allocate emergency relief funds from the AFL-CIO/PATCO Fund, an-other to oversee picket line duties, and a third to offer advice on benefits strikers might seek. (Later in August a committee was commonly established to seek job leads for fired controllers eager to return to a payroll—almost any payroll.) Locals sought opportunities to send speakers to personalize their cause and counter misunderstandings that everywhere damned their strike. Special attention was paid to area TV and radio talk shows, the meetings of nearby labor unions, and the newspaper columns of sympathetic feature writers.

Locals also set up food collection centers, many of which were run by a wives' committee. And these rapidly expanded to include clothing, odds and ends, and later, Christmas gifts. Equally significant was the presence of wives and older children on the picket line and at PATCO local meetings; certain wives set up their own phone networks and ran occasional "women-only" meetings to share advice, bolster their own morale, and much later, pass along leads to employment, for males or females alike.

But with the passage of weeks, and then of the months, locals naturally lost their ability to staff volunteer activities, even as the need for initial types of aid diminished. Many ex-controllers who "gave their all" back then look back now, years later, on this aspect of the 1981 strike with fond and proud memories. When the call came, they came through—and *that* can never be taken from them.

By mid-August, however, the mood began to shift:

> . . . this is a time of roller coaster emotions, of rising anxiety over shrink-ing bank balances, of trying to reassure wide-eyed children that every-thing will be all right when they themselves are beginning to wonder if anything will ever be right again.[22]

Strikers learned they were ineligible for unemployment benefits which most states ban to workers who have struck against the government. Even food stamps and public assistance were later denied by an October 1981 change in the law, and many social agencies were cool to the former controllers.

Summary.   By the arrival of the September Labor Day weekend (in the 100th anniversary year of the AFL's founding) the outcome of the largest recent strike of federal employees was clear, though both sides were still claiming victory. PATCO had drawn out over 13,000 of its 14,500 members, and had lost only about 1,650 to the President's demand that they break ranks and scurry back to work. The FAA *had* kept system turmoil to a minimum, put a secret flow control plan into effective operation, and avoided any significant mishaps while accommodating the unexpected loss of about 11,345 of its 16,000 controllers.

Taken all in all, however, the tally fell short of a PATCO triumph. The axiom of the union's Strike Plan notwithstanding, the system could, and did operate without the "indispensable" strikers. Huge, unprecedented financial losses were being absorbed; a slapdash, controller labor force had made do; and the luck of the FAA had held, while PATCO's star steadily set.

This strike did not have to happen; they would not talk to us. There is only so long that you can knock on a locked door.
Ronald Reagan (Explaining why, while he was President of the Screen Actors Guild, the union struck against the Film Studio.)

Chapter 8

WHAT WE WERE UP AGAINST*

Excerpts from the O'Keefe Survey: 1984

The FAA management backed us into the corner and did force us to strike. We had no choice. We just didn't realize how powerful and uncaring our government really was. We overplayed our hand. We had the best cards to start with. However, the government had more than we anticipated . . . up their sleeve. They didn't bluff us, they just bought the pot. They may lose the game, but they won the hand.

The news media killed us. Other unions deserted us. Strangers, even friends, say they are glad I was fired. I could not feel the same about my President, my country, or my job as a controller again.

USATCO or all ex-PATCO controllers need to contribute to pay for national TV time to tell the truth as to why two-thirds of the FAA's employees were fired! It wasn't money; it was the FAA's broken promises!

Someday, somehow, the true facts of this job action have to be given to the people. Also, the public deceit by the FAA regarding staffing, operational errors, etc., must be revealed. As well as the force known as the MSPB Hearings. Public opinion is a valuable tool (as we found out!), but, if the truth can be delivered to the public, I still believe their sentiment would be in our favor.

---

*by David Skocik.

No one could have believed that Reagan and Lewis would have been willing to set a new standard for abuse of government power—but they were and did!

It was the only way we could let the FAA know we were serious; they still don't believe that job is a killer.

I'm still amazed when I talk to union people in my present line of work (phone service sales) of how much they really misunderstood about our job action. They only remember the $10,000 raise and the 4-day work week.

Why Did We Think We Could Win?   The average layperson has no conception of the turmoil that continually went on in the facilities. (Recent newspaper accounts verify that much of the same feelings still exist today, even with a whole new nonunion work force.) People still ask me how PATCO could have so misjudged conditions in the country prior to its fatal strike. How did the air traffic keep moving?

One point which must be understood is that PATCO *should* have *won* the strike. The union's biggest mistake was in assuming that the other side would play by the rules. As simplistic as that sounds, it is the truth. By "rules" I mean not only the accepted historic guidelines for treatment of illegally striking workers, but also the rules of air traffic control. The administration honored neither.

The main reason PATCO decided 80 percent would have to agree to participate in any strike was that it would be impossible to run the system with that amount of experience on the streets. Knowledge of the system and its myriad safety rules told anyone the system could not be safely run without a large percentage of the experienced work force in place. That proposition was never in question during PATCO's strike planning. Its main concern was safely shutting the system down at a given time. No aircraft was to be left stranded, and any job action was to commence on a Monday morning with plenty of advance notice and before air traffic could build up.

No PATCO member believed the FAA would be irresponsible enough to try to run the system with the manpower left. They were wrong. PATCO members monitoring radio frequencies that first day were horrified at the number of incidents occurring in the New York area alone. Only because the weather was so clear (the clearest August in some 25 years) pilots could cooperate by separating themselves visually. Lists of medically retired, unqualified, and disqualified controllers who were working live traffic in the facilities were compiled and turned over to the media. They went unreported.

(This philosophy seems to have carried over into present-day operations. In mid-1985, after releasing glowing reports of how the number of near misses and incidents were below 1981 levels, the FAA was exposed by ABC News as having reported only half the actual incidents. Red-faced, the FAA admitted it had undercounted due to administrative errors which had allowed the rest to "slip between the cracks." What a convenience.)

Stabbed in the Back.   It would have been easy to cry "collusion" between the government and ALPA to make the system look better than it was. But it was not that simple. It is true that a pilot's paycheck is a big incentive to keep the system running. But what of safety? It is a maxim that the pilot is the first one at the scene of an accident. What is money if you can't spend it? I believe that many commercial pilots really wanted to believe things were better than before and bent over backwards to make them so. Past frustrations with the system became the fault of the ex-controllers; since they were no longer around, things had to be better.

Perhaps the biggest sellout came from ALPA, the Airline Pilot's Association. Before the strike it seemed pilots went out of their way to let PATCO controllers know that they wouldn't fly if it wasn't safe. That was an indirect, yet safe way of saying the union had their support. Or so it seemed.

Initially, neither pilots nor controllers had to worry about the flying. At the beginning of the strike traffic was curtailed by more than 70 percent at many airports, and that figure represented commercial aviation; small civil aircraft just weren't flying. But within several days it became increasingly obvious to those monitoring frequencies that pilots were indeed scrambling to get into the cockpit and even bending over backwards to downplay or outright ignore nonstandard operations and even near misses. It was as though some sort of deal had been cut between the FAA and pilots to keep the public believing that things were in the Administration's words, "better than ever." ALPA couldn't agree more. Some pilots even went out of their way to vilify the fired controllers as malcontents who ought to be removed from the system. Praise for the remaining controllers flowed like honey.

A Cruel Hoax.   By early December 1981, pressure was mounting on the President to show the former union members who had been so badly beaten some Christmas spirit by possibly offering them the opportunity to return to work.

Secretary of Transportation Drew Lewis was due in from Japan that evening, and the speculation was that the fate of the ex-controllers was up to him. But even more ominous was the word that FAA Administrator Helms had threatened to resign if even one of the fired controllers were rehired. That iced it. On December 9 the decision was reflected in a memorandum from the President: Controllers were to remain debarred from employment in the FAA; but they could apply for jobs in other federal agencies.

While the Teamsters, in an orchestrated response, proclaimed what a generous man the President was, Bob Poli summed up in three words what the offer amounted to—"a cruel hoax!" The fact was that there were no jobs. Federal agencies had been ordered to cut back their number of employees. At least one controller who because of his outstanding record had been accepted back into the postal service in California was terminated in early 1982. When he asked the postmaster why, he was told by directive from Washington, D.C. So much for the December 9 memorandum.

Blacklisting. Those who considered moving overseas to practice their livelihood found that as early as 5 weeks after their firings, the U.S. State Department apparently had intervened to deny them jobs in Saudi Arabia. My files contain letters of rejection sent to several former controllers by the Bendix Field Engineering Corp. (then under contract with the Saudi government), informing them that the Saudis would not accept terminated controllers. (This policy changed the following month, and applicants were sent form letters advising that they could reapply.)

Apparently, the same sort of blacklisting pressure was ongoing in the U.S. Several ex-controllers who had applied to a major moving van line to become owner-operators were rejected because of Administration input. One in Indiana and one in Michigan each recounted his experience in a letter to PATCO officials. Both state that they were told that government pressure (references to military contracts) was being brought to bear not to hire fired PATCO members. (One man, in the interest of accuracy, taped the conversation with a company representative and provided a transcript. The reference to government pressure is unmistakable.)

Neither did the FAA spare any attempt to apply what pressure it could bring to bear as a parting shot. Those controllers who had transferred into a facility within a year of the strike were ordered to refund all moving expenses. (In one case, a man who had spent 51 of the required 52 weeks in the New York TRACON was sent a bill for $15,951.09; no proration for the 51 weeks served—just send a check for the full amount. They finally deducted it from his retirement account.)

Shades of McCarthyism. Any doubt remaining as to the Reagan Administration's attitude toward those who dared defy it was erased in March 1982. A detailed questionnaire from the Justice Department arrived at the residence of each former employee. The cover sheet stated the interrogatories were for the "convenience" of those appellants "who do not have counsel." It also demanded that the interrogatories "shall be answered under oath." Therefore the appellant was required to swear before a notary public that his answers were complete. The phrasing of the first question was particularly significant: *"Are you now, or have you ever been a member of PATCO?"*

A chill ran down the spine of anyone familiar with the paranoia of 30 years earlier. Anyone who didn't agree with a certain senator's views was labeled a Communist, or "fellow traveller"—"disloyal." The remaining 27 questions on the Justice Department questionnaire were equally sinister. The government wanted to know not only the time and place of all union meetings where strike activity had been discussed, but also *who was there, and what was discussed.* The penalty proposed for not answering each question fully was automatic dismissal of any and all current and future appeals for job reinstatement.

The significance of this extraordinary document was certainly not lost on its recipients. Its wording was chosen deliberately. In the wake of the initial shock and disbelief came a sense of revulsion, followed by a wave of anger. Job or no job, what right did anyone have to question the protected rights, and more importantly, the loyalty of U.S. citizens? Despite the fact that the great majority of ex-controllers were Vietnam era veterans, membership in PATCO seemed to justify massive retaliation and ongoing psychological warfare. The majority of the questions were later ruled blatant violations of the First and Fifth amendments by a federal court.

Smearing the Strikers.   Part of the argument advanced for the President's stern stance was that "no group had the right to hold the country hostage." Such language was carefully selected as a reminder of the Iranian hostage crisis which had served candidate Reagan so well. Such rhetoric, combined with the "bearded radicals" terminology bandied about early on by Administration spokesmen, was designed to equate American workers with foreign terrorists who deserved the hatred and contempt of all America.

Disinformation.   It did not take anyone inside long to realize that the union was up against the biggest propaganda machine outside of the Kremlin: one that worked 24 hours a day to convince the public that everything the Administration did was good and everything PATCO did was bad. As with any skillful propaganda, the theme was kept simple: 1) the controllers violated a sacred oath, and 2) the skies are safer than they've ever been. Although always anxious to make use of the mass media to spread its simple gospel of the "good news of aviation," the FAA always dodged any program with PATCO spokesmen, whom it knew would be armed with contrary evidence.

Particularly during the first year after the firings, the indication that the airlines were being severely hurt was everywhere: flights were down and even with the reduction of scheduled air carriers and the drastic curtailment of general and corporate aviation, delays were common. General aviation, at least that part of it wanting to be in the air traffic system, was almost nonexistent, especially around busy hub airports. The controller shortage was certainly having its effects, whether or not the Administration admitted it.

Amnesty?   No one in the union ever believed American workers would be permanently fired or blacklisted. The rhetoric which preceded the walkout was heated, as is generally the case in a labor dispute. It did, however, reflect the deep-seated hostility between labor and management which had

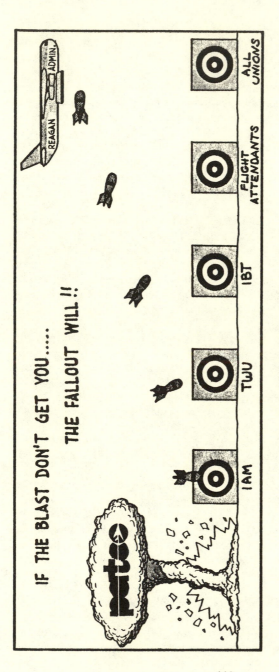

THE PATCO STRIKE:
FACT AND FICTION

The Reagan Administration, the airline companies, and ALPA have cut deals and flooded the media with misinformation about the current PATCO strike. This misinformation is intended to help the airlines cut their "dead wood" and blame it on PATCO. Your job may well depend on your ability to separate FACT from FICTION.

FICTION: Controllers have it easy. They make "big money," work "short hours," and have "great benefits."

FACT: Controllers work eight hour shifts with government regulations which exclude lunch periods and breaks.

FACT: Controllers are assigned mandatory overtime, up to 20 additional hours per week. Some of that overtime is paid at less than the normal hourly wage.

FACT: Controllers pay 2/3 of their own medical benefits, have no dental or optical plan, and pay a nominal fee for life insurance benefits.

FACT: Controllers pay a higher percentage into their own retirement than most workers pay into social security.

FACT: The controllers' job is a young person's game. 89% never make it to a normal retirement age because of rotating shifts and high stress. Some collect a 40% disability retirement. Most just quit.

FACT: A controller starts at $15,000 per year or less. It takes a controller, with the right transfer opportunities, a minimum of 7 years to advance to $29,000 per year.

FICTION: PATCO didn't give the government enough time to negotiate.

FACT: PATCO submitted our contract proposals in January of 1981.

FACT: The FAA addressed only 4 of our 99 proposals in the first 27 weeks of negotiations.

FACT: The final $40 million offer by the D.O.T. equaled about $2,300 in pay and benefits per each of our 12,000 members over a three year period.

FACT: The FAA (Drew Lewis) would not budge from their "offer."

119

FICTION: PATCO crossed airline mechanics' picket lines in 1965.

FACT: Air traffic controllers were not organized in 1965. PATCO was formed in 1969.

FACT: In spite of government restrictions, PATCO members have openly supported other airport unions, including a recent flight attendants' strike.

FICTION: Reagan says controllers violated an oath and jeopardized public safety.

FACT: In 1969, a Federal District Court ruled that any oath as a condition for employment is unconstitutional. Yet Reagan continues to insist that we broke the law.

FACT: Over the last three years, the FAA has violated several major articles in our contract.

FACT: Candidate Reagan violated his written promise to improve the "deplorable state of our nation's air traffic control system" in which "too few people are working unreasonable hours with obsolete equipment." Even before the strike, Reagan acknowledged that the system "placed the nation's air travelers in unwarranted danger." (Letter to PATCO President Poli from Ronald Reagan, Oct. 20, 1980)

FACT: The main thrust of PATCO's contract demands center on improvements in safety, not money.

FACT: It is the government, not PATCO, that is jeopardizing the public safety.

FICTION: Reagan is promoting "jobs, jobs, and more jobs."

FACT: Reagan's economic program has already eliminated more than one million jobs.

FACT: Reagan's union-busting tactics has opened the door for airline management to eliminate 20,000 jobs to date, with 63,000 more lost jobs projected.

FACT: The Reagan Administration has already spent over three billion taxpayer dollars (your dollars) just to break one union of 12,000 strikers.

120

Reprinted with permission of Los Angeles PATCO activist Charles Sheehan, whose local prepared and distributed this leaflet in the Summer and Fall of 1981.

FICTION: The PATCO strike is over.

FACT: 75% of the air traffic controllers are still on strike and holding firm.

FACT: The system is not normal, traffic volume is down by 50%, and the bad weather is yet to come.

PATCO is just the first step. By attacking PATCO, the government and big business have an excuse to force massive layoffs and contract concessions in the airline industry. The need for unity among all airport and airline workers is imperative to bring out the truth and achieve better working conditions for all.

SUPPORT GROUPS ARE BEING FORMED BY CONCERNED UNION MEMBERS. IF YOU ARE INTERESTED IN MORE INFORMATION AND/OR BECOMING INVOLVED, PLEASE CONTACT OUR HEAD-QUARTERS, 8639 LINCOLN BLVD., SUITE 204 (NEAR MAN-CHESTER BLVD.), L.A. 90045, (213) 670-8183, 670-8184, 670-8185. OUR PHONE AND OFFICE ARE OPEN 24 HOURS.

patco
PROFESSIONAL AIR TRAFFIC CONTROLLERS ORGANIZATION
Affiliated with M.E.B.A. (AFL-CIO)
PH. (213) 420-1191
LAKEWOOD, CA 90712
3871 PIMLICO

121

been brewing for years. It was not until the President gave his Monday morning ultimatum in the Rose Garden that union members even considered him an adversary. Until that time the strike was, in PATCO's view, strictly against an unfair employer, the FAA. Precedent in past strikes, even in other Free World countries, was that top leadership did not become involved until after the initial dust settled and cooler heads had prevailed.

Of course we all knew it was against the law for federal employees to strike, but plenty of illegal strikes had taken place in the past in our great country. Threats, injunctions, and jailings may have happened during such strikes, but upon their resolution, matters were always worked out. Arrangements were made to punish the ringleaders, and they were generally of a face-saving nature. Many of the very supervisors who were taking our places had themselves participated in illegal strikes in the late sixties. (In the resolution stage, the Nixon Administration referred to them as "sick-outs" rather than strikes.)

As with any technically illegal strike, when government leaders bend the rules, violation of the law becomes a technical point. But PATCO leaders banked on the notion that the common man is also given such consideration when he is an obvious winner. The powers-that-be would pick several scapegoats to suspend or fire, but *things would work out*. They always had in PATCO's past. For instance, in March, 1970, some 3,000 controllers struck for 20 days after the FAA involuntarily transferred three union organizers from Baton Rouge, Louisiana, Tower. During the confrontation, 52 controllers were fired, but *all* 46 who reapplied when the political smoke cleared 2 years later were rehired. And the improper transfers for union activity were negated.

Now, however, all of us were to be permanently blacklisted from our means of livelihood (unless we chose to emigrate). Further actions, such as denial even of unemployment benefits, food stamps, and extensions of FHA/VA mortgages were taken. Never in U.S. history had the awesome power of the Presidency been used with such vindictiveness against American workers.*

---

*See the appendix interviews with a Chicago activist and his wife.

Chapter 9

A BREED APART . . . FAR APART

Nobody will win the air traffic controllers strike, and both sides should share the blame for this unparalleled labor dispute . . . almost anything beats a no-win strike.
Joann S. Lublin, "Both Sides Made Mistakes in Controllers' Strike." *Wall Street Journal*, September 15, 1981, p. 28.

We are not being the least bit smug. I don't see ourselves as winning . . . There really are no winners. The implications are long-reaching.
Drew Lewis, *Philadelphia Inquirer*, October 14, 1981, p. 5-B; *Evening Bulletin*, September 25, 1981, p. B-10.

There are no draws in the game of power.
Earl Shorris, "Reflections on Power," *Harper's*, July 1985, p. 51.

Losing Ground . . . Daily. Within a week of the strike's start Secretary of Transportation Drew Lewis declared that his August 5 firing of 11,345 strikers had effectively ended the PATCO job action:

> None of these people will ever be permitted to come back. We don't want these people back. . . . It's taken 200 years for this democracy to develop, and it's developed as a system of law, and we just can't see that deteriorate based on a few people that just want to make more money.
>
> As far as we are concerned, this is a nonstrike situation, and we're rebuilding the system . . . it's over with.[1]

From the White House an exuberant spokesman declared "this is Day One of the rebuilding of a new system!"[2]

1) Looking to Reagan . . . Again.   Efforts to resolve the strike began the day after it began, but promoting them was not easy, for many powerful board members around Poli wanted to concede little and demand more, while resistance grew firmer daily from key people around the President who sensed a total victory in the making.

PATCO leaders feared betrayal, and their free-floating distrust of the government further complicated the negotiations. Convinced that the Justice Department and/or the FAA had legal or illegal taps on their phones, various PATCO officers took to making vital calls from phone booths, encouraged callers from the field not to discuss vital matters in calls to the PATCO office, and regularly explored the office for hidden "bugs." Persuaded that FBI and/or Secret Service agents had been assigned to spy on them, various PATCO officers took to maneuvers designed to shake off their mysterious shadows. And many PATCO militants could describe in detail the appearance and mannerisms of the individuals they took for spies assigned to their case. Convinced also that their mail was being opened and read, various PATCO officers urged all correspondents to find some safer method of communicating with the national office.

When combined with a long-standing certitude that the FAA had its own spies inside PATCO, the distrust with which the union operated undermined its ability to take risks in the covert negotiations or trust the word of would-be intermediaries.

While overtures were made by PATCO to possible sources of support, the union early on received unsolicited offers of intermediary aid from three former secretaries of labor—John T. Dunlop and W.J. Usery, Jr., who had served in the Ford administration, and James D. Hodgson, a member of the Nixon Administration. Others, including Congressman Jack Kemp and the Rev. Jesse Jackson, also offered to help in any appropriate way.

Poli listened appreciatively, but in some cases remained suspicious of the motives of certain uninvited friends, and specified that PATCO would only cooperate when the details of a face-saving deal were presented in writing over the signature of a high-level official clearly able to make them good.

At least one member of the executive board received an unsolicited call in mid-August from a distant acquaintance, a distinguished gray-haired mediator. After stipulating anonymity, he laid out the terms of a deal he was confident the Reagan White House would accept:

1) Poli was to call off the strike immediately.

2) Poli was to vacate the union presidency—at least temporarily.

3) Poli was to apologize publicly for the strike, and thereby re-inforce Reagan's prestige.
4) Poli was to order the strikers back to work, but warn them that their jobs were not guaranteed.
5) Poli was to ask the FAA to initiate an orderly reinstatement, one that might take 6 months to a year.

When the phone call was discussed the next day with Poli, he allegedly explained he couldn't sell it, since his people still felt they could win; and, in any case, he would have to have it first in writing.

A few days later the mediator called the PATCO board member to learn the union's response. When told of the rejection he reminded his union contact that the "package" included a pledge of no retaliation against Poli or PATCO, and he emphasized that it was the *only* way the strikers would get their jobs back.

A third call in mid-September repeated the offer, but warned that hope of selling it in the White House was rapidly dwindling. When this tone of urgency was conveyed to Poli, he allegedly repeated his original response, adding that he did not have enough support on the board to call the strike off even if he personally agreed the situation was getting desperate.

When word of the phone offers spread, the board member serving as intermediary was castigated as a "wimp" and worse for viewing the strike as lost, and the time come to "cut a deal." No further calls came from the distinguished gray-haired mediator (who may remain satisfied that he tried, tried, and tried again).

2) Decertification . . . Again.   Perhaps the most dramatic and revealing of all the salvage efforts was the one made to avoid the decertification of the union, an act so drastic and final as to galvanize the AFL-CIO into a major effort to prevent it, or at least constrain its occurrence. "Decert" would mean PATCO would lose its right to represent its members under the protective umbrella of federal labor law, and the FAA would be free to ignore it completely or treat it as it chose. Worse still, "decert" would set as a precedent likely to intimidate other unions of government workers for years to come.

While PATCO militants were fond of reminding everyone that the controllers union had suffered this fate once before (1970), and had come roaring back to life, the AFL-CIO leaders were convinced it would be different this time around: With the failure of covert efforts to soften the anti-PATCO hard line of the White House, the labor leaders suspected "decert" in 1981 would be permanent—and despite the "We can take it!" bravado of the PATCO executive board, the AFL-CIO set out to try to sidetrack the "decert" penalty.

Personal "Lobbying."   One revealing measure of the seriousness with which all of this was taken by concerned unionists—if not by the crowd around Poli—involved a furor over alleged efforts to exert illegal influence over the votes of the FLRA. Two union presidents, Al Shanker of the Teachers Union, and Ken Blaylock of the Government Employees Union, apparently went out of their way to discuss the PATCO matter with two members of the 3-man FLRA, a bold and controversial move that got both unionists censured, but exonerated, in court-ordered 1982 inquiries into these contacts.[2]

Tilting at the Bar.   On September 17 at an FLRA hearing the union based its plea not to be decertified on two characteristically quixotic arguments. PATCO's attorneys insisted the government had failed to prove the union had called or participated in a nationwide strike since August 3. PATCO suggested that punishment be waived in favor of an order that the parties start negotiating by September 23; with an independent arbitrator resolving any differences remaining after 30 days.

The FAA scoffed at the first bit of legalistic nonsense. And it claimed that FLRA order to resume negotiations would sanction strikes by federal employees. Demanding nothing short of PATCO's permanent decertification, the FAA advised the FLRA not even to consider the question of renewing bargaining talks, but to focus only on the most appropriate punishment for PATCO.

One Last Deal . . . Denied.   After this hearing, and before the October 22 date scheduled for the rendering of the FLRA verdict on "decert," one last covert operation was attempted—with the fate of PATCO fully at stake.

According to highly placed PATCO insiders who have since become strongly critical of Poli's leadership (or lack thereof), a critical series of events began late Thursday, October 22, that just might have kept the union hanging in—if only by its fingernails, and just might have kept reinstatement prospects alive—though on the terms and timetable of a gloating FAA.

AFL-CIO President Lane Kirkland allegedly called John Leyden, and told him to bring Poli to a meeting that evening at AFL-CIO headquarters. The discussion, both cordial and serious, had Poli concede that the situation appeared fairly hopeless. Kirkland, however, indicated decertification might be avoided, and some strikers might regain their jobs, if PATCO would agree to three conditions:

1)   PATCO must unconditionally call off the strike at a well publicized press conference;

2)   PATCO must accept full responsibility for the strike, indicting no other party (not the FAA nor the White House); and must appear humble and contrite;

3) PATCO must pledge never again to break the law through its use of an illegal job action.

If these conditions were met, the FLRA could put off a decision on decertification until such a time as tempers had cooled, inflicting a far less severe penalty on PATCO. The FAA would also stop hiring off-the-street replacements for the strikers, and strikers without flagrant records of picket line abuse, etc., would eventually be reinstated by seniority. While this process might take 12 to 18 months, nearly all of the strikers would be able to resume their ATC careers, strict seniority being honored in the process (much as the AFL-CIO preferred).

Leyden recalls that he gave Poli a typed copy of these terms the next day (the only written record of this critical session), and a seemingly receptive Poli promised to convey his Board's decision in time to influence the impending FLRA meeting.

On Monday morning Poli allegedly briefed the PATCO board, and, as often before (as in Chicago in 1980 over Leyden vs. Poli; and in Chicago again in 1981 over the Poli-Lewis agreement), the meeting was dramatic, stormy, and decisive. Only two voices were raised in favor of accepting the Kirkland terms, on the grounds that the strike was a lost cause. They urged focus on regaining controller jobs, thereby rebuilding PATCO from within a system ripe for poststrike changes (the media and Congress might be expected to force the FAA to mend at least the worst of its ways, as the strike had exposed them). Denounced as defeatists by the seven other board members, including Poli, the pro-Kirkland pair were voted down. The day was carried by undaunted board members who allegedly declared:

> the strike had *not* been lost;
>
> the strike *would* not be lost—the calendar was beginning now to work in PATCO's favor: stormy winter weather and heavy holiday air travel would soon demonstrate the indispensability of the strikers—and the FAA would be forced to come to terms and reinstate victorious PATCO backers;
>
> Lewis's last offer remained as insulting and unacceptable in October as it had been in August; the FAA and Congress could and *must* come up with more;
>
> the union should insist *all* win reinstatement or *none* would go back; PATCO would not abandon the militants whom the FAA would blacklist and leave "twisting in the breeze";

it was still possible that an amendment Congressman William Ford was willing to attach to a Department of Transportation funding bill would force the FAA to begin reinstating certain strikers;

PATCO's friend in the Oval Office could not remain under the influence of anti-PATCO advisers indefinitely; Reagan should soon see the error of his Rose Garden ways, and make some restitution to those who had backed his presidential candidacy; and

PATCO should cut no deal that did not include the forced resignation of FAA Administrator J. Lynn Helms, and his public acceptance of blame for causing the strike to occur in the first place.

Above all, the Board should recognize that out in the hinterland many PATCO rank and filers remained committed to "the cause" and what was left of the strike effort: They would not take kindly to an abject surrender by distant headquarters types, and would certainly expect far more in White House trade-offs than was allegedly contained in the Kirkland deal.

Other objections were raised, including the failure of the deal to specify exactly how many strikers might regain their FAA jobs, and the Board let Kirkland's deadline pass without a signal of PATCO concurrence. In short order the FLRA voted to decertify the 13-year-old union of air traffic controllers: the first time the authority had stripped a union of government workers of its bargaining rights.

When Will They Ever Learn?   Labor insiders recall that when Kirkland was later told PATCO had not only scoffed at his hard-fought deal, but also had the audacity to set terms of its own, including a demand for the forced resignation of Helms, he is said to have exploded over the lunacy of the PATCO leadership. AFL-CIO and international union heads concluded from this failed covert campaign that Poli was unable to deliver his own board, and was no longer in control, if he had ever been.

Relations thereafter between Labor and PATCO chilled considerably, though Poli was given a standing ovation 3 weeks later at the November 19 Convention of the AFL-CIO. He apologized for failing to consult other union leaders before ordering the August 3 strike, and won the passage of a convention resolution urging reinstatement. The convention declined, however, to pass a key resolution calling for a nationwide 1-day strike of all AFL-CIO unionists to demonstrate their solidarity with the striking controllers.

Reagan Unmoved.   Early in November the Secretary of Transportation, Drew Lewis, summed up the Administration's position:

> Sure, my job would be a lot easier if we took back, say, 3,000 controllers. But we have concluded that it would not be worth it.
>
> It would not be worth it as a matter of principle. And it would not be fair to the people on the job who don't want to be associated with the people who walked out; there would be a serious morale problem and disruptions that could affect safety.[3]

Lewis, the FAA, and the White House never let up on the specter of facility turmoil, though Poli insisted rehiring would not lead to intolerable friction (unlike the situation in 1974, when returning strikers "punished" those who had ignored PATCO's call).

So heated became speculation about whether nonstrikers and strikers could coexist in the same facility that Congress funded a secret survey of nonstrikers in December of 1981 to get their views on the topic, a survey Poli requested a month before. But before the survey data could be considered, the FAA was reiterating the Administration's unswerving opposition:

> . . . strikers and nonstrikers would have to work shoulder-to-shoulder in concert and harmony to ensure safety in the air. That's not a very realistic expectation given the bitterness, hostility, and mistrust generated over the past four months.
>
> . . . under any kind of general amnesty, the strikers would outnumber the nonstrikers by two to one, and in some facilities, by 10 or 15 to one.
>
> . . . the government's opposition to returning the fired controllers to their old jobs is based solely on its concern for the safety of the air traveler and its moral commitment to the controllers who remained on the job.[4]

PATCO insisted the enmity issue was vastly overblown, and argued antagonism had faded over time, and was quite manageable—even if the record of job action returnees in the 1970s gave more support to FAA fears than to PATCO reassurances.

Pulling Out the Stops.   Pressure was kept up, of course, and the reinstatement promoters began to warn that even the passage of years would not provide a trustworthy system. Graduates of the FAA Academy would receive hands-on training from weary nonstrikers who had been working months and years of overtime shifts, and who would undoubtedly harbor their own grievances with the "union-free" climate enjoyed by authoritarian FAA types. Similarly, the passage of years of FAA domination of airline schedules would prove anticompetitive in the extreme: "If put into effect, it would cancel the deregulatory gains in passenger service of the last 5 years, and that can scarcely be very efficient."[5]

Another tack had five prominent union leaders, including Kenneth Blaylock, join with Ralph Nader and the head of the Consumer Federation of America in filing suit to require the federal government to rehire the strikers. The union leaders charged that the Administration's ban was in violation of the 1958 Air Transportation Act that required the Government to provide "efficient, comprehensive, and timely passenger and cargo air transportation under conditions of maximum safety." While the suit got nowhere in the courts, the publicity added pressure on the White House to reassess its position.

Just before the White House staff was scheduled to consider amnesty for the PATCO strikers the widely syndicated *Washington Post* columnist William Raspberry wrote a fine column on behalf of reinstatement. A second column of his soon after, however, took note of an outpouring of calls and letters opposing reinstatement. And, to PATCO's great dismay, Raspberry reversed his position, explaining that it now seemed to him the public was not yet ready for clemency and the rehiring of the ex-controllers.

PATCO leaders believe to this day that Raspberry's switch, and his justification of his final antistriker position, was prominently cited in an ensuing Oval Office decision making session. In any case, the session ended with a "no amnesty" nod from the President, and Christmas of 1981 bore no gift to the strikers from PATCO's 1980 nominee for the presidency.

Buying Time—Perhaps.   In late November PATCO filed for protection under Chapter 11 of the Federal Bankruptcy Act. This was to free the union from the threat of creditors' lawsuits, and halt all pending litigation involving $150 million in fines and other assessments until the union could develop a rehabilitation plan to put its finances in order. Better yet, a Chapter 11 order would enable other unions to make donations (these were previously subject to attachment because of damage suits brought against the union by the airlines). PATCO stressed that it was seeking not to liquidate, but to reorganize, within the 120 court-monitored days.

Consistent with this decision, PATCO agreed in December to pay 14 airlines $28,900,000 in damages for the August 3–5 period, and thereby avoid the legal costs of a trial. PATCO accepted the net profit loss claimed by the Air Transport Association on behalf of the carriers, and assured the airlines they would receive a large portion of whatever assets a Chapter 11 reorganization determined the union to have.[6]

While fleet-footed in both matters, the union was jolted anew before the month's end by an assault from an unexpected quarter. On December 31, a group of working controllers, who called themselves CATCO (Concerned Air Traffic Controllers), declared war on PATCO and indicated their intention to win legal control over $3,500,000 in PATCO assets frozen since the strike, and to block Poli or any successor from remaining in command of the union. Claiming to speak for 3,200 nonstriking controllers, CATCO accused

PATCO of a "breach of trust" in having ever called the August 3 strike: "Those who struck were in direct contravention of PATCO's constitution, and have effectively resigned."[7] Asserting that they were "the only legitimate members of PATCO," CATCO said it would seek government recognition as bargaining agent for 6,100 working controllers, a role left vacant by PATCO's October decertification.

Ringing Down the Curtain. Maneuvers persisted to somehow avoid the union's annihilation, though priorities and perspective differed.

On December 30 a threat emerged of the first public break in the unity of the PATCO executive board and the union's strike policy. Up to this point PATCO had insisted that *all* strikers be reinstated, or *none* would go back. A dissident board member told Poli of his intention to hold a press conference on December 31 and announce the availability of fired controllers in his region to return, one man at a time, on the terms of the FAA.

Poli called a nationwide teleconference, and the PATCO board directed withering criticism at the dissident, who insisted in rebuttal that the strike was long since lost, and the goal now should be the regaining of any jobs possible, along with the rebuilding of PATCO from inside. Board members spurned this analysis, and called for the dissident's resignation, which he refused to submit. By the end of the 2-hour conference call, the dissident held to his intention to pull his region out of the strike—unless Poli resigned immediately and his successor launched a new effort to earn reinstatement for any controllers the FAA would accept.

On December 31 Robert E. Poli resigned as PATCO president, explaining "I have always stated that if I believed I was an impediment to a solution of the strike I would step down. That time has come. . . . I hope my resignation is a signal to take the fired controllers back. I am the symbol of the strike. There's no question about that." Poli said he was deliberately removing himself as a "stumbling block" to reinstatement. But the FAA retorted, "The controllers were fired for breaking the law. We can't see how Mr. Poli's resignation changes any of this."[8]

On January 1, in a very close election, the dissident who had threatened to pull his region out of the strike lost the election to succeed Poli to a Poli-backer, former Central Region vice president Gary Eads. The new PATCO leader said he understood that "Washington won't have a brass band waiting to greet me . . . I know our backs are against the wall. But as bad as things have been, I still have faith in the system . . . that this will be resolved in the best interest of everyone."

Eads agreed that his main goal of getting strikers rehired would not be easy, "but I'm going to do everything I can to avoid the antagonistic rhetoric between the Reagan Administration and our union. Hopefully, that will lead to something positive."[9] Eads was quick to establish a new and cordial relationship with the board dissident, and others started calling that longtime PATCO activist "brother" again.

Five months later the Circuit Court of Appeals upheld the decertification decision of the FLRA, and in July 1982, PATCO—the organization Poli had said was not a union as much as it was a religion—stopped being at least an operating union.[10] Its lawyers asked that its request for reorganization be converted to Chapter 7 bankruptcy, which called for liquidation of its assets. As it was down to only $1 million in assets, and was in debt to the airlines for fines of $33,400,000, the fourth and last PATCO president told reporters "it is over for PATCO. The union is gone."*

We were right then, and we are right now . . . We are still PATCO, and we are still proud.
Robert Poli, on learning of the "decert" vote; *Philadelphia Inquirer*, October 23, 1981, p. 24-A.

PATCO was open and flagrant in its violation, demonstrating a willful defiance of law as well as court mandate in a situation wherein the strike critically impacted on the public interest.
                              FLRA Decertification Order, October 22, 1981.

----

*See the appendix interview with Leo Perlis, a PATCO intermediary in the 1981 strike.

Part IV

MAKING THE BEST OF IT

Excerpts from the O'Keefe Survey: 1984

I'm a Vietnam veteran. I consider the PATCO strike a civil disobedience. It set my conscience free. Morally, the best thing to have happened to me.

Only chance to make it [ATC] a true profession; now it never will be!

The average American feels like the bearded Pied Piper led us into the sea. It was the rank and file of PATCO that told our leadership what we wanted. I stand proud and can look back without shame for my participation in the strike.

Extremely proud to be a part of this pioneer stance against all conceivable odds—the government, the press, media, public, etc. Have never for a moment had even a hint of regret, and never will. Would fight for first in line to do it again!

I went on strike to definitely establish the (unequivocal) right of federal employees to exercise their rights.

The FAA management backed us in the corner and did force us to strike. We had no choice. We just didn't realize how powerful and uncaring our government really was. We overplayed our hand. We had the best cards to start with. However, the government had more than we anticipated . . . up their sleeve. They didn't bluff us, they just bought the pot. They may lose the game, but they won the hand.

I feel our leadership did not have the will to win. Being under restraint is no way to deal with scabs. Bricks and violence would have settled the strike in short order. Candy-ass methods are for prima donnas.

I stand behind my husband—and I am so proud—of us all. We'll win, it's just gonna take a little longer. And if we don't win—we'll know we gave it our best shot!

(*USATCO Newsletter*, February 1983.)

Over the years I have spent working on this book no aspect of it has stirred as much interest as the post-1981 fate of the 11,345 fired controllers. Three separate, though clearly related sets of questions are involved:

1) *Reemployment*: What sort of jobs had they secured? How did their earnings compare with their ATC income? How interested did they remain in regaining their ATC posts and careers?

2) *Quality of Life*: How were the ex-controllers and their families faring? Was their standard of living very different?—Their personal health and mental well-being?—Their politics or political philosophy?

3) *Strike Reflections*: How did they feel now about the work stoppage, PATCO, the FAA, the federal government, and the strategies on which they had so heavily relied?

In sum, how did they now add it up? Would they do it over, if they had known then what they know now? Had the 1981 experience become a source years later of regret or of pride, of embarrassment or honor—or, some ambivalent and volatile mix of these elements?

In this section I briefly discuss each of these questions, conscious of their complexity and subtleties, and within the severe constraints of the only available national survey data, the little-known 1984 O'Keefe/USATCO* research project. Obliged by the requirements of his undergraduate degree program to complete an original piece of field research, Stephen A. O'Keefe, sought and received USATCO's cooperation in mailing a survey to its 2,400 members. His 900 survey returns now constitute the largest collection available of questionnaire responses from a self-selected bloc of fired controllers.

I was sent a first draft of the survey by USATCO officers who asked me to assess it and advise them about its usefulness. Delighted to find a kindred researcher willing to tackle this formidable mail survey task, I added four questions about strike impacts of special interest to me, and urged USATCO to cooperate. After O'Keefe finished his 28-page research paper, he sent it and his entire pool of 900 questionnaires to USATCO. Since that time I have been able to conduct several types of analysis of my own (see page 137). There is, of course, reason to suspect that USATCO members who bothered to complete and return the survey (as 62 percent did not) were probably pro-PATCO, pro-strike loyalists—a type whose answers would tend to accent the positive and downgrade the negative about the strike and their lives since.

---

*United States Air Traffic Controllers' Organization, the successor to PATCO

Even with this caveat, the fact remains that there is no comparable body of nationwide material. When used prudently, acknowledging its unverifiable character, the O'Keefe survey analysis can provide guess-estimates of considerable import to our reflections.*

Statistics are human beings with the tears wiped off.
Paul Brodeur, *Outrageous Misconduct: the Asbestos Industry on Trial* (1985).

---

* See the appendix interview with Steve O'Keefe

Chapter 10

REEMPLOYMENT

Strangers in a Strange Labor Market

If the truth is ever exposed, they will give us a "medal." I am still slightly annoyed at the way we were treated. Being blackballed in your own country is an interesting experience.
> Former Air-Traffic Controller, O'Keefe Survey, February 1984.

Hang in there, it is not over yet! Suffering produces endurance, and endurance produces character, and character produces hope, and hope does not disappoint us.
> Former Air Traffic Controller, O'Keefe Survey, February 1984.

My life may never be right until this thing is over. It is always on my mind, and I don't want to take it to my grave. It is not the money or the job. We were dumped in a foreign land. And we may never go home.
> Former Air Traffic Controller, O'Keefe Survey, February 1984.

How did the fired controllers do as reluctant job hunters? As recession-year pavement-pounders? As men privately hoping for an FAA callback, for some kind of White House amnesty that might enable them to return to a job many deeply wanted to regain—but only on PATCO-like terms?

Given their mean age of thirty-seven, and their modal G-S level 14 rank, with its average salary of $34,000 (1981), O'Keefe's respondents were a young middle-aged, promotion-winning, well-paid, and very secure bloc of civil service careerists—middle-class types unprepared for the overnight loss of job, career, compensation, security, status, and, in the worst cases of all, self-esteem.

Getting fired in August 1981, meant searching for reemployment under the worst possible conditions, especially for men without college diplomas and with many previous years of job security. Recession-based unemployment levels moved up rapidly in 1981–1983 to post-Depression records, and joblessness of 10 to 20 percent was noted in many areas; plant closings, business bankruptcies, layoffs, and a freeze on hiring confronted ex-controllers everywhere they turned. Many ex-controllers had never worked for any organization other than the federal government (either as servicemen or FAA employees), and were unfamiliar with private sector labor market realities. Many had less formal education than employers preferred (77 percent did not have a college degree, and only 3 percent had earned a masters or MBA degree). Many were older than employers preferred (25 percent were over forty-one, and another 39 percent were thirty-six to forty years old).

Whatever success the job-hunters had was credited by most to extraordinary effort—following every lead, looking in distant locations, and following up on tips provided by the USATCO network. Every day a prerecorded phone tape from USATCO advised callers of fresh employment possibilities, and the USATCO newsletter featured the details of long-standing job opportunities. Members of PATCO locals phoned one another with flash news of just-posted openings, and as soon as one striker gained entry he would begin to recommend union brothers to his new employer.

To judge cautiously from their job titles, the former controllers wound up accepting jobs quite different in content, and lower in status and compensation than what they had just lost:

Professional—	3%
Managers—	5%
Sales—	18%
White Collar—	26%
Self-Employed—	10%
Blue-Collar—	22%
ATC (here and abroad)—	11%
Unemployed—	6%
	(N = 100)

One in five wound up doing manual labor (electrician, truck driver, repairman), while the largest number secured entry-level clerical posts (administrative assistant, file clerk, data-entry clerk), and another 18 percent took jobs selling Amway products, cars, insurance, real estate, or the like.

As the O'Keefe questionnaire asked nothing about levels of current job satisfaction, Dave and I have only the survey's volunteered comments, the articles of others, and our own interviews to draw on in this regard—though even this slim resource base resonates with an oft-repeated theme: Once you have known the thrill of "moving traffic," it is very hard to find comparable rewards in other lines of work.

To be sure, a majority of the men we talked with accented the positive. Former controllers now working for themselves (10 percent) exulted in finally "liking" the boss and getting out from under the heel of the FAA. Other job satisfactions elsewhere were highlighted by many relieved ex-controllers:

> *Mail Carrier*: I now have every night off and every Sunday. My health is far better by my being relaxed and on a regular schedule.

> *Software Developer*: I am employed in a "survivable occupation" with a great future by an employer who cares about me as a person, not like the FAA considered me. I want an occupation which I can work on past fifty-six!

These testimonies notwithstanding, it is well to reiterate that four out of five strikers seemed to prefer their previous ATC jobs over anything they had (at least as of February 1984, when they completed the O'Keefe questionnaire). Their explanations varied greatly in detail, but an underlying message about unfinished business was common:

> It has been very hard to adjust to "civilian" life after spending all my working life with the government. I have been unable to find a job or position that offers the same excitement and personal satisfaction that controlling aircraft did. It's hard to rationalize being the best at a job you love, and then be told "we no longer want you" because you were a bad boy once. Most criminals are given more than once chance.

> Personally, I didn't walk out to walk away!! It was, as I've heard said, a strike of passion or love for the damn job—the saddest thing is that we have so much to do to get back to any kind of norm when we get back—and those that are still fighting will get that chance, I am certain.

> I am an air traffic controller by profession. I simply want to return to my profession under any conditions. The lessons learned in nearly 3 years will, I believe, enable me to live, work, and deal with FAA mismanagement, etc. We are the ones who can change things. We need to go back if we care about the system. I will not be subject to FAA humiliation, however.

Overall, the largest number of our interviewees slipped easily into nostalgia about their ATC careers—as if nothing held as much excitement, challenge, and electricity—nothing else seemed quite so real, or made the workday (and the workman) seem quite so special.

Not surprisingly, 80 percent indicated a willingness to consider dropping whatever they had secured and return to their ATC careers. Some 11 percent wanted this so much they attached no conditions, a revealing index of poststrike malaise. Two in three, however, took what O'Keefe, an ex-controller himself, termed a "hard stand" on reemployment conditions:

68% would not be willing to forfeit any of the seniority.

60% would not accept a position with a lower GS rating than their former position.

43% would insist on a back pay award.

14% would not accept an assignment to any locale other than the last one they had worked on; and

21% were uncertain on this last point.

O'Keefe believes "one may infer [from these percentages] that an attitude of defiance still exists among a substantial segment of the fired controller population, regardless of the financial losses they have experienced . . . respondents are a long way from unconditional acceptance of any government 'return to work' offer, and would be likely to carefully weigh the terms of any such offer before returning to FAA."

Naturally, therefore, some who desire reinstatement dream of renewing the 1981 struggle, and reviving PATCO:

I would return as a union organizer to create the changes we deserved, or to lead the next job action—this time, to win! . . . I would not return to the job because of my desire to control airplanes anymore, but only for the chance to make it a better place to work for everyone (yes, even scabs).

My primary concern for returning to work is the rebuilding of another union. If another union could not be rebuilt, and I had to put up with the FAA without a union, and the type of employee who would not want to put a union in place, then I don't think I would be interested in staying on the job.

Overall, one respondent summed up the mission of many when he wrote, "Would love to get back at FAA by having them hire me," even as another promised, "If we could get our jobs back, I would fight those *bastards* from the inside."

It should be noted that O'Keefe's respondents also evidenced a good bit of *pro*-employment flexibility:

45% set no cut-off date after which they would not consider accepting certain FAA reinstatement terms (and 43% were uncertain).

> 34% would not insist on a back pay award (and another
> 22% were uncertain).
>
> 34% would accept a lower paying position.

However motivations differed, all seemed to agree that ATC work, once experienced, was exceedingly hard to forget.

When all was said and done, however, the strikers in the O'Keefe sample finally took a very cautious view of their reinstatement chances:

> *Question 29.* How do you regard USATCO's chances of affecting a reinstatement for dismissed controllers?
>
> | | |
> |---|---|
> | Reasonably good | 15% |
> | Very hard to say | 38% |
> | Highly unlikely | 44% |
> | Other | 3% |
> | | (N = 300) |

Much of this skepticism was clarified in comments handwritten in the "other" column:

> Except for 3 to 6 thousand that want to return to work no one really cares, and I doubt that the situation will ever change. I still have hope, but less with every day that passes.
>
> . . . with the hard hearted/headed president we have, little hope of reemployment prevails while this Administration is in power. Without a surge of "front page" crashes with great loss of life, nobody will know how unsafe the system is and how overworked the controllers are today.

On the other hand, the hopeful view of a very small minority of terminated controllers was put best by a striker who wrote "Stranger things have happened," and another who insisted "Our time will come again," and a third who continues to believe "We'll win yet!"

Summary. Traumatically cut off from the most invigorating and rewarding jobs they could ever imagine filling, many ex-controllers found little solace or reward in the recession-marred labor market. While almost all regained employment, few seem inclined to keep it if their ATC jobs were soon offered back on honorable terms. Still proud and even defiant, their post-strike experience in the labor market brings to mind the summation of an O'Keefe respondent: "I feel I did what had to be done; I got knocked to my knees, but I'm not flat on my face."

Table 10-1
Reemployment of Former Controllers by Education, Standard of Living, and Gender*

	Schooling Completed	Change in Standard of Living	Sex
1. ATC - Australia	A.A.	Lower	M
2. ATC - Saudi Arabia	B.A.	Lower	M
3. ATC - Middle East	17	Much Lower	M
4. ATC - Middle East	3 yrs. College	Higher	M
5. ATC - Papua, New Guinea	2 yrs. College	Much Lower	M
6. ATC - USA	15	Same	M
7. Chief installer, custom auto shop	13	Lower	M
8. Corporate pilot	14	Higher	M
9. Service Mgr., auto dealership	2 yrs. College	Much Lower	M
10. Helicopter pilot	14	Lower	M
11. Aircraft mechanic	13	Lower	M
12. Shipper, receiver	12	Much Lower	M
13. Manufacturer of display booths	2 yrs. College	Lower	M
14. Deputy registrar (Ohio)	14	Same	M
15. Training coordinator, computer firm	14	Lower	F
16. 7-11 Store, assistant manager	12	Much Lower	M
17. Sales representative	B.A.	Same	M
18. Sales/bartender	13	Same	M
19. Owner of seasonal campground	13	Same	M
20. Auto mechanic	2 yrs. College	Higher	M
21. Heavy coil winder	B.A.	Lower	M
22. Satellite network controller	12	Lower	M
23. Network controller/Goddard Space Center		Much Lower	M
24. Government employee	Soph.	Much Lower	M
25. Software consultant	16	Much Higher	M
26. Chimney sweeper	B.A.-Psych.	Lower	M
27. Full-time student	14	Lower	M
28. School bus driver	13	Much Lower	M
29. Telephone equipment installer	2 yrs. College	Lower	M
30. Cabinetmaker (self-employed)	16	Same	M
31. Computer programmer	14	Lower	M
32. Lawn company employee	12	Lower	M
33. Flight dispatcher	2 yrs. College	Lower	M
34. Self-employed	12	Same	M
35. Bill collector	13	Lower	M
36. Carpenter	2 yrs. College	Lower	M
37. Zoning condemnation specialist	12	Much Lower	M
38. Transport driver (Oil Co.)	12	Lower	M
39. Utility worker (Sewer Co.)	12	Lower	M
40. Satellite network controller	MBA	Lower	M
41. Senior administrative secretary	14	Higher	F
42. Secretary	B.S.	Much Lower	F
43. Sales auditor	B.S.	Lower	F
44. Equipment specialist (army)	3 yrs. College	Much Lower	M
45. Purchasing agent	3 yrs. College	Lower	M
46. Purchasing	A.A. + 4 yrs. College	Much Lower	M
47. Appraisor for county assessor	12	Lower	M
48. Delivery truck driver	14	Much Lower	M
49. Police records clerk	12	Lower	M
50. Telephone sales fund-raising for veterans organizations	12	Lower	M

*Drawn randomly from the O'Keefe Survey. Used by permission.

As of the Spring of 1986, perhaps 500 strikers *had* won reinstatement, another 300 or so were employed at ATCs overseas, and perhaps 200 were doing ATC work for private firms. About 650 were still in graduate or professional school, and 100 or less were still jobless (55 months after the strike). Close to 9,500 other former controllers were earning paychecks elsewhere, making the best of a labor force with a persistently high unemployment level, a quizzical view of "suicidal oath-breakers," and a cynical devaluation of employees who had lost all in a strike the public had come to scorn.*

---

*See the appendix interview with a Ft. Lauderdale activist.

Chapter 11

QUALITY OF LIFE

Regaining Control

Life after the strike has been difficult only because I loved air traffic control and the money I made. I hated working for the government and the FAA. My health is better now. My family life is better. If we make a go of our business, we'll be O.K. There is life after the FAA!

Former Air Traffic Controller, O'Keefe Survey, February 1984

The only part of the whole experience I regret are the hardships imposed upon people's families. Being forced to survive for a change is good for one's sense of values . . . Everyone who lands on his feet will have learned from the experience. I'm sorry for those who won't.

Former Air Traffic Controller, O'Keefe Survey, February 1984.

. . . I've learned more about life and reality in the last 2½ years than any scab or boss will ever know or appreciate. I've learned the meaning of family life. I've also learned more about the value of the dollar . . . I feel better now, my attitude and outlook on life is much more positive, and it took the FAA to show me what I was missing. The FAA is the real "Snidley Whiplash"!

Former Air Traffic Controller, O'Keefe Survey, February 1984.

Income Changes. As the details on poststrike employment in an earlier chapter would suggest, the income record of strikers whose ATC earnings in 1981 averaged $34,000 per annum went in only one direction . . . and that wasn't up. Despite often heroic efforts at reducing family costs and expanding income, only one in three former controllers preserved his 1981 income level, and barely 7 percent raised it—in 30 months—to a new high. Instead, a large majority (59 percent) found themselves struggling to get by in 1984 on family incomes substantially lower than those they judged inadequate as (pre-1981) air traffic controllers.

Family Response.   Not surprisingly, the impact of a 50 percent salary cut on middle-income families ($25,000 to $50,000) sent many a striker household into shock, and posed a trying adjustment challenge. When O'Keefe asked another of my tag-on questions the answers revealed much hardship:

Question 25. Overall, what has been the impact of your dismissal on your immediate family?

Took it very hard; very difficult adjustment	39%
Took it hard; relatively quick adjustment	29%
Took it in stride; no real upset	28%
Cannot say	5%
	(N = 200)

Nearly 4 in 5 families "took it hard" or "very hard," a statistic consistent with a handwritten note of one striker who observed, "In some ways, we are still adjusting."

To judge very cautiously from the ratios above, over twice as large a bloc of families had been bowled over as had taken the strike in stride—a distribution that helps explain the wide currency among ex-controllers of rumors about spouse and child abuse, desertion, divorce, destructive drinking, and suicide.

Remaining jobless for an average of 8 months (though 18% went over 1½ years!), many strikers resorted to defensive measures with a high psychic price. Some sold homes they could no longer afford, and moved reluctantly to smaller quarters in less desirable areas. Many used up the nest egg of their FAA retirement fund cash settlement, and began also to wear down family savings they had put aside for a dire emergency. Most drew up stringent new budgets, and scaled back Christmas and vacation spending as never before. Cheaper cuts of meat, diligent use of discount food coupons, stealthy shopping for secondhand items at a Salvation Army outlet, and other humbling adaptations became commonplace.

Some put off expensive medical care, and either ran up large bills with dentists, eye doctors, and other specialists, or simply went without treatment. Many turned with embarrassment and hesitation to close relatives for loans to help tide them over. Especially across the first jobless episode of nearly a year's duration, family tensions and trauma often stretched bonds close to the breaking point, and, in divorce cases well known in the gossip network of the strikers, beyond.

Far commoner, however, by a ratio of 10 to 1, were handwritten expressions of pride in family response:

> ... I regained a family that I had lost by working weekends, holidays, and night shifts. I have learned to communicate with my family now, as I had no time for family life as an air traffic controller. My wife and children have relayed to me many times now how [much] easier I am to get along with ... that goes a long way with me. The pressure is less. However, I do miss the challenge!

> The strike has solidified my marriage, made me aware of the needs of others, brought home the importance of economizing, and given me my health back.

> Family situation vastly improved. Am now a pre-law student, and have never been happier, more relaxed, and self-satisfied.

> It was the best thing that ever happened to me, because I bettered myself and my family's outlook on life.

Indeed, much of the credit for recovery and renewal appears owed to the rallying of loved ones, or so our interviewees testified.

Expectations.   When O'Keefe asked another of the questions I added to his survey, the answers were exceedingly bleak:

Question 26. Compared to your standard of living as an air traffic controller, would you estimate your 1984 standard of living to be-

Much higher	3%
Higher	5%
Same	16%
Lower	46%
Much lower	30%
Don't know	0%
	(N = 300)

When Dave and I probed the question indirectly in our lengthy and widely-scattered interviews, we learned that the strikers had at least eight separate, but related sets of figures in mind when they reflected on their standard of living: Many were thinking about their new net income in terms of its adequacy to meet the bills of the entire family, its regularity, and its reflection of the value private employers put on their person. They also drew comparisons to what they had been earning as ATCs, to what they would now be earning if still ATCs, to what they heard working controllers were now making, what close relatives and friends of the same marketability were earning, and to what they had privately dreamed they might be making at this point in their lives.

Processed over and over again with the aid of an esoteric and confidential formula, one that commonly placed greatest weight on "adequacy to meet bills," the eight variable equation left 3 out of 4 strikers disappointed in the results. Overall, the inability of 3 in 4 to expect a rising standard of living in the current year—an expectation that most adult Americans regard almost as their due (or did so before the 1981–1983 recession)—remains a grim measure of the lingering harm done in 1981.

Personal Health.   On the brighter side, the answers to *Ques. 7, "How would you describe your present health?"* were decidedly upbeat. To judge very tentatively from the self-reports of O'Keefe's USATCO respondents, 60 percent either maintained or moved up to an "excellent" state of health after being fired, and only 5 percent believed their personal health had suffered since that event (while another 28 percent remained at or moved up to the middle level). Put another way, 28 percent felt their health had improved, 66 percent reported no change, and only 5 percent seemed worried now about a decline.

Very few respondents choose to comment one way or another about the matter, though most who wrote took pride in their poststrike well-being:

> I probably added 10 years to my life!

> I have truly found a better way of life. I no longer look forward to vacation.

> . . . the intangibles, such as an excellent mental attitude towards the whole world, are so much better that I can't place a value on them.

Overall, the health reports were far more often positive than negative, and this note, along with claims of family togetherness, stands out as the rare bright spot in the entire poststrike story.

Political Response.   The O'Keefe survey asked nothing directly about the pre- and poststrike political philosophy of the strikers. Second only to the subject of PATCO's mistakes, however, this drew the largest number of volunteered comments. In a ratio of 12 to 1, the respondents expressed surprise, disenchantment, and even outrage at the government's treatment of striking air traffic controllers. Many had not expected their sole employer, one they had served for over a decade on the average (military plus FAA years), to demonstrate the attitude they encountered:

. . . a miscarriage of justice. We were dealt with too harshly, with no regard for the fact that many of us saved people's lives, and most are good American veterans, many of whom served in Vietnam in a difficult time to stand up and defend your country. Why didn't the country defend us with at least some FAIRNESS?

I feel the court is the only shot, but we got a real eye opener of how this government really works. It's crooked, corrupt, and works in the interest of the very few, with the masses gullible enough to take it.

Had more faith in Government than should have that it would do the just thing.

I had little faith in our Government before the strike; now I have none.

Very few of our politicians in Washington gave us any support. They said what we wanted to hear, but their actions were not equal to their lip service.

Looking back, it's still hard to believe the cold harshness displayed by the government. There is no doubt in my mind that union-busting held a high priority. It turned my stomach to hear the Reagan Administration praise the union Solidarity in Poland, and place its own union people in jail. I have little to no respect left for our Government and judicial system, and often question the statement that we live in a democratic society.

My patriotism has gone down the tubes. Can't say that I'd ever fight for this country again as I once did in Vietnam.

This experience has greatly shaken my trust in our government, and in people in general. To be a Vietnam veteran who came back to indifference; then to serve another 8 years in the government, only to get "crucified" for one mistake, is almost more than I can handle emotionally.

The FAA and the Government have no hesitation about telling bald-faced lies.

One spoke for many when he wrote, "My biggest disappointment was my naivete about the character of the government."

Searching for explanations for the government's harshness, the O'Keefe respondents focused on ethical and moral duplicity more often than class conflict:

No one could have believed that Reagan and Lewis would have been willing to set a new standard for abuse of government power, but they were and did!

I made several errors in judgment. Those errors concerned the administration's total and absolute commitment to destroy all us rats. My faith in Mom, God, Country, and Apple Pie is destroyed. I should have remembered my experience in Vietnam and post-Vietnam.

Made the mistake of believing our government was honest. We were used by our government for political reasons. Our problems were ignored, justice was a paper formality, propaganda was inherent to the Reagan Administration. Who were the *real* losers of this fight? PATCO or the people of these United States?

I have only one real problem: Polish union members are praised by Reagan, and he had our people sent to prison. Justice and equality, my butt!

We did what had to be done, but we were naive to the fact that right and wrong mean nothing in this country anymore. The only thing that creates change is *money/politics*.

We did not give enough thought as to just how corrupt our system of government can be—how shortsighted they are.

Here, and elsewhere in our personal interviews, Dave and I were struck by the relative absence of class conflict analysis, and a focus instead on nonpolitical matters of honesty and integrity—a type of apolitical analysis that dilutes the ability of the post-1981 experience to radicalize these once-Republican-voting, middle-class, mainstream Americans. Expressions of militancy were evident, to be sure, in a very small number of responses:

I was cheering for the Czechs in the Czech vs. USA Olympic Hockey game, if that tells you anything. I know we were right in '81 . . . and I'd do it again!

I wasn't militant before the strike, but I am now!

Never again will I sit on my hands and let others manipulate me. I will take an active part in all decisions concerning my future. This, to me, was the greatest lesson learned from the strike.

We never had a chance—the leadership and we ourselves did not know what we were up against. We all believed that justice was inherent in the American Governmental system—Wrong! Unless the American people and their governmental "representatives" reject the current American shift towards neo-Fascism, none of us will ever have a chance at a decent, honorable, productive, and rewarding work environment.

Consistent, however, with a disinclination to "go to the barricades," the militancy of even outraged former controllers diffused and deflated without impact—lacking, as it did, any firm grounding in political philosophy—left, right, or otherwise.

Overall, and to draw now especially on our crosscountry interviews, Dave and I have the impression that even an eye-opening and possibly embittering experience like this one has not—at least, not yet—radicalized any significant number of former controllers. Indeed, it may have turned many more off politics than it has stirred any new interest in the theories of the Left or Right.

A plurality of PATCO members in 1981 were Reagan supporters, and the fact that PATCO was one of only three AFL-CIO unions to back the Republican candidate was congenial to the rank and file. Now thoroughly alienated from the Reagan presidency, the strikers seem to lean toward "a plague on all your houses!" cynicism, a defensive retreat from giving their trust soon again to politicians of any political stripe.

As for the wishful thinking of some on the Democratic Left who believe these strikers may soon interpret the FAA-PATCO clash in historic class conflict terms, Dave and I consider this a very faint possibility. Socialized by years of upward status mobility, patriotic military service, and civil service tenure experience, the ex-controllers, their lingering post-1981 grievances not withstanding, impressed us with their commitment to mainstream, conventional, and even suprapatriotic politics.

Bewildered by the treatment they met, and are still suffering at the government's hands, the strikers pin responsibility on the current President and his FAA leadership cadre. Most lack ideological motivation to construe their plight in broader political terms. While it seems true that the situation has whetted the political interest of some, raised new doubts about mainstream media with most, and stirred the militancy of a very few, turning this to political account seems a doubtful prospect, especially as once-vivid strike memories fade with every passing year.

Until the political vistas and vision of the strikers are expanded and enriched beyond anything now evident, their political reaction to the greatest labor movement clash ever in federal employee relations is likely to disappoint those on the Left and on the Right, any whose ideology argues that such an event should have galvanzied and radicalized its victims.

Summary. What can we say about the 1981–1984 quality of life of O'Keefe's USATCO respondents? As often before in these three chapters we can say nothing quite as well as do the men themselves:

> I like to think that I was the best there was at what I did, as most controllers probably do. But I can honestly say that I don't miss it. I am a survivor, and I will be the best there is at whatever I decide to do, with the help of the Lord . . . what we did was correct, and the Lord will look favorably upon us all, because we stood up for what we believed in.

> I do not regret the strike; too many people prostitute themselves for the dollar. But I am sorry for the trauma that has been inflicted upon so many good people.

> This was the greatest thing I have ever done for my family . . . We get along better. No drinking problem. Health problems have disappeared. Better relationship with friends, and new friends are easier to make.

The news media killed us. Other unions deserted us. Strangers, even friends, say they are glad I was fired. I could not feel the same about my President, my country, or my job as a controller again.

—To which another striker adds his seasoned valediction: "Hang in there! Life doesn't end when the paycheck stops, even though it feels that way."*

_____

*See the appendix interview with a Philadelphia activist and his family, and the contributed essay, "Post-Strike Lives of Boston Area Controllers," by Britta Fischer.

Chapter 12

STRIKE REFLECTIONS

Hindsight Wisdom and Lingering Hopes

. . . I don't think there is a member of this union who wants to go to jail . . . However, . . . there comes a time in everyone's life . . . that you must take a position morally on something you really believe in . . . there is a time when they must make a moral decision.
Robert Poli, PATCO President, congressional testimony, June 19, 1981, p. 89.

If 12,000 controllers had gone crawling back in when Reagan threatened us, everyone would have been convinced that we were just money-hungry crybabies with no real cause. We proved this was more than just an economic strike, and that the problems in the FAA were serious enough to force 12,000 people (give or take a few weak-kneed jack-offs) to make a tremendous sacrifice.
Former Air Traffic Controller, O'Keefe Survey, February 1984.

I've never blamed anyone for our failure, except maybe myself for not trying harder. I don't blame PATCO, the pilots, or the government. It's like playing poker. We had a good hand and played it out. We had maybe a good full house. But they had 4 of a kind!
Former Air Traffic Controller, O'Keefe Survey, February 1984.

When Steve O'Keefe asked one of the four questions I tagged onto his survey—"How do you now feel about the strike?"—his USATCO respondents gave it their overwhelming endorsement: only 34 percent felt it "never should have occurred and was mistaken from the start." A 43 percent plurality

151

thought it had been a "proper choice; dismissals could not have been fore-
seen." And 23 percent thought it had been the "only chance we had." (Consistent with their reputation as independent thinkers, 27 percent also chose to
write in an original point of view, which, on close scrutiny, gave often be-
grudging support to the 1981 strike.)

Why do nearly seven out of ten former controllers continue to speak and
think positively about a strike that cost them their careers, their union, and
their standing with the American public? To understand prostrike attitudes
here is to appreciate underlying ideas about the strike's sponsorship, its character, PATCO's many-faceted record, and Robert Poli's controversial leadership.

1. Strike Sponsorship.   A small number of ex-controllers believe they
were railroaded into the strike, one the new Reagan Administration viewed as
giving it a rare opportunity to "send a message" to easily-intimidated unions
across the land:

> I fear we were forced into the strike by the Government. It was a long-
> range plan that had nothing to do with us. But we were a vehicle to break
> a union on TV and thru the media. The dominoes were lined up; all they
> had to do was push the first over, ours . . . I feel if we wouldn't have gone
> on strike the FAA would have fired half of us anyway. They had this thing
> planned for too long.

> The Government forced the confrontation by ignoring all reasonable ef-
> fort to reconcile differences on the issues; therefore, the strike was inevit-
> able.

Explanations of this sort led many into harsh criticisms of Reagan's political
philosophy, and many worries about organized labor's near-future.

Allied to this was the view that the strike's origins could more accurately
be blamed on FAA leaders who were smarting from nearly 20 years of
steadily-escalating war with workplace insurgents:

> The strike was inevitable. Unavoidable. I still feel anger and resentment at
> the FAA itself. I am convinced that the lockout, blacklisting, and destruc-
> tion of PATCO was the FAA's objective from the start. They were over-
> joyed when Reagan said "Fire them!" As usual, the safety compromised,
> the millions of dollars lost, the careers destroyed, were a secondary con-
> sideration.

> Bottom line is we underestimated the FAA and overestimated ourselves.
> The FAA wanted this more than we did (as it turns out).

Those of this persuasion—just over one in ten of the O'Keefe respondents—
would probably agree with the striker who grimly wrote, "The strike was encouraged by the FAA; they set a trap, and we walked in, waving our banners."

Far more, perhaps 60 percent, now view the strike as inevitable and un-avoidable, a natural and even necessary outgrowth of irreconcilable differences:

> At the time it was the right thing to do. It was coming, one way or another, we all agreed.

> I must say I expected the dismissals, even told my family we'd all get fired, but it still had to be done.

> In my opinion, it was the only chance we had, since we had already tried every other legal avenue.

> I believe the strike was our only option. I believe the Government encouraged the strike by 1) not allowing a mediator to come in; and 2) by making each offer less attractive than the previous one. I believe that if Reagan really wanted us to return to work, things would have been handled differently. I think the Administration saw a way to give a warning to Labor while reducing the controller workforce (mainly the ones that cared the most about the system) and winding up with a compliant group that would do anything they're told without question.

Many link their inability to avoid this particular crash—something that goes against the grain—to a sort of call to honor, an obligation they had to meet:

> It was doomed from the start; it was the only correct choice . . . even though I firmly believe "you can't fight City Hall," that did not relieve me of the responsibility to do so.

> Had no interest in striking. Just seen a lot of darn good men ready to give it all up, and felt perhaps their reason was good enough for me to put my 12 years in a job that was love, not work, on the line . . . no regrets!

> I did see the possibility of dismissal. Had to try to change the course of the profession at some time; why not now?

Pensive and hard on themselves, tempted to see how it *ought* to have been done, the strikers take consolation in the notion that nothing could have prevented the 1981 clash, and since that was how it had to be, most take pride in how they conducted themselves throughout, though the price was unexpectedly and excruciatingly high.

2. With Heads Held High. As hard as the general public may find it to understand, or to empathize with, over one in four USATCO respondents to O'Keefe survey regarded some aspect of the 1981 strike as a high point in their lives:

> . . . we were right in what we did, and I will always be proud to have been a part of our actions.

> I'm a Vietnam veteran. I consider the PATCO strike a civil disobedience.
> It set my conscious free. Morally, it was the best thing to have happened to
> me.

> I found new friendships and strengthened existing scores during this or-
> deal, becoming closer to my fellow "firees" than any other group of peo-
> ple I've known.

Over and again in our personal interviews Dave and I heard proud men af-
firm their participation: Most wrung what satisfaction the strike offered from
a sense of having answered the call, having come through when it counted.

Some unusual strikers were inclined to put their own record under scrutiny, and to assume responsibility for personal shortcomings they linked to
the strike's outcome. A remarkable example of such unsparing candor accompanied an O'Keefe questionnaire from a thirty-three-year-old former
controller:

> I hired into the FAA in 1977; it rapidly became apparent to me that a
> 1981 strike date was already virtually etched in stone. The PATCO leader-
> ship, as observed by me in local and regional seminars, and in the printed
> matter distributed to the membership, seemed to me intelligent, articu-
> late, and perceptive. For this reason I was content to be a foot soldier in-
> stead of a leader—an unusual step for me, and a measure of the trust I
> had in PATCO. Although I was thoroughly *aware* of developments, I did
> not try to *shape* them . . . the strike did not seem an unreasonable or un-
> principled course of action, and I certainly did not foresee the dismissals.

> In retrospect, I do not regret what happened to me personally. I would
> not want to be working today at the cost of having betrayed my friends
> and coworkers; such a compromise in principle and commitment is un-
> thinkable to me. Nonetheless, I wish I had done things differently: I
> should have been more involved in shaping PATCO policy; I should have
> made much more of an effort to verify the working assumptions upon
> which PATCO strategy was based. I like to think that if I had done so, I
> would have been able to shape a more flexible approach to confronting
> the FAA, or at least have had a sound basis for appraising PATCO and
> my coworkers—from the outset—that I did not believe an inflexible
> strike plan would succeed, and that I would not commit myself to such a
> course of action.

Dave and I found many more such men in our interviewing, and left these
encounters having learned much of value from each of these former controllers.

3. PATCO's Record.   Much more complex a factor in explaining pro-
strike attitudes is how USATCO members now assess the preparation, maneuvers, and competency of the union they followed . . . over the cliff's edge.

While only 13 percent damn the strike outright and regret its ever having occurred, far more—82 percent of those who offered handwritten comments (or 56 percent of all)—had some heartfelt criticisms to make of an aspect of PATCO's conduct before, during, and since the fatal clash: In order of decreasing mentions, the ex-controllers had complaints about the strike's timing, the failure of PATCO to line up AFL-CIO and union support, the gaps in data provided the rank and file; the inadequacies of PATCO's public relations, the failure of PATCO to anticipate the Reagan Administration's hard line, the failure of PATCO to "play dirty," and the PATCO decision not to order the strikers to return within the White House 48-hour "window."

What we seem to have far more resembles a lover's quarrel than a bitter parting of the ways. Many, for example, who now wonder if it would have been wiser to hoist the white flag and return to work often have PATCO's preservation and the persistence of pressure on the FAA foremost in mind:

> PATCO leadership made the mistake of not having prepared to accept defeat and try to save a greater portion of the membership which could have taken care of the rest.

> A strike would have come sooner or later anyhow. The mistake made was not ordering the controllers back within the 48 hours. It would have been much easier and more effective to continue the fight from within instead of being on the outside.

> . . . our leadership should have ordered us back to work in compliance with Reagan's deadline. We would have made our point, and still been around to kick ass later.

Ex-controllers of this persuasion imagine continuing the strike from inside, a scenario of ceaseless guerrilla war and hit-and-run tactics—far too like a rerun of PATCO's previous 13 years to win many adherents among now-or-never strikers.

The point remains, however, that the 82 percent of note-adding respondents who volunteered a criticism of this or that aspect of the PATCO record appear to have done so with more positive than negative feelings, on balance, for that vanquished organization:

> . . . I am sad that so many good people were hurt so badly, but I *am*, and shall be whilst I breathe, *proud* to be a PATCO man!

> The strike was justified, but we should have bided our time and waited for a better moment. Hindsight is always the best, however, and I have no bitterness toward any of our former organization.

> The FAA was, or wanted to be, a paramilitary organization. There's nothing wrong with that, except the FAA forgot one key ingredient—*leadership*! We had a lot of supervisors in the FAA, but no leaders. They were in PATCO!

Sensitive about media and man-in-the-street derision of "Poli's Last Stand" and PATCO members of "Rev. Jones' Kool Aid drinkers," these strikers reaffirm their pro-PATCO identification and loyalty . . . albeit discreetly, in a land that derides losers.

4. *Poli's Leadership—Pro and Con.*   No aspect of the strike so divides the rank and file as the question of the quality of Robert Poli's leadership—or lack of it. Negative comments outran positives ones by a 16 to 1 ratio, and covered a broad range of issues:

> The only mistake made was when Poli let his personality conflict get in the way of rational thought processes.

> Enough mistakes to go around for both sides. Union was poorly prepared for absolute dismissals; should have been an out. Poli should have been given lessons in portraying a less arrogant personality.

> Dismissals could have been avoided if Poli and national officers would have been in constant talks with the Administration, the Secretary of Labor, and the AFL-CIO. 11,500 of us went it alone and got killed. . . . Had Poli been better in tune with the Administration this all could have been prevented.

> We were misled; we were lied to about the numbers. Once the numbers [of strikers] fell below the mandate we should have been ordered back to work by Poli. Had extremely poor to nil public relations. Lack of prior coordination with labor leaders, and too many glory seekers killed our chances of winning anything. Too many good, honest controllers were betrayed. Being a facility rep and organizer, I saw these shortcomings, but no one would listen, especially Poli.

Others, however, with whom Dave and I have talked across the country—especially PATCO local officers—continue as loyal admirers of Poli's assertiveness, charisma, and fierce dedication to the cause. Most would appreciate the view of a respondent who holds "absolutely no hard feelings towards Bob Poli as a lot of people seem to. He did exactly as *we* directed him to do."

5. *Embittered Losers.*   A minority of 13 percent, it will be recalled, feel the 1981 strike never should have occurred, and their views warrant brief exploration—since their ranks may grow should reinstatement continue to fade as a real possibility.

Some of the strikers explain their seemingly anomalous participation in very personal terms:

> I could have retired at reduced annuity 8 May 1982. Obviously, striking was a stupid move for me careerwise, but I could not tell younger men to strike while I continued to work. I gave 29 years, 3 months, and 19 days to

my brothers in PATCO, and I doubt that there is much gratitude felt on the part of my brothers.

I felt from the beginning that a strike was not the answer. I foresaw the possibility of dismissals and I made that plain to several people in my local. I'm out here with them because I know if the union got the numbers they were looking for, I wouldn't last very long inside anyway. However, I strongly believe the controllers of this country deserve much more than they have received.

Far more typical, however, of those who resent the strike they lost are ex-controllers angry at themselves or at the union principle:

The strike was a big mistake! The majority of controllers I know still can't believe that we gave up a job we loved so much for reasons we really never cared about and damn sure can't remember. I think my lifelong opinion of unions was correct: They have outlived their usefulness and are no longer looking out for the mass, but for the few.

. . . I made the biggest mistake of my life by listening to union bull. So far I lost a job I loved and have been totally blackballed from a profession I loved, all for reasons that are moot at best.

Much of this was well summarized by the respondent who wrote, "Either way, strike or no strike, was a no-win situation for us."

6. *Embittered Strikers.*   In bringing this overview of poststrike reflections to a close, it is important to note the many targets of the former controllers's persisting animosity. Strike breakers naturally lead the list:

I despise the "sprinters"; they walked on our back.

I still have some bad feelings for the controllers who ran back to work after the 48 hr. time deadline. *I always will!*

"Experts" who may have let PATCO down come in for a mention or two:

We got misled by our lawyers!! But not our PATCO leaders.

I believe we were "set up" by the Reagan Administration. We were told by the legal people these "things" could not happen to us, ever! Not only wasn't that correct, but everything "hit the fan!" right away. Then our legal people basically abandoned us. It wasn't their fight, unless we had more money. Bitter against some people? Yes!

Finally, some revealing disaffection with certain fellow strikers shows up in the O'Keefe commentaries:

> I can't even get reinstated controllers to join USATCO. Even former PATCO members don't give a shit about their former coworkers. *Sad*, but true.

> We thought some would be dismissed; that's why we had the strike fund. But the controllers did not stick together when Reagan threatened them with dismissal.

> My regrets and frustrations do not lie with PATCO or being fired, but with my fellow workers and those that have dropped out of the struggle. We were a 100% striking facility Aug. 3rd. Now I'm the only one that has bothered to join USATCO and stay in touch. My disappointment is in my fellow controllers who obviously had only a commitment to gamble for $10,000, and none for improving their chosen career. Frustrating to lose your job and ego, but no excuse for turning your back on the Cause.

Should this sort of disaffection and disillusionment grow—and with the shutdown of USATCO, it may—the years ahead may see an erosion of the feeling and commitment that now still helps a sizeable minority of ex-controllers stay in touch with one another.

Summary.   To judge cautiously, then, from the inability of USATCO ever to attract more than one-fourth of the 11,345 strikers into membership, the large majority of dismissed controllers seem to have put the matter effectively behind them, and have "vectored" a new life course altogether. To judge cautiously from O'Keefe's sample of USATCO members—and our extensive interviews with strikers in and outside of that PATCO successor—a small number of other ex-controllers *continue* on "strike," at least in terms of its never-ending salience in their lives.

These strikers, by and large, continue to believe the strike was unavoidable, moral, and honorable, albeit seemingly mismanaged and fatally flawed before undertaken. Many have the benefit of 20/20 hindsight in believing that this or that option would have improved the outcome, though most remain loyal to PATCO's vision even while second-guessing its methods. A very few are deep in regrets and recriminations, a fate that may befall more if reinstatement fades as a viable policy outcome. Overall, however, the 1981 strike remains for most strikers an event for which they offer no apologies, and derision of which they do not accept. Many regard themselves as better and braver for having carried it out, for as one wrote, "Sometimes, you just have to 'go for it!'"*

> *It was the only chance we thought we had—we were young and ignorant of the Labor Movement and the struggles of working and poor people in general. It's rather obvious other choices were available, but I would do it all over again tomorrow.*
> Former Controller, O'Keefe Survey, February 1984.

---

*See the appendix interview with a San Antonio activist.

Part V

FORMER CONTROLLERS: A BREED
BACK TOGETHER

. . . my mind is etched with the memory of those [1970 sick-out] air traffic controllers who sacrificed so much for the PATCO cause. This organization and you, the controllers who make it a brotherhood of people, owe those 1970 path-finders an eternal debt of gratitude . . .

Robert E. Poli, *PATCO Newsletter*, March 25, 1980, p. 4.

I loved my job, . . . , and I want it back with all my heart. I want to go back with my head held high, arm-in-arm with the people I left with. I believe we were right, that we had no other option, and that USATCO is the avenue to return all of us that want to return. I just wish we could convince everyone else.

USATCO Newsletter, January 1983.

We are an organization on the mend . . . the avenue through which all members, past, present, and future, can become united once again. As long as USATCO is there, no one should feel alone.

USATCO Newsletter, March 1984.

Live your life so if you lose you are still ahead.

Will Rogers

Chapter 13

UNITED STATES AIR TRAFFIC CONTROLLERS ORGANIZATION (USATCO)

On How to Help Bind the Wounds, 1982-1984

. . . And let's not forget one very important thing: we've come a long way together, further than anyone gave us credit for being able to, and we've done that because we didn't give up . . . there's still much that can be done for a group of people who deserve every chance there is.
Editorial, *USATCO Newsletter*, November 1983.

From July 1982, through November 1984, the United States Air Traffic Control Organization (USATCO), sought support from the White House, Congress, the FAA, the media, and the public in one of the most unusual and revealing strike recovery efforts of modern times. What it asked for, finally settled for, and why, are discussed below, for in the USATCO record are lessons of considerable value to all concerned with labor's poststrike possibilities and problems.

1.) Why Bother? In my role as a frequent research visitor to its small Washington, D.C. headquarters (known affectionately as "the bunker"), I often explored with its half-dozen leaders the question of whether their precarious venture made any real sense at all.

An overwhelming majority, 75 percent or more of the fired strikers, seemed intent on putting their ATC careers and PATCO participation behind them. None of the apparent victors—the Reagan forces or the FAA hierarchy—gave any evidence of softening opposition to rehiring the strikers. Why then, I would ask, had the bunker crowd formed a penniless successor to a bankrupt PATCO a week after its demise, and why would they persist in a struggle so many knowledgeable others dismissed as a dead issue?

From the outset, USATCO was clear about an ambitious agenda that stretched resources across three major sets of objectives:

Vocational Goals

1) Promote a policy-shaping link between the need for reinstatement and the need for the safety of air travel;

2) Talk up reinstatement at every relevant congressional hearing and reception ("If USATCO doesn't work, it won't be because I didn't talk to somebody." President Eads, *USATCO Newsletter*, February 1983);

3) Boost morale among USATCO members with news of court and FAA reinstatement gains;

4) Provide low-cost legal support for strikers pursuing their legal rights to reinstatement; and

5) Publicize job openings referred to it by reemployed ex-controllers, business-owning ex-controllers, and AFL-CIO locals.

Political and Media Goals

6) Weigh the ideas advanced by knowledgeable parties for new movement in the current impasse (such as expressions of White House interest in privatization of the system); and

7) Speak for the strikers on the occasion of media interest in their poststrike lives *and* the 1981 issues (". . . ensure that those reasons for which we have all sacrificed so much are not distorted by those who will do it if they are not challenged.");

Personal Goals

8) Rebuild the fraternal community of former controllers through the publication of upbeat notes and personal news from USATCO members ("Our principal role here at the national office is to try and bring our family back together.");

9) Maintain a phone counseling service for troubled strikers, and a phone hot line for updates on poststrike developments; and—

10) Remind strikers that the PATCO job action was basically about "the principles of aviation safety and the betterment of the air traffic control profession."

Above all, the half-dozen former controllers who dreamed up, formalized, and maintained USATCO did so to make the point that what they called "the lockout and blacklisting" *had* to give way to the rebuilding of the air traffic control system—if the safety of the public was soon to be assured. Only the reinstatement of the strikers, America's truly professional controllers, could achieve this rapidly and economically. Accordingly, the PATCO struggle to rehabilitate the ATC system was *not* done for. (As one O'Keefe respondent wrote, "The opera ain't over until the Fat Lady sings.")

2.) "Making Do" in the Bunker.   With dues set at $20 a month ($240 per annum), and the membership hovering between 1200 and a high of 2,400, dues receipts should have reached $24,000 to $48,000 a month. But, with many members financially strapped, USATCO averaged little more than $11,000 a month from about 800 members.

While a long list warrants review, a few membership services of the dollar-short group particularly stand out: USATCO made a special effort to promote outreach among its members. It offered an invaluable type of legal aid. It provided a phone counseling service of crucial importance to users. And it published a monthly newsletter so rich and varied that it is discussed in a separate part of this chapter.

Perhaps the second most important personal service (after publication of the *USATCO Newsletter*) was USATCO's Legal Services Program:

> . . . we wanted to ensure that any fired controller would be able to keep his or her legal appeal alive for as long as possible by assisting in retaining competent legal representation at reasonable rates and by making information available on how to carry on.

Over time, the Legal Program drew 3,000 or so users impressed by the experience of USATCO's firm and its comparatively low fees, so reasonable that members not taking part were able to use it as a bench mark when negotiating with their own attorney. (The average cost to process an appeal to the MSPB was about $750 per case, and to a federal court, about $1,000.)

A third service of note involved the art of phone counseling with what therapists call "the third ear." Especially in the months right after the strike, USATCO received scores of calls weekly from members in need of a patient, responsive listener, someone who had "been there" himself.

Another major and related service involved providing what USATCO called "ammunition," or the wherewithal to counter the most telling of arguments made against reinstatement. When the FAA, for example, insisted that working controllers would refuse to take the strikers back, or that returning strikers would need 6 months or more to regain proficiency, USATCO urged members to note that 500 strikers had quietly won appeals that got them their old ATC posts with no fuss and very rapid renewal of satisfactory performance. Similarly, when PATCO's prediction of doom was discredited by the absence of major air crashes after the strike, USATCO helped its members learn to rebut with an explanation that highlighted controller error in a rising number of well publicized near misses.

3.) Membership Services (General).   In a far more impersonal, but no less valuable way, USATCO tried to serve its members by realigning with labor and renewing the political activism of this type of American. Particular pride was taken in USATCO's effort to mend fences and "build bridges" where organized labor was concerned. At the start of 1983, for example, 618 information packages were mailed to labor editors throughout the country, many of whom subscribed to the USATCO *Newsletter.* Since the combined circulation of the AFL-CIO affiliated publications was over 15 million, USATCO hoped in this way to clear up strike-based misunderstandings, secure financial donations for its legal efforts, and possibly even learn of job openings for its members.

USATCO explained to members that thousands of strikers who were not able to keep their appeals alive had *one* hope for reinstatement: "The only remedy remaining . . . is a political one . . ." And, "in those cases where we haven't been able to change the attitude of the incumbent, we've got to be ready to change the incumbent. Our turn will come." (March 1984) While many USATCO officers eventually worked overtime on behalf of Mondale, the organization was careful to suggest President Reagan "stood to lose nothing politically, but could gain everything by taking back the controllers." He could "make amends with organized labor, show he has compassion, that situations change, that there is no reason to persecute people forever," and, not incidentally, earn the votes of grateful USATCO families (*Newsletter,* August 1984).

4.) USATCO Newsletter.   Outstanding in both personal and impersonal service to the membership was the organization's monthly newsletter, perhaps the most popular of all of USATCO's efforts. Sensitively geared to long-term, as well as to pressing interests of its readers, a typical issue would feature a spirit-lifting editorial, a prostriker explanation of recent legislative and judicial developments, capsule rewrites of AP/UP and local newspaper treatment of poststrike issues, relevant comments from air industry magazines, and a very large cross-section of letters from USATCO members.

Consistent with the themes of caring, concern, and commitment the *Newsletter* featured "good and welfare" notes of an urgent nature, such as the need for donations to help the two-year-old daughter of a striker with cancer-treatment medical expenses, a striker severely burned in a home accident, and the family of a striker in a hospital intensive care unit. Moving notes of appreciation from recipients helped round out the tale, and confirmed the sense of a community of concern nurtured by USATCO.

Naturally, the *Newsletter* was used to give public thanks to overseas ATC unions that sent donations and took out group memberships: the honor roll included ATC brothers and sisters in Australia, Britain, Denmark, France, Germany, and Sweden. American labor organizations honored included MEBA (the PATCO sponsor), PASS (a union of the FAA's technical work-force), the American Postal Workers, the Machinists Union, the American Federation of Government Employees, and the AFL-CIO. (Over 100 separate locals of these unions, and also of AFSME, AFT, the Carpenters, CWA, IBEW, ITU, Laborers, NFL Players Association, Teamsters, and others made contributions.)

The *Newsletter* also featured detailed accounts of helpful services fired controllers might not otherwise know about, such as that the Veteran's Administration had new funds for vocational schooling for unskilled, hardcore unemployed, and some of its members might qualify; dismissed controllers might qualify for retirement benefits under Public Law 92-297, and were advised to contact a USATCO brother in Texas who specialized in detailed advice on successful appeals; and USATCO had knowledge of 67 businesses in 26 states started by strikers eager for orders from other strikers; a directory would soon be mailed to 3,000 on the *Newsletter* subscription list.

Beginning with the March 1984 issue the *Newsletter* spotlighted job openings, and invited readers to mail in resumes to facilitate matchup phone call referrals from the USATCO office. Typical of the openings cited was a Virginia call for an ANP mechanic with jet experience, 60 GS-4 positions with the Federal Protective Service, and many ATC positions overseas (Abu Shabi, Australia, Papua New Guinea, Saudi Arabia, etc.).

This list still does not cover all of the *Newsletter*'s helpful features, such as its critique of FAA computer uses in ATC work, its inclusion of informal reports from USATCO regional directors, and its occasional use of aphorisms from Cesar Chavez, James Michener, Jesse Jackson, and the like. Thanks to its imaginative range of material its readers often told Dave and me they looked forward to its arrival, read it from cover to cover, shared it with other former controllers, and valued it as a service of substantial worth.

5.) Expectations of the Rank and File.   USATCO never stopped asking its members to act, the political area being only one aspect: Social gatherings, phone networks, and Strike Anniversary reunions were urged to help "defeat the isolated feeling and ensure that everyone has the latest information." Volunteers were sought by USATCO district directors and the national office to make lobbying phone calls, assist in large mailings, and so on. An update package was available for members willing to make a written or personal presentation to labor in their area. Everyone was urged to patronize businesses started by USATCO members, listed in the *Directory*.

Here as elsewhere in its operation, USATCO emphasized that its most important expectation of its members was that they share mutual support—would contact, and assist one another (as their oral history notes they had before 1981).

6.) *Organizing the Strikers.*   Considerable time and effort in the bunker went into the design and execution of efforts to expand the roles of USATCO members, but to little avail. Discouraged by this lack of response, the organization traced its problems to six unwelcome types:

> *"Bummed-Out" Victims,"* or those in such bad shape they could barely help themselves, let alone anyone else.

> *"Long Gone" Emigrants,* or "those who had cut themselves off so effectively, they probably no longer knew what's happening."

> *Shell-Shocked Officers,* those ex-leaders "so preoccupied with their own wounded egos they can't be bothered with someone else's need."

> *Self-Centered "Winners,"* those doing so well that "they don't need this anymore, they're through with it, 'never going back.'"

> *USATCO Detractors,* "those who will tell you that they just can't support anything or anyone through USATCO, because the organization offends them. Don't ask them what they're doing; they can only tell why they won't."

> *Global Negators,* "those who are so busy blaming everything and everyone else for what's happening that they're unable to see that their mistake may be the worst of all."

At every opportunity Eads and other *Newsletter* writers pleaded with nonjoiners not to "turn your back on our history, our heritage, the fact that we have stood together despite the odds. It's the one important asset that no one, certainly not the FAA nor their bureaucracy, can take away from us."

7.) *Reasons for Dissension.*   Despite the voluntary nature of the organization, USATCO had its normal share of disagreements within the ranks. Some members never quite forgave the organization for starting out as a nonprofit corporation rather than as a bona fide labor union, a branch of MEBA (as PATCO had been) or perhaps a branch of the American Federation of Government Employees (which began to organize working controllers in 1984). In this way, former controllers would have stayed aligned with organized labor despite PATCO's termination. And the FAA, the media, the AFL-CIO, and the public would have better understood USATCO's nature and intent from the outset.

The other side pointed out that USATCO had had little choice in the matter. Lawyers warned its founders to avoid any move that could render it liable to charges of being a legal "alter ego" for PATCO—and for about $35 million in damages and criminal fines assessed against PATCO. Furthermore, an unknown, but possibly large number of alienated strikers were believed disinclined to join any sort of labor union so soon again, given the meager strike aid provided by the AFL-CIO and its constituent unions. Therefore USATCO started out as a nonprofit organization, only to seek IRS recognition months later as a "labor union" when the PATCO link and antilabor liabilities seemed manageable.

A related rift focused on the character of the new organization, especially after its conversion to a labor union format. To help promote an image of the dismissed controllers as upright, mainstream, and level-headed types, rather than as radical and unreliable oath-breakers, the USATCO officers adopted conventional attire, a low-key, businesslike approach, and the restrained language and comportment thought likely to make the best impression on Washington movers and shakers.

Certain USATCO activists disparaged this organizational culture from the start, and grew more vociferous as its victories were slow in coming. As they explained their position to Dave and me, they preferred a more aggressive and risk-taking style. USATCO should have knocked loudly on the doors of policy shapers, rather than merely indicated its availability to explain the case for reinstatement at any time of day or night. USATCO should have told various unions exactly what help it needed in the way of loaned or donated office equipment and supplies; it should have gotten its anti-FAA demonstrators on nightly TV news shows after every near miss or FAA foulup. And USATCO should have shed its "Mr. Nice Guy" role in favor of a much more colorful, macho, and virile self-representation—a brand of high-risk advice the bunker-ites resisted to the very end.

A third, and perhaps most costly of all the rifts also concerned a decision made early on. USATCO's leadership cadre was divided over the wisdom and justice of offering membership to working controllers. No one doubted that some were pro-PATCO loyalists with sound reasons for appearing to have scabbed on the strike; nor that valuable confidential information might come to USATCO through this channel. And some shared a generous concern to "help the families of those fired and the new controllers who are not confident of their futures" (*USATCO Newsletter*, February 1983, p. 12).

But many others believed the animosity strikers felt toward working controllers was so unyielding that USATCO should steer clear of these potential
enrollers. (Even a USATCO officer, Bill Taylor, was quoted in the press in
1983 as declaring bitterly, "They worked and got paychecks, and were called
loyalists. Many of us lost our homes, lost all our finances, and we were called
outlaws.") This position lost out, however, and a dozen or so working controllers signed up, at a cost their opposition put in terms of hundreds of antago-
nized former controllers who thereafter declined to join USATCO.

Some who supported insider membership briefly thought themselves
vindicated when certain discontented worker controllers began to seek re-
unionization. Concerned parties in and outside USATCO assumed Eads was
privately directing the drive, and that USATCO might soon be back in as
PATCO's full-fledged descendant, a recognized union dealing in a direct col-
lective-bargaining relationship with the FAA.

Considerable dismay met clarifications that put USATCO entirely on the
sidelines. To be sure, USATCO had originally intended to seek representation elections at one or a few key facilities, relying on former PATCO activists
who had won their jobs back. Bill Taylor explained, "Our people who are going back will help us a lot. We'll have people inside who know what it is to
have a contract and to stand up to management. They're going to be the key
to organizing."

Problems, however, threatened to sidetrack this objective from the outset. The Federal Labor Relations Authority, which had decertified PATCO,
indicated it would oppose USATCO if it felt the new union was PATCO under another name. And the limited funds and manpower of USATCO had
never built up to meet the needs of an adequate organizing campaign.

Where USATCO had once intended to operate stood an old ally and do-
nor, the American Federation of Government Employees (AFGE), backed by
a few PATCO activists it had added to its organizing staff. Eads explained to
disappointed USATCO members that their organization was hard-pressed
to fight for reinstatement, let alone take on the FAA in a organizing campaign. Some listeners grumbled that ATCs would always shun a general
membership outfit like AFGE, preferring an exclusive "club" like PATCO or
USATCO. Others originally ambivalent about welcoming scabs into membership now saw even less reason to, and other feisty types deplored missing an
opportunity to once again "kick ass."

As if these disputes were not costly enough, USATCO also suffered from
its direct lineage back to PATCO and Robert Poli. Some members, and far
more nonmembers, judged PATCO and Poli harshly. Editorials in the *Newsletter* seldom mentioned PATCO, and Poli never. PATCO was not cited as a
model of how to do or run anything, which did not stop certain members
from complaining to Dave and me that Eads had been too close to Poli, and
that certain key officers were ex-PATCO "Kool Aid drinkers" (fanatical mili-

tants whose hatred of the FAA had led to 11,345 career suicides, a metaphor drawn from the then-current Jonestown tragedy).

On the other hand, we also heard from USATCO members who regretted the organization's failure to be more PATCO-like. They were offended by its alleged wallowing and pleading (as in the instance of a USATCO letter to a southern newspaper that ended: "Isn't three years of lost homes, broken marriages, employment blacklisting, financial ruin, and families being torn apart enough punishment?").

Finally, the membership was split over the question of when and why to throw in the towel. Certain illusionless members worried that more harm than good came from sustaining reinstatement hopes when one development after another blighted that prospect. They thought it did an injustice to former controllers to distract them from the urgent need to build non-ATC lives. With resignations, inactivity, and dues arrears, they signaled USATCO to shut up shop—long before the bunker regulars or *Newsletter* letter writers thought the cause or the reinstatement dream lost.

8.) *When the Fat Lady Finally Sang.*   With the unexpectedly harsh judgment against reinstatement from the Federal Circuit Court in May 1984, and the reelection of President Reagan 7 months later, USATCO's two major reasons to exist—the hope for either judicial or political support—disappeared. At about the same time the bunker crew noted a significant falloff in the need of members for phone counseling, rumor clarification, job leads, and learning about one another. By October 1984 the number of members sending in dues was down to about 400 from a high of 800 in 1983, and bills began to run far ahead of receipts.

Throughout 1983, USATCO had felt that the biggest problem its members had was uncertainty about their ATC prospects. Bill Taylor explained, "There's one thing that all the dismissed controllers share. You don't know whether to get on with your life. You can't plan tomorrow, you can't plan next week . . . We're anxious for some answers after all this time." By November 1984, the answers were in, and they were uniformly negative on reinstatement.

Bunker leaders had been growing increasingly weary, and the strain on their own families was beginning to tell. A departing coworker had written of

> . . . watching, on a day-to-day basis, the people that I love and care for burning out, and having all this take a terrible toll on their lives, and on the lives of those in their families . . . these guys had to face the trauma of the strike just like 11,400 others. The difference is they have to relive that pain every day through each and every call or letter. They can't crawl into a corner and forget. They have to face it head on every day, and they seldom complain. (November 1983)

With the failure of the Mondale campaign, and the resounding "NO!" of the Circuit Court decision, the bunker crowd began to face homeward, and on November 30, 1984, USATCO was officially dissolved.

A letter to the membership cited exhaustion of funds as the primary reason for USATCO's end, and saluted readers whose efforts forever made the leaders "proud to have been counted among you." No excuses were offered, or final shots taken at any old adversaries. One brief paragraph reviewed the April 1982–November 1984 accomplishments, all consistent with USATCO's founding objectives; and President Gary Eads closed with a fitting epitaph:

> While this hurts a lot, there is, at the same time, a great feeling of pride in knowing what we have stood for. Few people will ever understand; we do, and that's the important part. For us, it was worth every minute of it.

Earlier, on the occasion of the third anniversary of the strike, a note had been struck in the *Newsletter* which Dave and I will always associate with USATCO: "The pain's still there, just as the struggle remains, but at least we can be proud that, despite the loss of our jobs, we stood by our profession. No group we know can be prouder than that."

Summary. Ambitious and hopeful, USATCO transformed itself into a unique labor union (without a contract or an employer), a unique self-help movement (without a staff of professional mental health specialists), and a unique advocacy and lobbying operation (without the employ of Washington wheeler and dealers). Run by gifted and dedicated amateurs, it demonstrated the considerable ability the 11,345 fired controllers possessed in their ranks, and underscored the extraordinary talent the FAA and the nation was throwing away. Above all, USATCO provided the modern labor movement with a sound and rewarding example of how to help bind the wounds—in the aftermath of a plant closing, a decertification loss, an organizing campaign loss, or, as in the case of the controllers, the mass firing of nearly an entire labor force. USATCO's example, warts and all, warrants replication if labor is to prove it has heart, a shoulder to lean on, and a "third ear" with which to listen—along with the more traditional assets of brawn and brains expected by the rank and file.

. . . I am still optimistic that when real justice prevails and the "fat lady has sung," those of us who wish to, will be back putting the system in proper order.
Letter from USATCO member doing ATC work in Saudi Arabia, August 1983.

Chapter 14

PATCO LIVES

1985 to Date

To the surprise of no one who knew Bill Taylor's dedication to the cause and his concern about fellow strikers, USATCO's Director of Communications found he could not give it all up when USATCO ended. A month later, in January 1985, the first issue of a successor to the *USATCO Newsletter* appeared, this one entitled *PATCO Lives: The Lifeline.*

Designed as a bimonthly publication, the newsletter was to be the major, and possibly even the sole service of a one-person operation, PATCO LIVES, an organization "dedicated to the good and welfare of PATCO air traffic controllers and their families." Operating from "the bunker," USATCO's former office, the new organization differed from its predecessor in several revealing ways:

1) PATCO LIVES was not a labor organization, but more of a fraternal outfit and an "eyes and ears" in Washington for the strikers.

2) Much was made of pride in a PATCO heritage, and this link was no longer muted to avoid offending disaffected strikers still angry at PATCO.

3) A monthly budget was set at $5,000, a fraction of the $48,000 USATCO goal never approached.

4) The mailing list was expanded to 5,300, in contrast to USATCO's 2,500-person list.

5) An announcement was made of the scheduled production of T-shirts and bumper stickers to help raise consciousness of the unending campaign to win reinstatement.

6) Decisions would be made by a referendum run in the newsletter, but the final say would belong to the one person doing it all and taking on all the responsibility—Bill Taylor.

Shorn of the ambitious regional and local unit structure of USATCO, and unable to assume its multifaceted program (lobbying, PR, legal services, communications, counseling, etc.), the new operation focused on the "good and welfare" of its members, and not, as had USATCO, on the reinstatement possibility. Taylor wanted to "take them where they are," and tend to their immediate needs, rather than pursue a dream of renewing distant ATC careers.

When I asked Bill "why again?" knowing of his many personal sacrifices to help keep PATCO and then USATCO alive, his answers focused on his experiences over 29 months as a phone counselor in the bunker. Much that he heard, especially when he probed for the essence of the calls, left him persuaded that a significant number of strikers needed to believe "the cause" continued, and the "community" of former controllers remained an operational reality, aided and abetted by a communications center (PATCO LIVES) and a concerned veteran of the wars (Bill Taylor).

Accordingly, the first issue of the new newsletter featured an unprecedented discussion of striker suicides, "a subject too long avoided." Taylor wrote movingly of the self-destruction of a thirty-seven-year-old former controller, and used this tragedy to explain his motivation for attempting, once again, to help assuage the pain of losses stemming from 1981:

> The brooding, the drinking too much, the isolation, and the feeling that life is not worth living if we can't control airplanes anymore are all symptoms, not of a lost strike, but of a choice of how to react to it. We are hostages for only as long as we choose to be.

Taylor urged readers to see his newsletter, and, through it, continued contact with brothers and sisters in PATCO, as an indispensable aid: "Perhaps we will honor [our suicides] best by remembering that we are a lifeline for each other."

Consistent with this, and in replication of his earlier effort for USATCO, the new newsletter included many job leads, reprints of anti-FAA editorials from leading newspapers, updates of striker legal actions, details of new near miss incidents, and a letter from a couple urging readers to appreciate people as what makes life worthwhile:

> We have met some of the best through PATCO/USATCO and being involved with the strike. Good people. People who have touched our lives.

> It's not trying to live in the past as some people think, or the inability to get on with our lives because we want to stay in touch.

> Life is short, and when you are lucky enough to meet a group of people who are good, who care, and with whom you have shared a major experience, it's a wonderful thing to keep in touch.

The letter closed by thanking PATCO LIVES for "caring enough to work to make it all possible."

An insert with the premier issue of the newsletter reprinted other letters of endorsement:

> . . . PATCO lives in my heart as it does in yours. Perhaps not as the union we are familiar with, but as a brotherhood of caring, loving people who, if nothing else, at least can believe in each other.

> We are so happy to hear about PATCO LIVES—we are not ready to quit—we are as right today as we were on August 3, 1981.

> We feel that a tragic wrong will someday be righted, thanks to your unselfish efforts for all of us.

Taylor responded in the May/June 1985 issue by urging readers to mark the fourth anniversary of the strike by "remembering, sharing, and being proud of our journey together, through, perhaps, the greatest challenge of our lives."

Naturally, Dave and I have encountered doubters and detractors, some of whom believe USATCO's termination came at the right and proper time to end the entire matter. Others feel that lobbying, political action, and legal maneuvers could achieve more gains than Taylor's hand-holding, back-patting, and morale boosts: since PATCO LIVES cannot pursue the former, and focuses on the latter, these critics expect no significant gains. Finally, some feel that Taylor is unnecessarily delaying the start of his own non-PATCO life by "fooling around" with still another imitation PATCO.

Such misgivings notwithstanding, a small, but spirited core of 500 ex-controllers cheered at the outset—though receipts fell quickly behind the bills:

	Income	Contributors
January/Febuary (1985)	$10,320	552
March/April (1985)	$10,219	465
May/June (1985)	$ 5,689	230

Three months after its inception, PATCO LIVES drastically cut back on its mailing list, urged readers to beat the bushes for new members, announced its intention to ask Labor to help, and, not coincidentally, noted the smallest number of August 3 reunion announcements it had ever received since the 1981 strike.

As of March, 1986, PATCO LIVES was struggling along, with Bill Taylor still committed to providing the communications former controllers needed and deserved.

Part VI

WHAT CAN WE LEARN FROM PATCO's LEGACY?

General Aviation News: *The government had the right to fire PATCO. It doesn't have the right to sentence PATCO's former members to a lifetime of punishment and retribution. Now it is time the government did the logical, sensible, and decent thing: hire the most qualified people to fill these critical jobs. To continue doing otherwise is shameful.* (September 1984)

When I'm asked, "Do you want to go back?" I answer "NO, I never want to go back, I want to move forward. I want to move forward to the profession I love so dearly with the knowledge we have fought one hell of a battle and won."

Letter, *USATCO Newsletter*, August 1984.

Chapter 15

WAS THE STRIKE WON OR LOST?

Excerpts from the O'Keefe Survey: 1984

We won! The cost was high, but we told Reagan to shove the job, and we didn't crumble when threatened.

Sorry it took place, and sorry about the outcome, but still feel it was morally justified, what we did. Sometimes the price of righteousness comes high.

In talking with the people on the inside, nothing has changed in the attitude of management, and never will. We did the only thing that could have improved the system and working conditions.

Cannot believe the FAA would allow the Government, the airlines, and the country to lose so much money and cause so much hardships on everyone, and be able to cover it all up.

We don't dwell on what we've lost, but what we've gained. We have more time as a family, we've learned that money isn't everything, and we've seen the value of our friends. This can never be taken away . . . We don't regret August of 1981. We will never forget the issues . . .

As the wife of a former air traffic controller, I know it has been a long and bitter battle . . . be assured, we are still in there and tougher than ever. Everyone from this steel area we live in knows that steel, in order to be strong and durable, must be

177

forged in fire. We have felt the intense heat of injustice, and we're tougher and stronger for it.

Outcome predictable, however unreasonable. It's a bitch standing for what you believe, but still proud as my forefathers.

We're still a brotherhood, win or lose. I have few regrets. Air traffic control was my chosen profession, 12 years. I was really into my job. Aviation was my vocation and my avocation. I miss it.

On the surface the strike might seem a total loss, an impression encouraged by PATCO detractors, FAA admirers, elements hostile to the American labor movement, and, sadly enough, held by many former controllers themselves.[1]

The judgment seems obvious: Nearly 11,400 PATCO backers have been forced to make entirely new lives while nonstrikers, neophytes, and supervisors have taken over their careers. The FAA is no longer obliged to negotiate with an assertive union capable of scrutinizing and countering its every move. Unions of federal employees have been thoroughly intimidated, and much of the anxiety and uncertainty of labor union activists in the private sector can be traced to the beating taken in 1981 by PATCO and labor alike.[2]

On reflection, however, the PATCO 1981 strike proves to have accomplished far more than it is generally given credit for, and the strikers have far more to be proud of and to take comfort from than many have yet realized.

To his credit, PATCO president Robert E. Poli was emphatic on this score, although here, as often elsewhere, his argument failed to register. When Poli was asked about gains on December 31, 1981, the day he resigned from the PATCO presidency, he claimed two for the union:

> . . . the changes the FAA made to cope with the strike are changes we asked for for years: the metering of traffic, stretching the traffic out.
>
> There will be a closer look at the FAA as to how they run their operations, and are the traffic controllers being treated fairly.[3]

Flow control, and, FAA on the hot seat; two major accomplishments, without a doubt—though Poli was quick to acknowledge the strike "has had a toll on a number of innocent people who lost their jobs."[4]

While the media and the pundits chose to ignore or devalue Poli's positive claims, he was on sound ground in directing attention away from an overly simplified, single-factor, "winner-take-all!" perception of the strike's lasting significance. Far more enlightening is recognition of seven major criteria by which a strike may be assessed:

1. *Concerns*—Did the issues for which the rank and file risked everything fade rapidly into insignificance? Were they ex-

posed as trivial matters, hardly worth the risk run by the ill-fated strikers?

2. *Creativity*—Did the union adapt and invent techniques to augment its strength?

3. *Camaraderie*—Did the strike aid and abet the cause of labor solidarity?

4. *Care*—Did the strikers reach out to one another? Were bonds of fellowship forged and maintained?

5. *Claims*—Did union warnings about the impact of a one-sided "victory" by management prove reliable? Have the warnings been vindicated by related events?

6. *Clout*—Did the union have the right target and the soundest plan of operation? Was the union "on target" and in possession of enough leverage to attain its objectives?

7. *Continuity*—Did anything survive the seeming total loss of the strike? Did anything positive remain?

Consideration of these seven criteria adds perspective to the evaluation of a labor-management confrontation, and calls into play a full array of significant variables. While even this lengthy list bypasses other integral topics, it makes the point that a judgment or verdict on the 1981 strike is not self-evident.

1. Concerns. The assessment question here asks, Did the issues over which PATCO went down disappear on its demise, adding insult to injury? Do rank and filers now appear to have been pursuing phantom goals?

PATCO called a strike of its 14,500 members over four pressing concerns:

> Rank and filers maintained that their work was seriously undervalued and under-rewarded;

> that their work week was unreasonably long, especially in comparison to the hours worked by their overseas counterparts;

> that the FAA's approach to supervision and to union-management relations undermined morale and the safety of the system; and

> that the FAA neglected serious deficiencies in staffing levels and hardware reliability.

In the years that have passed since the strike, all four union concerns have persisted as major problems of the FAA—despite having carte blanche since 1981 with a nonunion work force at its mercy.

Where job rewards and work hours are concerned, the FAA successfully petitioned Congress in 1982 to extend the June 22 PATCO/FAA contract terms to its poststrike labor force. But the persistence of flare-ups over hours and mandatory overtime at far-flung facilities in 1983, 1984, and 1985 suggest that the original PATCO agenda remains unmet.

Similarly, where supervision is concerned, the FAA record since August 1981 does not appear a triumph. Censured first by Secretary of Transportation Drew Lewis, and then by his successor, Elizabeth Dole, for third-rate supervisory practices, the FAA has been forced to implement Human Relations Committees and Facility Advisory Boards.[5] Despite these efforts at mitigating its autocratic management style, the FAA has continued to earn adverse publicity for problems with inadequate staffing levels, excessive overwork, debilitating stress ill-designed resectorization, and unreliable quality assurance.

The second Jones Report in 1984, and an agencywide survey of its employees both suggest to congressional investigators that "human relations in the FAA have not improved since the strike, and working relationships are probably worse than they were in 1982."[6] Most damning of all is workplace dissatisfaction which leads working controllers openly to attempt re-unionization; hardly evidence that the FAA has resolved what PATCO had been complaining about.[7]

Finally, in the matter of staffing levels and hardware quality, the FAA has recently conceded that PATCO was right on both scores. After years of denying that it was grievously understaffed, as the strikers had long insisted, the FAA in September 1985 announced plans to add nearly 1,000 air traffic controllers over the next 2 years, to reach a level of 14,480. The plans come "after more than a dozen air crashes this year, an increase in near collisions on the ground and in the air, and growing concern in Congress over whether the incidents may reflect on the quality of traffic control. . . ."[8]

After years of insisting that its hardware was quite adequate to the task, the FAA in 1982 asked Congress to approve new taxes to cover as much as $20 billion in capital improvements over the next 20 years. The FAA conceded that existing equipment could not accommodate the expected doubling of the aircraft population in the next decade: "For the most part, these limitations are the result of an aging physical plant and inefficient techniques and procedures."[9] Particularly in need of replacement was a favorite PATCO target, or computers of 1960s-vintage at 20 traffic control centers.

PATCO had urged FAA administrators, Langhorne Bond in the 1970s and his successor J. Lynn Helms, to join the union in lobbying Congress for these overdue reforms to no avail. The FAA now is left to make the case alone—a case that knowledgeable parties recall they first heard from PATCO.

2. Creativity.   The assessment question here asks, Did the union venture beyond conventional tools and stratagems? Did it invent or improve any significant aids to the running of a strike? Did it try to enlarge acceptance of poorly understood demands of its members?

PATCO took advantage of the long lead time (1978-1981) that preceded its strike to prepare to use four novel aids. As Professor Richard Hurd explains elsewhere in this book, PATCO designed, debugged, and successfully implemented one of the finest communication systems ever used by labor in a nationwide job action. Thanks to counseling from former AFL-CIO specialist Leo Perlis, various PATCO locals made unprecedented and reasonable requests for strike aid from various "Community Chest" resources.

PATCO public relations officers were quick to seize an opportunity offered by comparing Reagan's fervor for Polish dissidents and his grim implacability toward striking controllers. Here and elsewhere, the PATCO "PR" effort was on the alert to focus favorable media attention. PATCO spouses and teenage children were sensitively drawn into local-level support activities, helping to boost the morale of strikers and dependents alike.

PATCO did not invent any of these tools, of course, but the union carried them farther than was customary at that time. And its model has since informed and strengthened many successful labor campaigns (the airline pilots strike against United Airlines in 1985, for example, appears to have drawn heavily on lessons from PATCO's use of telecommunication aids).

As for pioneering in bringing its case to concerned others, PATCO did its best to get across a novel concept, the workplace stress issue, to a sometimes baffled audience. People found it hard to understand exactly what was "bugging" the controllers—the constant pressure of making life-and-death decisions? The lack of margin for error? The need to rely on others in decision processing? The threat of equipment outages? The reluctance of the FAA to force airlines to smooth out peaks and valleys in the flow of traffic? The mandatory overtime? The toll shift work took on personal and family life? The high burnout rate and lack of a funded vocational retraining program? Or, all of these equally?

PATCO especially contended with the derision of FAA officials at the controller's stress-related problems. (So extreme has the FAA position been that as late as 1984 the FAA "refused to acknowledge stress or stress authorities" in congressional testimony.[10] A subcommittee's persistent probing that year of FAA witnesses "revealed that specific FAA activities had not seriously addressed the effects of stress on controllers."[11] Little wonder that in 1978 medical scientists at an FAA Aeromedical Institute in Oklahoma City were ordered to delete the word "stress" from their copies of a new $2.8 million controller health study.)[12]

Despite the opposition encountered, PATCO locals used their speakers' bureau, their picket line leaflets, and every other tool at their disposal to take the nation "to school" in this matter. Known increasingly as "the black lung of the technical classes," avoidable and abusive workplace stress was highlighted by PATCO in 1981; and labor-management discussions since should profit from the pioneering effort PATCO made to help legitimize the subject.[13]

3. Camaraderie.   The assessment question asks: Did the strike promote the cause of union solidarity? Has the labor movement been stronger since for its occurrence?

The strike record at first glance inspires little confidence in the ability or inclination of unions to extend themselves on behalf of one another: although PATCO asked 110 unions to honor its picket lines, they declined out of fear of violating legal bans against secondary strikes. PATCO welcomed and received financial and material aid from scores of unions here and abroad, but some PATCO activists criticized the $840,000 raised from AFL-CIO unions as paltry. PATCO was featured at 1981 Labor Day parades across the country, but some PATCO activists insist more than cheers was desperately necessary. Lane Kirkland, Ken Blaylock, and Al Shanker went out of their way to influence events in a pro-PATCO fashion. But some PATCO activists insist that more could and should have been done. Labor's detractors gloated that the strike exposed a paper tiger, encouraged employer opposition in negotiations, and deepened the public's considerable disillusionment with Organized Labor.

There is no gainsaying that PATCO was initially rebuffed by unions previously ignored by the controllers. An airline pilot offered this biting explanation to a journalist:

> Out here people of all employee groups have walked the picket lines— caterers, flight attendants, baggage handlers—and never once did we get any support from the air traffic controllers. Generally, they'd say it was because they were government employees. Well, they crossed everyone else's picket lines—as far as I'm concerned, Ronald Reagan did the right thing.[14]

As the weeks and months went by, however, this sort of vituperation was generally replaced by a more sympathetic and supportive attitude (although relations with the Pilots Union went from bad to worse).[15]

Far less publicized was a 50-state record of remarkable collaboration at the grass-roots level. Office space and equipment was donated by locals of the Machinists and Auto Workers Unions, MEBA, and the Independent Federation of Flight Attendants. The Longshoreman's local in Los Angeles set aside day work jobs on the docks for strikers in need of well-paid day labor. Locals everywhere welcomed PATCO speakers who explained the strike and took up a collection; locals everywhere created a job referral service to help ex-controllers make a new start. While little of this was judged newsworthy, and most of it remained known and valued only to rank and filers, thousands of grass-roots unionists got a new and valuable experience of "solidarity."

As for whether the entire PATCO experience left labor stronger or weaker, a case can be made for either proposition, suggesting that we may still be too close to the event to be sure. Those who believe it weakened labor cite the obvious humiliation of defeat: Had the pilots' union or the machinists' union backed PATCO, the controllers might have forced the White House to deal. If the AFL-CIO had persisted with mass picketing and a large-scale consumer boycott, the same happy result might have been achieved. Had a well publicized outpouring of moral and material support from labor swayed public opinion in PATCO's favor, victory was possible. But since none of this occurred, the labor movement seemed the weaker and more vulnerable in the aftermath.

Conversely, the PATCO strike can be given credit for four types of positive, if painful, impact. Labor activists were reminded once again of their need to research and constantly improve the mechanisms of interunion aid—the communication, fund-raising, and job referral links. Labor leaders were reminded once again of the advisability of forging alliances *before* taking a job action that could profit from a display of solidarity: PATCO's meager effort to mend fences and line up interunion aid before June 22 undermined the entire course of the strike. Labor lawyers and lawmakers were reminded once again of the legal deterrents to joint union action during a strike. Unless and until the legal regulations are revised in labor's favor it appears necessary to reduce rank and file expectations of what types of joint strike action are plausible. Labor activists were reminded once again of the toll taken by long-standing rifts and rivalries that divide unions from one another, and of the necessity to weld a higher allegiance to a collective known as the "labor movement." None of these reminders were brand new to the PATCO strike, of course. But even with their familiarity each could make a significant contribution to labor's renewal. PATCO's strike still could leave labor the stronger for the painful experience, if drawn on as a teaching source for strike management gains.

4. Care. The question asks: Did anyone give a damn—about one another? Did the strikers lend mutual support, or was it every man for himself? As the chapters in this book on USATCO and PATCO LIVES make clear, the record here is very bright. Over 3,000 strikers joined USATCO, and another 2,000 received its monthly mailings. These men and women lent one another moral support, job leads, survival tips, and other sensitive and invaluable forms of aid. While over half of the 11,345 strikers never joined either of the PATCO successors, many are known to have read and shared the publications of these groups. Reunions on August 3 regularly draw scores of ex-controllers together in warm and fraternal comradeship, even as informal phone networks still link local union stalwarts together years after the strike.

Always a close-knit group, one required by the nature of the job to rely more heavily on one another than is true in most occupations, the controllers carried their sense of "family" into the 1981 job action, where it stood them in good stead. Many kept the concept alive and strong long thereafter, and set up a model of fraternity well worth emulation by the rest of organized labor.

5. Claims.   The question asks: Have major warnings issued by the union about the dire consequences of its loss been borne out?

PATCO urged concerned parties to recognize that permitting total victory for the FAA could mean three unwelcome developments: The FAA might be tempted to falsify poststrike reportage to keep up appearances. It might ignore or reject evidence that its supervisory mistakes persist, despite efforts it might make at self-reform. It might refuse to acknowledge a serious decline in the safety level of the system. To judge from the August 1985 research report of an experienced congressional subcommittee, PATCO's warnings were correct on all scores.

Regarding the union warning of FAA misrepresentation of poststrike reportage, the House subcommittee has complained the FAA gives assurances that controllers are no longer being overworked, and the average workweek is only 40.9 hours. But hearings "showed that controllers were, and will likely continue to be, overtaxed for the foreseeable future. Broad system averages presented by FAA masked high overtime, and other conditions of controller overwork."[16] (Indeed, the FAA 40.9 hour figure included people who were not controlling traffic, but were working instead at FAA headquarters!)[17] Despite FAA assurances of a return to normal work conditions, the hearings included testimony of "extensive periods at the radar scopes without a break; first-line supervisors working as controllers; annual leave sometimes being limited to 1 week; disallowance of sick leave."[18]

In the same vein, the subcommittee expressed exasperation over the FAA's insistence it was on schedule in getting the controller work force back to normal, when it still had about 3,000 supervisors working the "boards"; had only 47 percent who were fully qualified among 14,000 controllers, as compared to 82 percent prestrike; and had 2,665 senior controllers becoming eligible to retire in 1985 .[19]

Perhaps the most troubling—and frightening—type of misrepresentation involved FAA reportage of operational errors, operational deviations, pilot deviations, and near midair collisions. In 1983 NTSB found that "numerous unreported operational errors and deviations are occurring daily in the ATC facility operations."[20] In the same year the Aviation Safety Institute insisted "there have been specific instances where there have been coverups."[21] In 1984 the FAA initially under-reported the number of near midair collisions by almost half. After the Aviation Consumer Action Project, a Nader af-filiate, found over 500 unreported near collisions, the FAA said many reports had inadvertently not been forwarded from regional offices.[22] Little wonder, accordingly, that the House subcommittee found it "dismaying" that the FAA "has not objectively monitored the safety of the ATC system and regularly re-ported on its status."[23]

Concerning the union warning that the FAA might misrepresent re-forms in its supervisory practices, the House subcommittee felt research and testimony confirmed the failure of the FAA to follow its own study recom-mendations and to treat controllers as professionals.[24]

More specifically, the hearings produced testimony critical of ongoing FAA reform efforts that had left "major problems with employee relations remaining long after the strike has been resolved."[25] The chairman of an FAA-funded task force that studied the subject twice after the strike found the FAA still paying insufficient attention to deep-seated workplace stres-sors.[26] One of his colleagues noted the persistent "absence of a collaborative, teamwork relationship between supervised and supervisors, between man-agement and employees."[27] Instead, extensive testimony led the congressio-nal subcommittee to conclude that "the feeling of 'us' [controllers] versus 'them' [FAA] has been reborn."[28]

FAA spokesmen naturally made much of several poststrike activities the agency had initiated to improve controller-management relations. Facility Advisory Boards to handle operational and technical concerns, and Human Relations Committees to deal with personnel matters had been established in all ATC facilities. Human resource specialists had been hired to advise and educate both management and staff on improving human relations. Manage-ment training had been improved, and now placed heavy emphasis on han-dling people. Job descriptions for managers had been revised to place em-phasis on the ability to manage people. And, an employee rights handbook had been developed. The subcommittee was not overly impressed, however, especially as the FAA strongly discouraged its new boards and committees from working across facility lines, even though most major issues in air traffic control have always been national in scope (staffing, overwork, etc.).

When the FAA surveyed its controllers (and nine other divisions) in 1984, the results were damning of its human relations gestures. When asked if management was generally committed to improving human relations, whether organizational authority and responsibility were appropriately shared, and whether they had seen any positive change in the FAA's empha-sis on managing people, working controllers gave the FAA the lowest ratings of any of the agency's 10 divisions.[29] Consistent with this vote of "no confi-dence," the House subcommittee warned the FAA that "human relations committees cannot substitute for sensitive participative management."[30]

Finally, on the union warning that the FAA might misrepresent post-

Table 15-1
System Changes: 1981, 1985*

	Strike Response (1981)	*1985*
1) *Traffic Volume*:	Down 25% from 1980 level	8% above prestrike levels, and growing!
2) *Size of Work Force*:	16,244 (of whom 13,205, or 80 percent; were fully qualified controllers)	12,500 (of whom 8,315, or 66 percent, were fully qualified controllers)
3) *Flow Control*:	Strictly instituted, with cooperation of airlines	Substantially liberalized in 1983 at insistence of airlines
4) *Overtime*:	377,000 hours; $8.1 million cost	908,000 hours; $28 million cost
5) *Slot Allocations*:	Strictly instituted at 22 major airports	Removed at all but one by April 1984
6) *Resectorization*:	Number of sectors was reduced from 721 to 558	Number of sectors is now 641
7) *Distance-in-Trail*:	Was increased 3 to 5 miles in terminal areas, 5 to 50 miles en route	Substantially lessened.

*Source: Adapted from the *Report* of the House Subcommittee on Investigations and Oversight of the Committee on Public Works and Transportation, 99th Congress, 1985; and the 1986 *Aviation Safety* Report of the General Accounting Office.

strike safety, the House subcommittee rejected all FAA assurances and "perceived a diminishing margin of safety. Stress, fatigue, staffing shortages, increasing traffic, lack of supervision, and an unseasoned work force have all impacted the margin of safety."[31]

Much was made of a 1983 report of the National Transportation Safety Board (NTSB) which questioned the wisdom of removing traffic restrictions *before* normal working conditions had been reestablished for controllers. The NTSB worried that "as flow restrictions are relaxed, in-trail restrictions reduced, and traffic volume increased, the controllers' work load is increased and the margin for error is reduced logarithmically . . ."[32]

PATCO, in short, had made three major claims: If the White House refused to negotiate and insisted on a "total victory" for the FAA, this could lead to a seriously overextended controller group, a persistently mismanaged situation, and the coverup of a significant decline in the safety of the system. Four years after the strike at least one body of knowledgeable students of ATC realities seems to agree that these warnings were well taken: another validation of the strike's lasting significance, and another reason for keeping reform pressure on the FAA.

6. *Clout.* The question here asks: Was PATCO on target? Was the strike based on a sound analysis of the issues, and could union clout therefore reasonably hope to succeed?

PATCO focused on traditional economic demands, and predicated its victory on the imposition of deep economic losses on the airline system. PATCO sought more to alleviate the effects of working conditions than to alter them. While the union originally put 95 to 99 demands on the table, the top three were compensation, reduced work hours, and an improved "early retirement" plan, or what could be termed an "unwork" solution to controller discontent.

At least three other approaches were possible, and proponents of each believe they would have made a union victory far more likely: PATCO could have focused on workplace politics, rather than on economics. It could have sought more power over the work process, rather than an "unwork" solution. In place of seeking less work PATCO could have sought *better* work — through a demand for the imposition of flow control, the hiring of many more controllers, the curbing of unregulated pleasure aircraft, the disciplining of authoritarian supervisors, and so on.[33]

PATCO could have focused on ideology, rather than on economics, and highlighted its rejection of the Government's no-strike pledge. That is, PATCO could have followed the tradition of the civil rights movement of the 1960s in urging the public to recognize "it is immoral to obey an immoral law." PATCO could have argued that its struggle for workplace justice and a livable job superseded unjust and repressive legislation and, in this bold and principled way, sought to checkmate the Reagan law and order theme.[34]

PATCO could have focused on organizational climate or culture, rather than on economics. It could have demanded an end to the most disreputable style of management in the entire federal service. Impartial researchers had long before exposed the FAA organizational climate as "uncaring, unconcerned for its people, uncommunicative, and unreceptive."[35] PATCO could have sought contract changes to compel the FAA to convert to a leadership style "based upon incremental influence (the persuasive, contagious effect of esteem, collaboration, warmth, trust, and respected expertise)."[36]

As labor critic Stanley Aronowitz notes, these alternative orientations were outside PATCO's frame of reference because labor still fails in this country to link its economic struggles to workplace politics and ideology. Instead, PATCO's critique of management prerogatives remained an action critique, rather than a theoretical, ideological, and political critique.

By separating economic from political relations, PATCO focused on a $10,000 demand and less work, rather than on techniques for genuine self-management in a thoroughly revamped work culture. To be sure, PATCO sought to escape from under the FAA, but the union only advocated the privatization of the ATC function, rather than the establishment of a worker-owned and operated substitute for the FAA (along the model of worker-owned or union-owned business). And PATCO sought an end to intolerable FAA supervision, but it had no alternative ideological guide to the direction of the work of 14,500 controllers. Instead, the union spent over 2 years preoccupied with the forthcoming strike as a primarily economic matter—and, as a result, PATCO was finally left with "no entry into the ideological and political context of public discussion except through its claim that it could bring the airline industry to its knees."[37]

PATCO thus was left with far less clout than might have been possible had it fought in 1981 on several fronts simultaneously, fought primarily for workplace self-determination, and fought harder for *better* rather than for *less* work.

7. Continuity.   Thanks to the superficial and short-lived attention of the media the impression was generated that PATCO "augured in" (as test pilots label a fatal crash), and the FAA lucked out. On closer inspection, however, the record shows more persistence by union stalwarts than is widely acknowledged.

For an organization believed routed, PATCO has contrived a miraculous sort of survival: As detailed in earlier chapters, PATCO was first resurrected in the form of the United States Air Traffic Controllers Organization (USATCO), an energetic, politically savvy, and warm and caring operation. Primarily focused on winning reinstatement and highlighting the safety and personnel problems of the poststrike system, USATCO's 2-year existence attests to the need several thousand strikers felt to keep the PATCO spirit and "cause" alive. When USATCO folded, its place was immediately taken by a direct descendant, PATCO LIVES. This one-man operation, guided and staffed by former PATCO and USATCO activist Bill Taylor, put together an even bigger mailing list of over 5,000 supportive ex-controllers . . . people who had retained a firm allegiance to what they believed the strike had been all about. To be sure, the union has gone out of formal existence, and its records molder in a locked storage van in Northern Virginia (Jack Maher purchased the rights to the logo for $400 from a bankruptcy referee to keep it from falling into the wrong hands). The *spirit* of PATCO, however, as distinct from the actual organization, persists, and this helps vindicate the strike effort and the union alike.

Summary.   Was the strike won or lost? Popular opinion, including that of many PATCO stalwarts who should know better, holds that the 1981 job action was an unqualified disaster, a complete wipeout, a loss without any redeeming aspect. This counsel of despair, however, does not withstand close examination.

The strike had losers, but none that one would recognize from media mishandling of the event. President Reagan was a loser in that he expected far more than only 10 percent of the strikers to heed his warning to return to work; he was also a loser in being revealed as an inflexible novice in federal labor-management relations. Congress was a loser, since years of focused hearings and reams of advice, threats, and requests failed to force the White House and the FAA to negotiate in good faith with PATCO, and to do everything possible to avoid the 1981 strike. The airline industry was a loser, for the strike proved the costliest in the history of aviation labor-management relations. The general aviation industry was a loser, since more rules and regulations were slapped on it by an enthusiastic FAA, using the excuse of the strike crisis, than ever before in aviation history. The airline passengers were losers, as delays, cancellations, and the loss of service to small cities all intensified. The AFL-CIO and its member unions were losers, for their disinclination to break the law and shut the airlines down left them the targets of public scorn and intimidation from emboldened anti-union employers.

The biggest loser of all, however, was the very outfit heralded as the winner—the FAA: On the contrary, the FAA actually left the 1981 strike deprived of 90 percent of its most valued experienced manpower; taxed with such impossible tasks as getting "up to steam" in a bare 2 years, with only raw Academy graduates and overworked, retirement-eager ATC veterans as their mainstay; sitting on a volcano of working controllers open to regaining some sort of union representation; and constantly "harassed" by congressional hearings and investigative journalists skeptical about FAA assurances of the safety of air travel and human relations improvements in ATC facilities. Another Pyrrhic victory like 1981 and the FAA would come apart.

The strike had one real winner, although once again, no one might realize it from the public impression of the event. PATCOs' strikers were the winners, for alone among all parties—the oath-upholding President and law-upholding Secretary of Transportation included—the 11,345 strikers took a personal stand from deeply held convictions, and remained steadfast when all sides railed against them. They recognized, as the President never did, that the oath required of them was inappropriate, just as the law against their strike was unreasonable in a democracy that respects a citizen's right to withhold nonstrategic labor services. They recognized, as the President did not, that PATCO's confinement to "collective begging" was untenable, and these controllers, as they loved controlling, had to try to win basic reforms in 1981 even by putting their careers on the line.*

---

*See the contributed essay in Appendix I, entitled "A Retrospective on the PATCO Strategy," by Rick Hurd.

Chapter 16

EPILOGUE*

Some Lessons Worth Pondering

. . . this is the kind of thing nobody wins. The travelers are losers; the government's a loser; and obviously, the union's a loser. And most importantly, we're going to lose a lot of very fine people that we'd like to have operating our system. Nobody wins this kind of thing.
Drew Lewis, August 5, 1981, *The McNeil-Lehrer Report*, TV transcript, p. 5.

. . . for years, the primary focus has been directed to the system's mechanical and technical aspects. Despite the attention to those elements, the air traffic control system is founded on the decision making capability of a human being—the air traffic controller. It is long past time that the controller work force receives the attention it so desperately deserves.
Robert E. Poli, PATCO President, in 1981 *Hearing* of the Committee on Post Office and Civil Service, House of Representatives, April 30, 1981, p. 15.

On a console at the Fort Lauderdale tower is a cartoon somebody clipped from a magazine. It shows a controller answering the phone in a tower. 'We're fatigued, stressed out, understaffed, overworked, and inexperienced. Would you mind calling back later?' the caption says.
Buddy Nevins, "How Safe are the Skies?", *Sunshine Sunday Magazine*, December 15, 1985, p. 12.

We will be years in extracting, assaying, and applying all we can learn of value from the White House-PATCO clash of 1981, but there are lessons that may help us better pursue the task.

1) *Reassessment of the governmental approach to strikes by its employees is imperative.* Reform here could begin with recognition that many types of federal employees do *not* perform services so indispensable that their temporary cessation is intolerable. As state courts are increasingly recognizing, the right of

---

*I draw here especially on the writing and ideas of Leo Perlis, an exceedingly perceptive and original student of these matters.

citizens to withdraw their labor services by striking is a precious entitlement in a democracy, one we outlaw in only the rarest of situations (as in the case of national security).[1] A strike of air traffic controllers clearly means inconvenience, and an enormous financial toll—two sets of reasons for PATCO and the FAA to have avoided such job actions whenever possible (as through the full-scale use of the impasse-breaking aid of the Federal Labor Relations Board, a service mysteriously ignored by everyone in 1981).

It is hard to agree, however, that prohibiting all such strikes was reasonable, especially when this left the controllers' union reliant on "collective begging" in its negotiations with a recalcitrant FAA. Little wonder, accordingly, that specialists in public sector labor relations insist "the federal government's policy of *simultaneously* rendering strikes illegal, and asserting the power unilaterally to fix terms and conditions of employment, is an offense to fundamental fairness, and constitutes a confiscatory infringement upon the associational economic interests and civil rights of public employees."[2]

Far wiser would be new legislation permitting a limited right to strike to certain federal employees, including controllers, and setting out a firm timetable of pro-resolution steps, such as a "last offer" choice made by an impartial arbitrator if no resolve is reached within 15 or 30 days. Only when employees have the right to strike can their union foster a climate of collaborative labor-management relations that cuts the likelihood of strikes.

2) *Redirection of the entire FAA management culture is imperative.* If many years of industrial conflict in ATC work suggest anything, it is that the FAA's management culture must be reconstituted if safety, productivity, and morale are to reach optimal levels. Or, as the FAA's Jones Committee concluded nearly a year after the 1981 strike, wide-ranging changes in management style and philosophy were desperately needed within the agency. Committee researcher David G. Bowers pointed out that "a less directive and bureaucratic style would have buffered the problem of the strike, and a participative style would have solved it."[3]

If the ATC work scene is ever to overcome the distrust and hostility attested to in 1984 and 1985 by disenchanted working controllers, redirection of the FAA will be required, one deeper reaching and faster paced than anything now underway.[4] It would help if congressional oversight committees and investigatory journalists kept FAA administrator Donald Engen on the hot seat. It would help even more if the White House immediately rescinded its unprecedented lifetime ban on the rehiring of fired controllers, many of whom could make a seasoned and constructive contribution to any honest FAA effort to implement a participative management approach.

3) *Reliance by unions on frank counsel is indispensable, especially during strike preparation and throughout the course of a strike.* As best as can be ascertained, PATCO essentially kept its own counsel while preparing for "the big one," and sought little or no advice from MEBA, IAM, AFGE, or other logical entities. Even after the strike began and got quickly into mortal difficulty, PATCO

decision makers essentially talked and listened to each other, giving short shrift to concerned and experienced labor leaders eager to share insights, and doing without lawyers with labor law expertise.

This leadership insularity fosters myopia, illusions, and an inability to reckon with realities. The PATCO record strongly recommends much closer communication among the leaders of interrelated unions: Very helpful here is the example of the AFL-CIO's Public Employees Department (headed by former PATCO president John F. Leyden), which alone of all such federation units *requires* its 32 union affiliates to discuss plans for any strike *before* the fact. In this way advice is offered when it can still make a difference, mutual aid can be planned, and the 32 unions can prepare an informed and common front.

4) *Recognition by labor of the strategic power of the media is imperative.* PATCO was very attentive to press relations, and a full-time media staffer tried in the late 1970s to shape public support for controller grievances. Among other things, PATCO commissioned a short film about controller duties in 1978, but the union declined to commission documentary films for rapid sharing with media representatives initially willing to hear PATCO's case for striking. Had such films been in the can and available in multiple copies for local TV station use around the country, it is possible that PATCO might not have suffered as it later did from negative public stereotyping and media pillorying. Writing off public opinion as irrelevant and inconsequential, a naive judgment of some inexperienced PATCO officers early in the strike, cost the union dearly and needlessly.

5) *Renewal of PATCO's pioneering focus on stress relief is imperative.* Prior to the effort PATCO made to expose the toll unnecessarily taken by workplace stress, little was heard about this problem in union-management negotiations. Public and media derision drowned out PATCO's many reform arguments here, but more and more current research backs PATCO's pioneer effort to draw remedial attention to this "invisible, silent killer." Labor can, and *must* keep this a high-priority in contract negotiations, using such topical reforms as "wellness programs"; on-site health, exercise, and nutrition projects; health problem screening efforts; and alcohol and drug abuse campaigns as key aids to the rapid and permanent relief of unnecessary debilitating stress.[5]

6) *Replication of USATCO and PATCO LIVES could substantially strengthen labor in future poststrike situations.* As demonstrated in 1985 by well publicized losses in the Continental Airlines and Phelps-Dodge strikes, many international unions are joining PATCO in experiencing defeat when least expected.[6] Like PATCO, many such unions are unprepared to cut their losses, cushion the blow to their strikers, and mitigate this setback.

If the AFL-CIO was to study USATCO and PATCO LIVES, and prepare an instructional videotape and manual based on transferable lessons from these PATCO successors, many unions would not have to "reinvent the wheel" in confronting strike setbacks. USATCO learned valuable techniques of lobbying, raising funds, and cultivating the media, even as PATCO LIVES learned much about communications, networking, and morale maintenance. Both organizations warrant replication, the better to demonstrate labor's cumulative advance, and its respect for the price ex-controllers paid learning poststrike lessons now available to guide other labor organizations.

7) *Reconsideration of the Man-Machine relationship in ATC work is imperative.* A dream of transferring decision-making autonomy away from a human controller and over to a "thinking machine," a supercomputer replete with "cutting edge" artificial intelligence, persists at the highest levels of the FAA, and grossly distorts employer-employee relations in ATC matters.[7]

PATCO disparaged the workerless notion of ATC-by-computer, and urged the FAA to side instead with advanced technologies to augment, rather than to replace human operators. PATCO insisted that ATC contingencies were so fast-changing, and the life-and-death responsibilities of the role so substantial, that no foreseeable, fail-safe, and affordable computer system could fill the bill. PATCO urged the FAA to open its eyes to the rule-bending creativity of topnotch controllers, and to applaud their adaptability and thoroughgoing dedication to the task—two attributes computers could never rival. (As PATCO put it: "Computers don't separate planes: controllers separate planes.")

What little response the FAA made generally took the form of a press conference to highlight still another megabuck contract to a computer vendor promising to produce yet another high-tech marvel. PATCO in turn would suggest that a "marvel" was already on the job, increasingly anxious about how long he or she might have a job to excel at.[8]

Until the FAA makes a commitment to put computers at the service of human controllers, and shelves its technocratic fantasy of replacing people with machines, a cloud of doubt will pervade ATC realities, and undermine safety, productivity, and morale. The illusion of being able to create an error-free system that operates with a high degree of certainty distracts the FAA from pragmatic remedies for long-standing human problems at work. The illusion of emancipation from human workers diverts the FAA from appreciation of the trained intuition and judgment of seasoned controllers, to the detriment of air control system operators and users alike.

Summary.   Every day, over 200,000 takeoffs and landings transport over 1 million air passengers, though the nation's ATC system has nearly 2,000 fewer controllers trying to handle about 10 percent more traffic than in 1981. Only 63 percent of all working controllers are fully accredited, as against 81 percent before the strike, a sharp falloff in experience level that may help explain why nearly 700 near-misses in 1985 outdid the 592 total in 1984—and was nearly double the 359 figure recorded in 1981.[9] The situation appears increasingly dangerous, a perception the public links uneasily with the fact that more lives were lost in 1985 in air fatalities than ever before in commercial aviation history.[10] Little wonder, accordingly, that seven senators and 78 congressmen urged the White House in December of 1985 to order the FAA to rehire some of the fired ex-controllers.[11]

With this in mind, we may ask once more the overriding question: "What is there to be learned from PATCO's legacy—from its 13-year struggle, its strike 'defeat,' and the refusal of a proud minority of its members to fade into obscurity?"[12]

Perhaps a two-part lesson offers the best counsel: On the one hand, it urges us to avoid falling victim to shortcomings of the 1981 participants; i.e., the harsh management style of the FAA; the unrealistic naïveté of PATCO; the inadequate response of organized labor; the belligerence of the White House, the superficial activities of the media; and the gullibility of the general public. On the other hand, the same two-part lesson offers the instructive example of ex-controllers who tried to rescue their profession, became better unionists, earned the support of loved ones, and went on to regain their equilibrium and momentum. As well, through USATCO and PATCO LIVES, many kept faith with the vision that helped their strike become an ennobling "cause."

If organized labor and the concerned public soon draw on lessons inherent in the FAA-PATCO clash, both from its shortcomings and its merit, we heighten our chances of achieving what PATCO was pursuing all along—a quality of worklife and a way of gaining it that honors us all.

POSTSCRIPT

In March 1986, new doubts were raised about the FAA's ability to ensure system safety. A study released by the General Accounting Office, a highly regarded congressional watchdog, concluded that the FAA "has not met its staffing goals for fully qualified controllers at many major facilities. . . ."[13] The GAO warned that "the growth in air traffic activity has caused the controller workload to reach a point where controllers are stretched too thin. . . ."[14]

To make matters even worse, of the 15 percent of controllers eligible to retire now or within 2 years, some 84 percent indicated their intention to leave as soon as possible; a much higher figure than the 14 percent projection the FAA uses to reassure uneasy congressmen.[15] Relevant here is the fact that the second most frequently selected reason for wanting to retire was dissatisfaction with FAA management (92 percent of all volunteered comments about agency management were negative).[16]

Not suprisingly, the GAO critique is being used to rally support for passage of a bill (H.R. 4003) that would require the FAA to rehire at least 500 experienced ex-controllers in each of the fiscal years 1986 and 1987.[17] Among others lining up behind this idea is the influential Airline Pilots' Union (ALPA), which has urged reinstatement to help "address inexperience in the ATC system . . . and counter some dangerous trends before we have an accident."[18]

At the request of the House Committee on Post Office and Civil Service, to which H.R. 4003 has been referred, the GAO has begun a new study to learn: (1) how many former controllers will accept reappointment; (2) how long it will take them to "check out"; and (3) how the current workforce might react to the rehiring of certain of the PATCO strikers. Due in September 1986, the second GAO report appears likely to stir even more controversy than has the first.

Complicating the scene is the unwelcome pressure of the Gramm Rudman Act. Under its harsh terms, the FAA might actually be required to cut $200 million from its budget, a down-sizing prospect that alarms many observers already convinced the agency needs far more, rather than fewer controllers.

Meanwhile, both AFGE and MEBA continue to invest funds and staff in competitive campaigns to reunionize disgruntled working controllers, a prospect enouraged by the March 1986 GAO finding that "morale problems are broad in scope and fairly serious at the major air traffic control facilities . . . controllers and their supervisors believe FAA management does not sufficiently consider or respond to their concerns."[19] First heard 5 years ago from PATCO strikers, this indictment is all the more telling for persisting today . . . and it helps assure continued turbulence in ATC matters for some time to come.

Part VII

APPENDICES

POST-STRIKE LIVES OF BOSTON AREA CONTROLLERS

Britta Fischer, Ph.D.
Department of Sociology
Emmanuel College
Boston, Massachusetts

The aftermath of the strike resulted in a protracted crisis, which has been recorded through interviews over a period of 4 years. Fifteen Boston area controllers were interviewed in their homes between January and June 1982, some 6 to 11 months after the start of the strike. At that time we* gathered information on a wide range of questions covering their experience as air traffic controllers, their views of PATCO and the government, their social background, training, and family situation, as well as their poststrike work or unemployment experience, and their plans for the future. Subsequently, in March 1984 and in June 1985, follow-up interviews were conducted by telephone focusing on job search, employment satisfaction, and current standard of living.

What can be learned from the experience of a convenience sample of 15 controllers? In order to answer this question it is helpful to look at the larger picture of air traffic controllers in the Boston area.

In 1981 the Boston cluster of PATCO, Local 215, included 114 members according to an address list supplied by the union leadership. Of these, 63

---

*In the initial background research and during the first round of interviews, I was assisted by a Faculty Development Grant from Emmanuel College and by five student volunteers: Marion Donahue, Margaret Lally, Carol Mulcahy, Mary Neagle, and Theresa Sardagnola.

had been employed prior to the strike at Logan Airport, a major facility. Fifty-one had been working at 5 lesser towers at surrounding locations. At the Boston tower of Logan Airport there had been 62 men and 1 woman. The lesser facilities, being the training ground for new blood, employed 36 men and 15 women. Both women and minorities were, because of recent recruitment efforts, concentrated in the towers requiring less experience and offering lower salaries.

More than three-quarters of the Boston area controllers lived in suburban communities: 14 lived in the Boston-Cambridge-Somerville area and another 7 came from medium-sized industrial cities.

Our group of 15 includes one white female and two male minority members. We interviewed 9 suburban and 6 urban residents. (The expense of travel and long-distance calls caused us to include a disproportionate number of city dwellers; but this does not seem to have adversely affected the representativeness of the group as a whole.) Of our controllers, 12 were from the Boston Tower and three from lower-level facilities. In terms of experience there were two with 2 to 3 years on the job, 10 who had put in 8 to 15 years, and two within reach of retirement after 22 and 23 years as controllers. Their salaries reflected this range of experience, but when averaged, the mean was $35,000, about as much as in the O'Keefe data.

For the 1981–1982 period we checked whether our 15 controllers shared commonalities with controllers nationwide by assembling accounts of the lives of striking and unemployed colleagues. There seemed to be no substantial differences, as will be detailed below. As media coverage fell off and coping strategies of unemployed air traffic controllers ceased to have novelty value, especially as several years had passed, it became impossible to check from newspapers whether our group shared or departed from the fate of others. At this juncture the O'Keefe data and interviews of Shostak in this book fill in the gap and allow us to conclude that the 15 individuals from the Boston area, whose activities we followed for nearly 4 years, reflect the range, though perhaps not the exact proportions, of the experience of PATCO members nationwide.

An official of Local 215 of PATCO, who has kept close track of all the Boston area members and of affairs nationally, confirms this assertion for the careers taken up by former controllers. However, there appears to be one deviation for the Boston group as a whole and for our sample within it as compared with controllers nationwide: Boston controllers have experienced what must appear as a remarkable degree of stability in their patterns of residence and in marital status. Few have moved from the area (perhaps 15), only about 10 have been lost from sight, and only 7 or 8 divorces have occurred.

It should nonetheless be kept in mind that what is presented here are the results not of a survey but a number of closely studied cases which are primarily valuable for the qualitative data they yield.

FIFTEEN BOSTON AREA CONTROLLERS

The purpose of the initial in-depth interviews in 1982 was to gather information about the impact of the strike and of unemployment, job search, and political outlook. The follow-up interviews in 1984 and 1985 were held to trace the efforts at career reconstruction and their effect on the families' standard of living. While the 1982 interviews reflected disillusionment as well as hopes, the later data provide some answers about the actual resolution of the crisis in the individual controllers' lives. Overall, the interviews give us a longitudinal picture of the unemployment experience and the coping mechanisms of which the controllers availed themselves.

Let us begin with portraits of two men who in several respects had similar backgrounds, but whose experiences since the strike have been quite different: David Thomas and Steve Sypek (the names have been altered). David Thomas was thirty-six years old at the time of the strike in 1981. He had a wife and three children and a well-appointed suburban home. Having served in the military for 4 years during the 1960s he was discharged as a trained air traffic controller and entered that line of work as a civilian. By 1981 he had 13 years experience of which 6 years had been at Logan Airport, the nation's ninth busiest airport. Thomas' income of $40,000 allowed his wife not to work, but the presence of small children and his irregular and long hours may have been equally compelling reasons for the spouse not to seek gainful employment outside the home.

Thomas' father had been a craftsman, his mother a practical nurse; his education included 3 years of college. A longtime member of PATCO, he had held leading positions in several locals and was a spokesman during the strike. Nearly a year after the strike, at the time of his first interview in June 1982, he was unequivocal in his support for the actions of his local and also of the national leadership of PATCO. The FAA's blatant disregard for the safety of airline passengers (by suppressing reports of near collisions in the air and sending the reporting controller to a psychiatrist) and for the well-being of working controllers (by demanding ever-rotating schedules and overtime and by allowing the use of faulty equipment), were Thomas' major reasons for supporting the strike. These complaints are consistent with his desire to be a responsible professional. The unresponsiveness of the FAA combined with President Reagan's summary firing of 11,500 controllers completely turned Thomas against the government—not only its leadership, but also against other government employees, whom he saw as unproductive and deserving of their negative reputation as pencil pushers. Wholesale disillusionment with the federal government set in when he realized that the FAA would not be forced to institute changes, even after its negligent practices had been publicly exposed.

Being independent, articulate, and resourceful, as well as finding moral support within his community and his family, Thomas sought work that would be as far removed as possible from the authoritarian organization from whose company he had just been painfully parted. After a few initial odd jobs he worked as a traveling salesman. In 1982, 10 months after the strike began, salesmanship suited Thomas very well, and it appeared that he would settle into that line of work. However, hints of other plans could be found in a comment such as "If sales don't work out, I might go north and work as a fisherman." Indeed, by the end of 1983 he had founded a completely new venture, a printing business in his own home, built up from scratch and highly successful by March 1984, when I checked with him again. At the time of the third interview in June 1985 the business was thriving, Thomas relished being his own boss, and in retrospect saw the strike as a blessing for him personally, because it had forced him to redesign his life and this had worked out for the best. He reflected on the strike's effect on the labor movement, the controller's profession, and the flying public, and concluded that for them the strike had been "horrible" and that the air traffic controllers' current situation shows that they "will never be a profession."

Steve Sypek's history as an air traffic controller closely parallels Thomas', as do the major personal data. The only difference in background information is that he is Thomas' junior by 5 years and hence served in the military 5 years later, which in his case involved a tour of duty in Vietnam. With less work experience as a civilian controller he earned approximately $10,000 less than Thomas. His father had been a fireman, and he, like Thomas, had slightly over 3 years of college. At the time of the strike his wife was not working and there were two children; a third was born since the strike. Sypek owns a home in a suburban section of Boston.

A loyal supporter of PATCO, he had been active in his local. He too had been incensed over dangerous and stressful incidents, such as managers trying to cover up problems. If, for example, a controller complained that icy runway conditions were not properly reported to pilots he would be labeled a troublemarker. His trust in the government has been severely shaken and bitterness toward the FAA lingers. Sypek's initial pro-union stance has suffered as a result of the strike. The AFL-CIO's lack of resolute support for PATCO was a disappointment to him, as was PATCO's own impotence as a union with no legitimate power to strike.

As a result of the strike Sypek's wife went to work as a nurse, which was difficult and upsetting because their children were still quite small. He obtained low-paying clerical work at a hospital and for a time cherished the idea of training to become a hospital administrator. However, by 1984 he had not begun any studies and was still working at the same job. More recently he had found employment in the maintenance department of a hotel, but in June 1985 he was looking forward to beginning work in an entry-level position at the post office. He had turned down a controller's job at a military facility in western Massachusetts in favor of the postal job, which he believed would give him more security.

The euphoria of Thomas contrasts with the downscaling of Sypek's expectations, yet both cases are quite typical. Economic hardship, in most cases we encountered, was limited to changes in lifestyle: cutting back on the food budget, taking children out of private school, and not buying the house one had saved for. The approximately $20,000 retirement funds from the federal government, which the strikers could request to be paid out, seem to have provided a cushion. But more importantly, the controllers whom we visited seem not to have lived beyond their means and often had savings in addition to the pension fund to fall back on. Qute a few said that they had experienced no economic hardship. These were largely the conditions of those who had found work, had working wives, and three children at most.

A larger family and some fairly ordinary "extraordinary" circumstances combined in one case into a quite different situation. Still paying off the bills from the hospitalization of several children, this family found itself having to survive on the wife's earnings as a cashier, food stamps, and welfare payments. From a combined family income of $47,000 in 1981 they survive on less than $30,000 per year in 1985. The husband has settled into manual assembly work while still studying for a technical degree; the wife provides daycare in the home.

Unemployment is not just an economic phenomenon. It affects self-esteem; the allocation of roles in the family, especially the father's authority; and social support systems in the community. It tests a family's moral resources in a way comparable to a severe illness. We came across a number of quite depressed men. One, a resident of Boston, whose wife was also not working, and who by the accounts of a colleague was a very good controller, was in such a state of despair and social isolation that he had become extremely taciturn and unwilling to elaborate in conversation in 1982, a response quite uncharacteristic of the generally very articulate and talkative controllers. By 1984 he was a technician taking engineering courses at night and looking back in 1985 at the strike experience with an "I'd do it again if I had to" attitude.

Community reaction does not seem to have been entirely negative, contrary to the public image propagated by the media which described an angry public that could muster no sympathy for the "selfish" PATCO strikers. The instances of harassment were limited to a few cases of ostracism and ignorant or hostile remarks, such as "I resent your husband. My husband has to fly and your husband is interfering with that." However, quite a few PATCO members avoided the risk of rejection by simply not bringing up the subject of their former occupation or by withdrawing from community activities, such as coaching a youth sports program.

Supportive sentiments were expressed in a church by individual members who offered help, by neighbors who didn't favor the strike but nonetheless brought food to a family, by a coach who arranged a waiver of the $200 fee for a controller's son to be part of a sports team. Then there is the controller-turned-salesman who knocked on 250 doors per week and who told everyone what work he'd done before and who received very few, perhaps three, negative comments.

In our group the predominant response of families to the strike was to move closer together; wives, especially, often got actively involved in strike support. Many wives sought and found full-time employment, which in several cases became the family's primary source of income, at least initially. Some men became house-husbands. For an older controller, who had previously not been involved with his teenage children, it was not the kind of rediscovery and joy that another man had experienced with his baby (*Boston Globe*, February 28, 1982; p. 74). Not having a place to go every day and having to chauffeur the children to activities, and to do the family's laundry undermined his self-esteem and set in motion a spiral of withdrawal behavior. He stopped going to church, avoided family gatherings, and the wife confessed that she had cried a lot and that her "work was a blessing. I didn't have to see him so depressed all the time." The only people with whom this man kept in contact were other air traffic controllers. He was in touch with them by phone and at the biweekly Sunday meetings at the union hall. That was the situation in 1982; by 1985 this controller was economically back on his feet, running his own franchise business, but the strike and its aftermath had left his personal life in shambles. His drinking had cost him his marriage. Now, in his fifties, he feels like an old man sapped of his physical strength. Just 4 years ago he had been within reach of retirement; now retirement is out of the picture because his funds went into the business and there is no pension plan waiting for him.

Others also mentioned the tremendous emotional upheavals they had undergone, yet many were able to retain some sense of optimism, both in their personal lives and for the resumption of a career. In this they may have been helped by their relative youth.

The Class Position of Air Traffic Controllers

The materials brought together in this book give a fairly consistent and clear picture of the poststrike experience of PATCO members. If one accepts their self-definition as professionals, albeit a not very highly educated and considerably regimented segment of the professions, then according to all the data available they have, as a group, experienced a fair amount of downward social mobility. In fact, I shall argue here that they have moved from a solidly middle-class to a predominantly working-class position.

A word is in order at this point about how I propose to define the much over- and misused categories of working class and middle class. Without getting highly technical, I have found it useful to distinguish as workers those whose conditions of work involve strict regimentation by management, and hence a considerable lack of freedom and of identification with the content of their work. These conditions of work run across traditional lines of blue collar and white collar as well as across productive and nonproductive work. They are, however, the conditions of work of approximately two-thirds of the American labor force (Braverman, 1974).

Where, then, do air traffic controllers belong? Their social origins, their relative lack of formal training, and the lack of control which "controllers" have over their own conditions of work might place them among the skilled levels of the working class such as machinists or "panel watchers" in automated industries. Nonetheless, I place them in the lower levels of the new middle class or salaried petty bourgeoisie for the following reasons: 1) their self-definition as professionals is not illusory; they have a high degree of responsibility and identification with their work as the quotes in this book amply testify. They love their work primarily for its variety, excitement, and social importance, rather than for the pay or friendship networks it provides. They accepted much hardship and personal sacrifice before the strike to do their work, which they saw as gratifying and worthwhile. 2) Their income level is a further indicator of the social standing which this line of work afforded. Controlling may not take much formal schooling, but it does take long years of experience to reach the highest levels of proficiency, which are required for modern aviation. 3) They were regimented, but unlike other workers, they saw this regimentation as an affront to their professional self-esteem, and they ultimately risked everything to regain control over important aspects of their work lives. They did not view their work as a means to an end, but fought to make it an end in itself by providing for the safety of countless others. In this desire they are not unlike nurses and teachers, who also occupy the lower end of the scale of the salaried petty bourgeoisie.

The history of PATCO, as so vividly described in this book, is an excellent example to illustrate the pitfalls and potentials of professional or middle-class based unions. Professional unions are different from working-class trade unions (Fischer, 1980, p. 201). The better they understand their strengths and weaknesses, the more successful they can be in a job action. By virtue of their position in the middle class, professionals tend to be independent-minded and individualistic. Their bonds of solidarity are strong among those whom they consider colleagues—other controllers. Solidarity with other union members is not a given. Neither the membership nor the leadership think of themselves primarily as union men or women. The leadership generally does not encourage the members to participate in the struggles of other trade unions. It does not call on other unions to support its struggles. Consequently it tends not to forge strong bonds with other unions on which it could call in hard times. In fact, the designation of "union" is usually consciously avoided in favor of "association" or "organization."

Leadership roles in professional unions take the professional away from his work, from chances for advancement; they are not seen as an avenue for social mobility to be held on to at all cost, as they are among working-class union leaders. This may in part explain why PATCO in its early years relied so heavily on outsiders to provide direction (e.g., F. Lee Bailey), for it is quite evident that they did not lack in leadership potential.

Professional unions give collective expression to their members' individualistic consciousness. The reasons they hesitate to seek support from blue-collar trade unions are the following: 1) They believe that their own particular occupation is so indispensable to the running of the industry in question, that a solo strike just by them *must* inevitably bring about its desired result. 2) They do not wish to be in a position where at some future point they owe support to a blue-collar union or to the labor movement in general, because as middle-class professionals they wish to differentiate themselves precisely from the working class. Neither reason is very wise, but a thorough examination of unions among engineers—a comparable group of technical professionals—shows that such behavior is as widespread as it is self-defeating. Some strengths of professional unionism, and certainly of PATCO, are the extraordinary dedication of its members in a period of crisis, their internal cohesion, and the pursuit of goals that also serve the larger community.

SUMMARY

Extraordinary circumstances disbanded the membership of PATCO and caused many individuals to fall back into the working class. It remains to be seen whether the occupation of air traffic controller, beset with difficulties as it may currently be and composed of different personnel, can maintain its middle-class position. To do so, of course, does not depend on an act of will on their part, but on the nature of the FAA's efforts at restructuring (*Business Week,* Jan. 18, 1982; Blum & Lobaco, 1985) their occupation.

A RETROSPECTIVE ON THE PATCO STRATEGY

Richard W. Hurd, Ph.D.
Associate Professor
Whittemore School of Business and Economics
University of New Hampshire

The destruction of PATCO has been written off by most labor leaders as the inevitable result of an ill-conceived challenge to an anti-union U.S. President. Although there is widespread sympathy for the rank and file members who lost their jobs in an attempt to exercise collective bargaining rights in the best tradition of the U.S. labor movement, there is at the same time much disdain for the actions of the national officers of PATCO, most notably President Bob Poli. Although the criticisms of the officers are at least partially valid, it is important to recognize that the strategic miscalculations they made were by no means unique. It is even more important to give PATCO's leaders and members credit for the implementation of a brilliantly conceived internal organizing campaign.

Critics of PATCO conveniently forget that it was a small union by AFL-CIO standards, with only 15,000 members. Furthermore, the membership was scattered across the country in some 400 different facilities. Although the regional flight control centers typically employed 200 to 400 air traffic controllers, the majority of PATCO members worked in airport towers and belonged to small locals. Under the circumstances, preparing for a possible strike was a logistical nightmare. The legal prohibition of job actions by federal employees made the task all the most difficult. PATCO's ability to stage a strike which was supported by 75 percent of its members even after President Reagan's firing deadline had passed was a truly remarkable feat. Unfortunately the internal organizing consumed virtually all of the attention of the national officers, and the strike was lost because of flaws in other aspects of the union's strategy.

PATCO's failure can be directly traced to the fact that its unsuccessful external relations were poor, and political activities were misguided. Another crucial weakness was a lack of understanding of economic factors, which led PATCO to overestimate its own strength. Because of the high visibility of the strike, these mistakes were magnified to such a degree that PATCO's officials were widely criticized (even within the labor movement) as bullheaded, inept, misguided, foolhardy, and worse.

Because the flaws in PATCO's strategy are not unique, it would be a mistake to ignore the experiences of this feisty little union. In the discussion that follows, the various aspects of PATCO's approach are considered with particular attention to the specific lessons which can be drawn from the experience. The most important and least discussed contribution of PATCO was its internal organizing program. After reviewing the implementation of this most positive part of the PATCO game plan, the discussion will turn to the components which were not handled as effectively.

I. Building Internal Solidarity[1]

In 1978 negotiations with the FAA, the only major improvement won by PATCO was overseas familiarization flights, essentially free trips abroad for members of the union. When the FAA failed to implement this plan because international airlines refused to honor the agreement, PATCO staged a series of largely unsuccessful slowdowns. Out of this experience came pressure from a group of rank and file militants to initiate changes within the union.

In order to assure that future job actions would be supported by the membership, a committee was appointed in the fall of 1978 to begin preparations for 1981 when the next contract would be negotiated. The "81 Committee" had seven members, one appointed by each of the union's seven regional vice presidents. The members of the 81 Committee, known within PATCO as "choirboys," were chosen for their leadership skills, popularity with the rank and file, and willingness to commit 3 years to the nitty-gritty task of organizing within the union in preparation for a possible strike.

The 81 Committee developed a strike contingency plan and explained it at regional meetings. Under the plan the union was organized geographically into 73 "clusters," with 1 to 12 locals per cluster. The idea behind this structure was to group smaller locals together with larger ones to reduce the feeling and reality of isolation. The 81 Committee selected a choirboy for each cluster to implement the strike plan locally. Eventually additional choirboys were selected so that there would be at least one at each facility, or over 400 nationally. All choirboys fit the same basic mold—they were organizers first and foremost, popular with the rank and file, and committed to strike if necessary.

The 81 Committee instructed the choirboy in charge of strike preparation at each cluster to organize seven committees: communications, security, picketing, motivation, headquarters, good and welfare, and solidarity. In the smaller clusters every union member was assigned to a committee. In the larger clusters committee membership was often voluntary, but the broadest possible participation was encouraged. The cluster choirboy selected leaders for each committee, chosing individuals with skills appropriate to the committee's tasks, but with a commitment to strike if necessary as prerequisite.

Although the 81 Committee did not specify the duties of the seven committees in detail, and as a result a fair amount of variability developed from one location to another, the general assignments were as follows:

(1)   communications—responsible for establishing a communication network locally (essentially a telephone tree), including an elaborate callback system for disseminating secret information;

(2)   security—responsible for protecting strike headquarters from unwelcome visitors, keeping track of strikebreakers, and hiding the local president and choirboy in case arrest warrants were issued;

(3)   picketing—responsible for setting up periodic informational picketing prior to the strike, and staffing picket lines during the strike;

(4)   motivation—responsible for building support for the strike, and maintaining morale during the strike;

(5)   headquarters—responsible for locating an appropriate strike headquarters, arranging for necessary supplies, and staffing the headquarters;

(6)   good and welfare—responsible for helping members and their families survive during the strike, especially by directing them to government agencies (food stamps, etc.) and charitable organizations;

(7)   solidarity—responsible for arranging social events for members and their families before and during the strike.

In addition to the seven required committees, each cluster choirboy was free to establish additional committees. The most common addition was a spouses committee which helped build family support for the strike, and often assisted other committees once the strike began. Some clusters also had a formal public relations committee and/or a political action committee. A final ingredient to the strike preparation plan was added by the 81 Committee as the strike deadline approached. In order to solidify the organizational structure and improve communication, the cluster choirboy selected an informed member from each work crew as an official contact. In some clusters these individuals were also referred to as choirboys.

More important than the details of the committee structure or the duties of the specific committees was the opportunity provided by this system for rank and file members to get involved in strike preparations. The committee system in a sense democratized PATCO—there was extensive delegation of authority, and a noticeable increase in membership involvement in the union throughout the country. The spiritual effect of this change was captured in the June 1981 issue of *High Cotton*, the newsletter of the Memphis cluster: "The decision to strike . . . will not be made by a few powerful union officials in back rooms with under the table deals, nor was the Choirboy Program itself developed in that manner; but by us . . . the individual professional air traffic controllers of the United States. We are the people who work the boards and we are the ones who know best what we want and how to achieve it."

The committee system was implemented in most clusters during 1980, although a few did not get organized until early 1981. In addition to committee meetings (often weekly, and more frequent as the strike approached) there were monthly local meetings and quarterly cluster meetings. As the committee system built momentum, attendance at local and cluster meetings increased dramatically. During the summer of 1981 there was a local or cluster meeting every week, and attendance approached 100 percent of those not on duty.

Another key component of the 81 Committee's plan was a requirement that 80 percent of all full performance air traffic controllers, or approximately 90 percent of PATCO members, vote in favor of a strike. The feeling was that a strike could only succeed with near unanimous participation by PATCO members. With this 80 percent rule built into the plan, cluster choirboys established detailed monitoring systems so that they could accurately gauge the level of strike support. Members whose willingness to strike was suspect were given special attention, with a careful attempt to motivate rather than intimidate recalcitrant individuals. For example, black controllers in many clusters were only marginally involved in strike preparations. Visits by members of PATCO's national Black Caucus often won their support. In other cases older controllers near retirement who were PATCO activists talked with their contemporaries who were reluctant to support a strike. In addition to this one-on-one organizing, teams of PATCO members from highly organized clusters would visit clusters that had been less successful to offer advice and give pep talks to the membership.

Although the degree of organization and level of participation in the committee system varied from one area to another, the very existence of the committees assured high visibility for strike preparation and offered every member a chance to contribute. Most PATCO members took advantage of the opportunity, and spent much of their own time involved in union activities during the spring and summer of 1981. It was this high degree of internal organization that enabled the 81 Committee and the national officers to hold the union together in the face of President Reagan's firing ultimatum. Clearly the extensive internal preparation was highly successful. Other unions should take note of the methods used and do more to involve their members in union affairs.

The only weakness in the 81 Committee's strategy was the exclusive focus of the cluster committees on *strike* preparation. The tight internal cohesiveness became so powerful that it developed a momentum of its own, making a strike almost inevitable. Had the same system been used to prepare for other aspects of the 1981 negotiations, particularly public relations and coordination with other unions, the chances of success would have been increased.

II. External Activities

A. Coordination with Other Unions.   Although the 81 Committee advised locals to get involved in state labor councils, there was no formal system installed to assure that this happened. Some locals did establish links with other unions in their areas, but most paid far more attention to internal strike preparation. Indeed, if the locals took the activities of the national office as an example to emulate, little or no contact would have occurred. PATCO decided to wage its illegal strike with no prior official contact with the AFL-CIO or individual unions who would be affected by the strike.

Communication with other public sector unions would have given PATCO leaders informed feedback on their planned course of action. This would have been especially useful given the general lack of experience of PATCO's national officials and the small professional staff of the union. Equally important, the larger public sector unions have extensive political influence which they could have used in PATCO's behalf.

The failure of PATCO to communicate with airline industry unions was primarily an act of poor courtesy. Had the strike succeeded, thousands of union members could have been out of work for its duration. As it was, the reduced flight schedules which were imposed when the strike began gave the airlines an excuse to demand wage and work rule concessions from their employees' unions.

All unions can benefit from cooperating with other labor organizations. For public sector unions such solidarity is crucial because of the strict limitations placed on their activities by federal and state public sector bargaining laws. With their own power severely constrained by legal restrictions on strikes, public sector unions should coordinate their activities closely with other unions to increase their leverage and bargaining power.

On a positive note, an important improvement in AFL-CIO policy was implemented as a direct result of the PATCO experience. The Public Employee Department now requires advance notification 15 days prior to any probable strike by a federal, state, or local affiliate. The rationale for notification is to improve the "quality and effectiveness" of "the support affiliated unions can give to and receive from each other during crisis situations."[2]

B. Public Relations.   To the general public, the PATCO strike seemed to be an example of another greedy union throwing its weight around without regard for who was hurt by its actions. The lack of sympathy for the strike stemmed in large part from the widely publicized PATCO demands, which certainly appeared to be excessive: a $10,000 annual pay raise (increasing the average salary to $40,000), a 32-hour work week, and full retirement after 20 years on the job. Although this package might have been appropriate in the context of the posturing which accompanies contract negotiations, the demands were extreme based on the work experiences of the average citizen. PATCO could have avoided a total public relations disaster simply by moderating its demands and focusing more attention on nonwage aspects of the dispute.

PATCO had at its disposal ample ammunition for an effective public relations campaign. Of particular relevance were the reports of two groups of outside consultants hired by the FAA to investigate labor-management relations, worker attitudes, job stress, and worker health in the air traffic control system. Both reports were openly critical of management practices. The 1970 Corson Report could have been used in conjunction with the 1978 Rose Report to demonstrate the persistence over time of management's inflexibility and insensitivity. The two reports were potentially valuable to PATCO because they provided objective evidence that the air traffic controllers had legitimate complaints with management, and legitimate concerns with health related issues such as stress and burnout.[3] In particular, this information could have been presented to the public to make an excellent case for a reduced work week and an improved retirement system.

Although most unions could benefit from more attention to public relations, this is an especially important issue for public sector unions. Because their members directly serve the public, and because government decision makers must ultimately answer to the electorate, it is crucial that popular support be aggressively pursued. PATCO had a good case, but by waiting until after the strike began before going to the public it allowed the Reagan Administration to set the framework of the debate. In fact, by reiterating its initial extreme bargaining demands when announcing the strike deadline,

PATCO played right into the Administration's hands. As Bog Poli later admitted, "Our own public relations efforts were about as successful as Qaddafi's."[4]

C. *Political Action.*   To its credit, PATCO recognized the importance of pursuing an aggressive political program. Legislation was introduced on the union's behalf in the House of Representatives, a coordinated lobbying campaign was conducted, and an apparently sympathetic candidate for president was endorsed with much fanfare. Unfortunately, there were two flaws in this program, one of them fatal.

First, the legislation was unrealistic and gave the opposition ammunition to use against PATCO. The combination of huge increases in salaries, future pay raises well in excess of inflation, reduced hours of work, and improved retirement made the proposal extremely expensive. When the Congressional Budget Office placed a $13 billion pricetag on the bill its defeat was guaranteed and PATCO's image as just another greedy union began to form.

The second and fatal mistake was to trust the assurances given by Ronald Reagan in return for PATCO's support of his candidacy. The endorsement followed a private meeting between Poli and Reagan and a subsequent letter from the candidate promising to "work very closely with you to bring about a spirit of cooperation between the President and the air traffic controllers."[5] This campaign pledge was accepted at face value with no apparent consideration given to the candidate's anti-union reputation. After taking office, Reagan reiterated his commitment to PATCO in a private February meeting with Poli, expressing sympathy for the air traffic controllers' desire for a reduced work week and improved retirement system.[6]

While Poli was being charmed by the "great communicator," the real Reagan strategy was quietly taking shape. In February 1981, the Department of Transportation hired Morgan, Lewis, and Bockius to handle the expected "volatile contract negotiations" with PATCO. This anti-union law firm, well known to the readers of the AFL-CIO *Report on Union Busters*, was eventually paid $376,000 for services directly related to the PATCO negotiations and strike.[7] In March, J. Lynn Helms was appointed FAA Administrator. While President of Piper Aircraft, Helms had personally coordinated campaigns to defeat union organizing drives in new plants, and to weaken locals in existing plants.[8]

During the summer another ingredient was added to the Administration's strategy. An original strike contingency plan developed by the Carter administration was discarded because it was too restrictive. It was secretly revised to allow for much higher levels of air traffic (approaching 75 percent of normal), more flexibility in scheduling, and more discretion for individual airlines regarding which flights to cancel. Airline representatives were involved in the planning process, and the FAA was assured of their cooperation in advance of the strike.[9] The final ingredient was added to the formula when Reagan issued his firing ultimatum with a 48-hour time limit. Subsequently, 3500 members of the union elected to cross picket lines and return to work, assuring the success of the strike contingency plan and the destruction of PATCO.

It is especially important that public sector unions recognize that their struggles may be won or lost in the political arena. The PATCO experience makes clear just how difficult it is to implement an effective political action program. Poli's apparent coup in gaining Reagan's assurance of cooperation eventually boomeranged. As should be obvious from what happened in this case, politicians who form an alliance based on the pragmatic goals of an election campaign are less reliable than politicians whose personal views are consistent with the interests of the labor movement. Furthermore, unions must be alert to the reality that the politician will become part of management once in office, and will inevitably view public employee unions differently than during the election campaign.

D. *Understanding Economic Factors.*   PATCO's leaders expected the strike to cause serious economic problems for the airline industry. If it had, there is little doubt that the airline companies would have pressured the Reagan Administration to settle the dispute. There were two reasons for the lack of significant economic impact. One was the revised strike response plan implemented by the Reagan Administration as discussed above. However, even this revised plan called for a 25 percent reduction in scheduled flights for an extended period of time. Such a major decline in business would normally be expected to be painful for any industry. But the airline companies were not operating in a "normal" environment in 1981.

The industry had been struggling ever since the Airline Deregulation Act of 1978. Increased competition had resulted in more flights, lower fares, and more empty seats. As a result, the industry lost a total of $200 million in the first half of 1981 alone.[10] Under the reduced mode dictated by the strike, the Airline Deregulation Act was essentially scrapped. The airlines were assigned quotas, but with significant flexibility to decide which flights got eliminated. The choice was obvious—nonprofitable routes were cancelled first. This enabled airlines to take inefficient aircraft out of service, save on fuel, lay off employees, win concessions from unions, and increase the all-important passenger load factor (the percent of seats occupied). Also, with fewer flights available there was less competition for passengers, allowing the elimination of discount rates. The major airline companies, then, stood to reap economic gains in the long run if the PATCO strike was not resolved. And the beauty of it from their standpoint was that the higher fares, reduced flights, and layoffs could all be blamed on PATCO.

PATCO's leaders had *assumed* that the strike would have a significant economic impact. Any careful analysis of the economic conditions prevailing in the airline industry would have cast immediate doubt on that assumption. The lesson here is that unions must be willing to conduct appropriate analysis before planning a strike. After all, strikes are primarily economic actions. They are seldom effective except in an environment where the economic impact is likely to be significant.

III. Reflections on the Strengths and Weaknesses of the PATCO Strategy

The leaders and members of PATCO deserve the highest praise for their internal organization. In spite of the geographic dispersion of the membership, an unprecedented degree of internal solidarity was cultivated by delegating authority and facilitating rank and file involvement. Every member had the opportunity to contribute, and most rose to the challenge. The AFL-CIO has recently encouraged affiliated unions "to provide additional opportunities for members to participate in union affairs."[11] Unions which take this charge seriously would benefit considerably from a careful review of the PATCO model.

Unfortunately, the brilliance of the internal strategy was not matched in the union's external activities. It is incumbent upon union leaders objectively to evaluate the economic and political environment, and to offer an accurate assessment to the rank and file. Leaders should also coordinate with reliable allies to maximize potential strength, and communicate the union's just concerns, grievances, and demands to the general public. In virtually every facet of its external affairs, the PATCO strategy was lacking.

In the final analysis, however, most of the criticism of the 1981 strike is misdirected. PATCO represented the ultimate in union democracy, and its actions accurately reflected the frustrations of the rank and file. Strategic errors were committed, but the air traffic controllers had legitimate gripes which were ignored by the Reagan administration. The goverment's hard line, noncompromising approach was unwarranted. The President challenged the pride and guts of an organization built on pride and guts. In the end a good union was needlessly destroyed.

INTERVIEWS WITH UNION LEADERS

1. JIMMY HAYS, FIRST PRESIDENT of PATCO
(MIAMI, FLORIDA, SPRING 1984)

"I would *never* do it again, *never!* We didn't accomplish anything, and it gets more dangerous now to fly every day. They have too few experienced controllers, too many overworked controllers, and over 2,000 retirements pending in 1985.

"It was crazy after we struck. Rumor control was terrible, and most of the goddamn rumors lifted our hopes—so when we went up and down 100 times, and wound up with nothing it led to a lot of depression.

"If I were offered my job back I'd grab it! I'd have no problems getting along with the scabs, though two or three of my friends inside tell me the basic management system is the same or worse than ever. Conditions are real good for reunionization, though I'd prefer something other than AFGE. We need a more professional-like union, one that can help set standards, and try to get along with the FAA. It will take the FAA at least 10 years to develop and install any kind of 'intelligent' guidance system, so they'll need us for at least that long a period.

"I spent 6 months looking for work, and found myself blackballed everywhere, in the government, the electric company, the phone company, the utility companies, everywhere. My wife had to get a job, at long hours, and our income still fell 50 percent. So now I work for a lawn service company, a

215

lot of dirty, backbreaking, hand work, which I *never* expected to find myself doing again.

"We should have gone back inside the 72-hour period. Hell, we were not out to degrade the President's office or to 'defeat' the country, though it is all so much easier to see clearly now than at the time. I don't discuss any of it with anyone, though none of our neighbors or any relatives ever showed any animosity over it.

"Frankly, I still have a problem with having broken my oath. That remains a difficult one for me. But I remind myself that the Constitution protects our right to withhold our services if we think we cannot get a redress of grievances—and we had tried for 10 years. Nobody seemed able to do enough, and everything seemed to be going in a *negative* direction.

"If you had the right personality, an *appropriate* personality, there was no better job in the world for you. I loved it! I loved the demands it made on me, and I loved seeing the accomplishments. I loved the flow of it, and my part in helping to make the system move efficiently. The guys at my facility were one of the best groups I've *ever* been associated with . . .

"Now, back when I was PATCO's president, we tried to bring our issues forward, the gripes we had with the conditions, like the overload of stress. But, we may have overdone it. because lots of people came to think our problems were too big, too overwhelming, to tackle.

"'81 was over *one* thing: our need to get a *survivable* occupation, one you can put your life into, and live through. . . . We needed an escape avenue, something like early retirement or retraining, so that when the time came to bow out, when the stress finally got to you, you had some place to go—that's what we were after, and they *still* need it today.

"Some people say we should have tried some violence, but I think that's just damn foolish talk! It would not ring true with what we were trying to accomplish, it would not be consistent with the people we were, and are . . .

"As for Poli, I'm not mad at him: he did his part, and really tried to help change things. But, too many people got hurt, and we've now lost all these years since '81 which could have gone into changing the system from inside . . ."

2. JOHN F. LEYDEN, SECOND PRESIDENT of PATCO
(SILVER SPRING, MARYLAND, SPRING 1984)

How far back did PATCO's problems go? "When I look back to 1970, and recall how a lot of gains came very swiftly to us, I think sometimes that may have contributed to PATCO's demise. We did so well so early that some of the guys thought we should continue to make progress without stop; they lost track of the importance of patience and persistence."

What sorts of mistakes did PATCO make after you left office? "They went out of their way to exacerbate tensions with the pilots and FAA management, and there was no good reason for that. They also went all the way to arbitration to win the right to wear a T-shirt at work giving the finger to the FAA! *Crazy!* Or, to win the right to wear shower clogs to work! What in hell did that shit have to do with anything? Looney-tune notions!"

What was the major hazard PATCO faced in '81? "Anarchy! The biggest risk we ran was losing control of the union to the crazies, like at O'Hare in '80. The militants out there began to write their own ticket, and there was no stopping them. I had stopped anarchy twice at New York and Chicago when I was in charge, but Poli was *not* the master of his own destiny."

Should a leader always implement the "will of the membership," as Poli promised? "No! Total democracy does not serve the best interest of a union, at least not in all cases at all times. A leader should take full responsibility for his actions, and show the way! A leader should lead, *not* follow; a leader should bring people along, *not* rush to do what he thinks the crowd wants him to do—for ultimately, the rank and file can reward or punish his leadership through the election process.

In PATCO, the choirboys were important and helpful at the start. But by '81 they were driving the organization, and that was all wrong! They were a fringe lunatic group that wanted to fight for the sheer sake of fighting, and a *real* leader would have separated himself from their suicidal, looney-tune nonsense."

When did 1981 first go wrong? "When Poli failed to understand that the June 22 agreement was *his* contract, and his credibility was at stake. Lewis and others who were important felt Bob had gone back on his word, and PATCO went downhill from that point on."

In 1981, was PATCO well-advised? "Hell no! The attorneys should have told them of the difficulties that lay ahead, and not that all the members could escape being hurt.

"When the union's regional VPs were in Washington, some would call me for advice. But most spoke only to Poli and one another, and that wasn't broad enough.

"What hurt the most was having Poli and his crowd oversell to the membership their contract demands, so that it became 'pie-in-the-sky' stuff, a wet dream they never could have made good on.

"I warned Bob the lemon was dry! I told him 'You've taken it to .the edge—one more step, and you go over!'

"After awhile, however, they were living in their self-made 'bunker,' and were only talking to one another—and there was nothing anyone could do with them."

How close to success did the secret deals come? "Much was going on! I've got 35 pages of memos, notes, and stuff that I'm saving to use in my own book, but I can tell you we had some openings and a lot of behind-the-scenes discussion. Some very highly placed people were willing to discuss a deal, but when the PATCO crazies were told, and fired back their terms—'the head of FAA had to resign, and the government had to declare there was no winner and no loser'—the window slammed shut. Those stupid bastards couldn't understand they had *lost*, and could not demand anything! . . . . There *were* opportunities to salvage something, to pull off a Dunkirk, but Taylor and others said, 'All go back or none go back!' And I said, 'No one will get back, in that case,' and I was right, unfortunately."

How serious were the charges your opponents leveled against you in 1980? "They said *crazy* things. I was considering leasing a plane which the PATCO Board and I could use in fact-finding visits to many of our locals across the country. We could have saved a considerable amount of money doing it that way. According to them, however, I was trying to rent a luxury jet to take myself, like some goddamn potentate, around the country . . . They said I was misusing funds, and a lot of shit like that, but none of it held up, and they knew it before they started!"

Was any deal offered to soften the loss of the presidency? "Bob came and offered me an emeritus title, and 'plastic.' He said I could use the credit cards to travel, buy things . . . I said 'no,' I was too proud for that sort of thing. I wanted no part of it. I'd had enough. Enough damage had been done . . . I would have won if I had run, but I had enough."

After leaving PATCO, you joined the FAA. What did that amount to? "What was it like? *Worst* time of my life! Sitting in a cubicle with one phone, no secretary, and everybody listening in to my calls. They assigned me to rewriting sections of the ATP manual which controllers used as their bible. Now, I was an English major in college, and I think I know a little about the King's English. So I worked hard, and submitted draft after draft, and they would come back with nit-picking little comments. Then, about the eighth draft I started to understand. So I submitted the original version they had given me to improve, and the bastards indicated I had finally gotten it right! I knew then what they were doing, and, what my FAA job really amounted to—worst time of my life!

"But the Poli crowd said it was a 'tit' job, a piece of cake! Said I had sold out, and was helping FAA prepare to wipe out PATCO. Hell, they didn't need any help doing that: PATCO would murder *itself*!"

3. STANLEY A. GORDON, PATCO SECRETARY-TREASURER and CHARTER MEMBER (SILVER SPRING, MARYLAND, FALL 1985)

"Through a series of circumstances, not motivation, I became an activist, and eventually one of the founders of PATCO. I was called on to lead, confront, and to be part of the top level of a new bureaucracy. In the past I had never had any experience with any of these roles, nor did I feel comfortable in exercising them.

"Right from the beginning I was given total financial responsibility for PATCO's affairs. In addition I began to travel around the country selling the union. I had to participate in press conferences, and help to run meetings. This was the first time in my career as an air traffic controller that I was involved in something else that I truly enjoyed. These new responsibilities, though, were accompanied by a great deal of fear, as I had no familiarity with this role.

"The structure in the early days of PATCO was very different from that of our FAA Center. There was no direct supervision. We had an appointed leader, Jimmy Hays, and a world-famous attorney, F. Lee Bailey, who gave directions, but informally. The board of directors, of which I was part, were equal members. The membership was so new that they provided neither direction nor leadership. Since there had not been a previous structure, and none of us had any administrative experience, we developed the structure and organizational culture as we went along.

"Socializing was part of every union meeting or conference. Expense-account living became a part of my life. The 'cause' was the primary factor surrounding everything I did. Someone else was always paying the bills for the meals and hotels. We were dealing with very high level company and government officials.

"Some of the stressors in my FAA/PATCO life might have been reduced or eliminated if—

1. FAA training had been more formalized, and progress had been related to merit;

2. Promotions had been based on merit (some sort of testing or evaluation would have been better than the buddy system then in existence);

3. Supervisors had been required to have clearcut standards, and employees had been treated evenhandedly;

4. 'Cause' and training in our PATCO organizing drive had been more closely integrated (Not only couldn't we train ourselves, but I don't believe our PATCO leaders were qualified to do it);

5. Social upheaval could have been anticipated (movement from a relatively normal life to instant "jet-setting" took a heavy toll on many); and—

6. Advisers had been sought with labor backgrounds, rather than lawyers and corporate executives (We eventually affiliated with MEBA, AFL-CIO, but much time was wasted before we made that move).

It is clear to me now that this era was the most interesting and exciting in my career, and probably in my entire lifetime."

4. Leo Perlis AFL-CIO Director of Community Services, Retired (Bay Harbor, Florida, Spring 1985)

"I've often reflected back on that entire experience, and it saddens me. I learned a lot then that really hurt. Here was confirmation once again that otherwise mature and competent adults, people in charge of the lives of many others, can make so *many* terrible, irrational errors—errors of omission and commission.

"I was a sort of liaison between PATCO and the White House. It was a sad kind of business, and I'm inclined now to fault *everyone* involved.

"It began for me in 1979 when PATCO asked me to lecture in their training program at the George Meany Center. They were gung-ho to learn about community service and strike assistance, and I spoke about our strike assistance program beginning with the 1945 auto strike approach I initiated, and how all kinds of voluntary and public resources can be used to aid strikers in need, on the basis of need.

"When I retired from the AFL-CIO in 1980, PATCO asked me to become a paid consultant. They wanted a plan to deal with alcoholism, drugs, stress, and emotional problems, that sort of thing. I did a proposal, but by the time I explained it to them at their 1980 Las Vegas convention they were preoccupied with strike preparations . . . My plan was outlined in PATCO publications. They paid me, and my consultancy ended.

"When I later read that Poli and the FAA had agreed on terms for a new contract I sent a telegram of congratulations, but I was premature.

"From clear out of the blue Poli called me 2 days after the mass firing, and asked if I could help. I put one condition down: I was not to get paid! They were on strike, and I would not take a penny. I insisted on paying for my own cabs, and the like.

"Poli asked me to intercede with the White House, and I agreed. But I told Poli that everything he told me, I would tell to the White House, and then later, I told the White House the same thing. I wanted everything up front, and I don't think they kept anything back from me.

"Things were bad from the start. While Donovan, the Secretary of Labor, was kept out of it, Lewis and Helms were in charge. I felt Reagan should have played a larger part and dealt directly with the issue.

"My message to the White House was—'Let's open the door: PATCO *is* willing to go back.' I called Rep. Jack Kemp to intercede and we had several conversations. Once he called me from his mother's home in California to tell me that, even though he himself was for reinstatement of the strikers and continued bargaining, the President was adamantly opposed to it for a number of reasons.

"The White House became nervous about the reactions of strikebreakers to any returning PATCO people. I tried to reassure the White House that PATCO could ease the inevitable tensions, and I emphasized the need for compassion and humanity—but there was none to be found in the White House. Of course, everyone was very courteous and polite, even amiable. And for the first 2 weeks I remained hopeful, and kept appealing to their humanity. But as it dragged on into 3, and then 4 weeks, I grew concerned . . .

"Sometime during that period my wife and I were invited to a dinner at a friend's house, and I found myself seated next to an admiral, a personal friend of the President's. We chatted a bit about the PATCO strike, and he warned me the President was stubborn, and did not change his mind easily or often.

"As time went by, my White House contacts never lied to me, or shut the door on me. They may have led me on, but none of us could persuade the President to reconsider.

"I turned my attention to Poli, a very nice and moderate man, if a bit vain. I urged him to resign, claim all responsibility, and offer to go to jail as a sacrificial lamb. To his credit he did not wince and said he might. I never made this offer to my White House contacts, however, as Poli never told me he was *actually* willing to go through with it.

"At lunch one day soon afterwards, I urged other PATCO leaders to get Bob to resign, even if it took holding a big, fancy dinner in his honor, but nothing came of it.

"Overall, as a consultant I feel I made a mistake in not warning PATCO beforehand of the full and awesome risk it was running. But they were only asking me about the community relief aspects of the subject, and it was *not* my role to offer advice they had not requested . . . it was truly a sad kind of business, one from which we've *got* to gain knowledge. It was a tragedy of errors."

5. JACK MAHER, CO-FOUNDER of PATCO
(POMPANO BEACH, FLORIDA,
FALL 1985)

What was it like at the outset? "Many of us performed our work in isolation, especially those of us who worked in black-light centers. There you only talked to dots on the scope; many, many dots. With PATCO we became a 'society,' and our work became a 'calling.' After 1978, we finally succeeded in becoming a 'family,' and we dedicated ourselves to preserving a sense of craft.

"But we also developed a sense of 'Us' against the 'World.' Earlier the idea had been—'I'm gonna beat the shit out of that traffic!' Later it became —'We're gonna take on this whole goddamn system, and *change* it!'"

What was the prestrike goal? "We wanted to create a 'Big Bomb' equivalent, something so frightening, potentially dev..stating, to the FAA that PATCO would never have to use it. We wanted to get so well prepared, and have so many graduates of our training center out there, along with our 'choirboys,' that the FAA would know we meant business, and would hesitate to take us on. We did not *need* to strike, and if our 'Big Bomb' frightened them into signing the contract we wanted, so much the better—our people were our 'Bomb'! But we were finally left with no choice except to use our bomb and both sides and the bystanders as well have been suffering through a 'nuclear winter' ever since."

How was the timing? "Bad, real bad . . . the Iranian hostages had just been released in January 1981, and the country was in no mood to be held hostage again, by PATCO or anybody else. As if that wasn't bad enough, a long base-ball strike created resentment against any disruption of what the public had come to count on, of what was normal and expected, like uninterrupted air travel—and we walked right into that. America needed to kick the shit out of someone and politically it was expedient to do just that. The pricetag for this shit-kicking contest has yet to be tabulated."

When was the decision made to strike? "In early July, when Poli called a 2-day meeting at 2000 'N' St. of about 20 choirboys, the die was cast. They looked over the June 22 contract, which had not addressed the key issues and it was judged second-rate, completely unacceptable.

"I felt the choirboys were pressured into acting with too much speed, but they did get Poli to fund four or five of them to travel around in an attempt to build up our strike force, though the time was *too* brief.

"The really deadly move made at this meeting was the decision to dilute the three-tier vote-weighing system we had written to prevent overriding the will of the membership. This safeguard was negated or minimized and this move made the strike inevitable."

Were the crazies really crazy? "Hell no, and I resent a lot of that kind of talk. The people now being put down as 'crazies' were really well-schooled and *very* disciplined! They actually kept some of the 'dirty trick' types under lock and key, and are owed credit for a lot of the good accomplished by locals when the going got tough. Now, after the first month of the strike, some of the discipline and good sense frayed, but until then the 'crazies' were anything but! They were intensely dedicated to changes which were necessary 20 years ago, and in 1981, and still today. They loved their profession enough to risk losing it."

Why didn't PATCO demand flow control? "For one thing, the FAA warned us it was a management prerogative, and a right of theirs to do as they pleased. In practical application, many of our people used their own form of flow control individually, and we thrived on the challenge. And your self-esteem, your ego encouraged you to tackle the peaks in a love-hate relationship. When you beat the peak traffic down, you could be good, *real* good! Not necessarily an intellectual choice, but more of an emotional 'we can handle any kind of thing!' And, if a bad bind resulted, you could blame your supervisor for the lousy peak-and-valley situation. So, it was a win-win type of situation, and that's why PATCO kind of left it all alone."

What were the deals like? "In the fourth or fifth week two overtures were underway: A Cabinet-level Commission was under consideration, one which might have investigated what the strike was all about. And another type of top-secret discussion had AFGE's Ken Blaylock in touch with people either on Reagan's staff or with the Civil Service Commission. They were considering a *broad* settlement, one which might have included a shorter work week and early retirement, but also Poli resigning in disgrace to help Reagan look good. Unfortunately, just when things got interesting, the Secretary of Labor, Ray Donovan, let the discussions out in some offhand comment, and the press got *very* excited about the possibility. So the White House broke off negotiations, and we were left with just another tragedy."

Why was the Kirkland deal rejected at Baltimore? "I was not there, but as best as I can make out, most of the board members insisted on having a *written* guarantee, and would not take anybody's word for the details, *no matter what their credentials.* They also had *no* sense of urgency about surrender terms, because most felt PATCO was beating the shit out of the FAA. They would tell one another—'Back in my hometown half the planes are grounded! And those companies will either go bankrupt soon, or force the FAA to come to terms with us!' So, this mass illusion that we could still kick ass kept almost everyone in Baltimore from seeing the value of cutting a deal at that time. They thought they were fighting the FAA, but it had gone well beyond that."

Was PATCO prepared to cut its losses? "No, not very well at all! Before the strike we left its timing and politics, etc., to the top leadership while a PATCO 'War Board' focused on getting the machinery oiled and ready. Our job as we saw it was to give them the firepower. Now, in hindsight, I think we should have had many more planning groups, such as one focused on political relations. And another one concerned with interunion coordination. Another one to protect our three-tier plan. And still others that could have served as a kind of checks-and-balances on what the guys at headquarters were doing to make best use of the 'army.' And of course more time to build, to heal, and to maneuver.

"In this way our complete and total reliance on the sword, on our ability to use might, would have been reduced. We had taken the sword, but we couldn't find a way to put it back in the scabbard. Even before we walked we thought about planning how to lose. But we excluded any of this planning from our documents, because we worried that its presence would confuse and demoralize our people. Or that it would be perceived as negative thinking. I feel this was right, but still think we could have thought more deeply about it."

Was the strike utterly lost? "No, not unless you assume the current ATC system works, which it doesn't. They changed all the rules, and passed the cost and inconvenience along to the public, and the numbers they boast about don't make any sense with PATCO as a safety watchdog eliminated. Nor was it lost in terms of what happened to Poli. Sure, nobody loves a loser, and he was a leader of a losing cause, but attacks on him are vastly overdone.

"What should have been lost was the charter ALPA had from the AFL-CIO. It should have been lifted because of the way they treated us in their own self-interest. Incredible! They are historically aviation's greatest strike-busters."

What sort of regrets do you have now? "Well, I think I should have backed the staff employees union more when Bob turned on it. I didn't speak up, and let too few know how much I disagreed with his union-busting move. This act foreshadowed and masked very deep leadership problems. And I should have spoken up when I realized they were not using the three-tier voting plan I had written into the '81 blueprint. If they had stuck to the blueprint there would not have been a strike! I knew they wouldn't get the numbers, and they didn't! But I didn't say anything . . .

"And I probably should have said something to someone when I heard rumors about the deal we could have struck to get some of the guys back, deals that Poli never really pursued—but I kept quiet about that, too.

"I guess you could kind of say I let too much go by thinking it was for the good of the organization, though if I had it all to do over again, I still don't know that I would do it much different. And of course the strikers and their families certainly deserve better than they have received to date, victims of overkill. I regret their ignominy and salute them all."

INTERVIEWS WITH UNION ACTIVISTS*

1. Philadelphia Activist and Family (Spring 1984)

What impact did the strike and mass firing have? Consider the story be-low of a family that lost its suburban home to foreclosure, went nearly 30 months without the ex-controller earning a paycheck, learned to rely on recycle stores and hand-me-downs from concerned neighbors, split com-pletely with close relatives, and in many other ways, really suffered. Neverthe-less, when interviewed in March of 1984, the former controller claimed the entire experience had helped him gain the greatest peace of mind possible. His wife felt their children were better off for their suffering, and the couple were now charismatic Catholics, closer to the Lord than either had ever be-fore thought possible. A staunch union supporter during and since the strike, this former controller deeply missed his job, but would only return to a tower if he could help unionize his coworkers inside. Otherwise, he was grimly pre-pared never to "move traffic again," a prospect that still caused his eyes to mist over.

What impact did the strike and mass firing have? Consider a story of shock and of recovery, of heartbreak and of balm, and of one family's search for and discovery of the "right stuff" at home, where it really counts.

Shortly before my colleagues and I arrived for our first discussion with this family, the woman at its head, a thirty-five-year-old mother of three, asked her children to stay home that night to talk with us. Donna's oldest, her

---

*With the exception of interviews 1 and 6, the names of all interviewees and locales have been changed.

fifteen-year-old son, reminded everyone he had basketball practice, although he volunteered a cogent thought about his family's 30-month PATCO strike experience. As Donna later recalled, the boy said with great intensity: "Mom, if you promise not to get angry with my words, I'll tell you what I *really* think —I think the strike sucked!" Donna welcomed us at the door of her home with this anecdote, and it foreshadowed much that we learned in the 3-hour dialogue that followed.

"Doc" Livingston, a thirty-eight-year-old former controller, joined all of us a minute or two later, having dropped their oldest son off at a nearby basketball gym, and listened to Donna's repetition of the anecdote. "Yes," he sighed, "the strike took a helluva lot out of all of us, and the kids have every reason in the world to be bitter. They hate the way the government treated me, and they hate the way Donna and me got into arguments over money. And they were denied many things other kids were getting, things they should have had."

After asking our approval, the parents called in Desiree, their thirteen-year-old middle child, a bright and affable youngster who quickly warmed up to the subject. Only ten and a half years old when the August 1981 strike had been called, she remembered the pain of hearing former playmates curse her father as an outlaw and lawbreaker. TV had helped inject some fun by making brief celebrities of Doc, Donna, and their three children, but the fun had faded very rapidly after President Reagan fired the strikers. And days, weeks, and months of just plain being scared were the child's strongest lasting impression of the past 30 months.

Along with the youngsters of other PATCO strikers, Desiree had put much time and effort into a short-lived ad hoc group called C-PATCO (Children's PATCO). Boys and girls dreamed up and prepared their own picket signs, marching proudly alongside their folks in the hopeful early phase of the strike. Nowadays, however, all contact among C-PATCO members had ended, though Desiree took pride in her well-handled newspaper clippings, photos, and other momentoes of the lost campaign.

"When I got into fights at school," the thirteen-year-old recalled, "the other kid would shout—'At least my dad's working!'" On one occasion, a run-of-the-mill tussle with a neighbor's child ended with that eleven-year-old boy screaming - "Your dad should get a job! Maybe he could become a cop, 'cause they also get on TV, and they are more honest and protective than the damn controllers!" Teachers often took the sting out of encounters like these with friendly questions of concern, but, overall, Desiree said she wanted to put it behind her—and soon lapsed into attentive silence, moving in and out of our room over the next 2½ hours.

Reflecting later on their daughter's familiar words and feelings, both Doc and Donna dwelt on their admiration of the youngster. A steady earner as a much sought-after babysitter, Desiree had often helped keep groceries on the table: "It was especially nice because we didn't have to ask. Whenever we needed money for gasoline, or milk, or food, she'd come up with it, or just go down to the store and buy whatever was necessary." Overhearing some of this, the child rushed to remind her folks that her older brother, then eleven and a half, had taken up a paper delivery route to also contribute to the dollar crunch. And in the summers the boy had worked from 6a.m. to 5p.m. to bring home about $75 a week.

Both parents were firm in their belief that their three children were better off as a result of the entire experience. The older two, and even the youngest, who had been only seven and a half at the strike's onset, appreciated life and material goods much more keenly now than ever before: "We used to get our things in really good places. Now we have to shop in discount stores and recycle stores, and we accept hand-me-downs from one or two *really* good neighbor families. But the kids don't seem to mind. They never give us lists at Christmas; we have to wait until it is almost too late before we can get any idea of what they might want—we make them 'dream.' However, we make them understand that we will make it all up to them someday, tenfold! We do *not* dwell on the past, but we urge them to dream instead about moving soon to a better house and better neighborhood."

Some sort of move is actually in the offing, since the suburban home they have occupied since 1980 has been foreclosed, and Doc and Donna have watched daily for an eviction notice ever since the sheriff's sale 6 months ago. Donna recalled accepting a sister-in-law's recent invitation to go apartment-hunting in the parish area, but freezing when the car stopped in front of the first halfway-decent, nearby rental complex. Through sobs, she swore that she would not go back to apartment-renting. Having promised the children they would remain in the same parish and attend the same Catholic schools, Doc and Donna are hard-pressed to know where an affordable home can be found to rent nearby, but.they.trust "something will come up."

Little surprise, therefore, that Donna would occasionally reflect aloud, though mostly to herself, "Sometimes I want to scream—and yet, sometimes I understand."

Doc's long history of PATCO activism was something Donna particularly understood: At two FAA towers he had worked prior to their 1977 arrival in the Philadelphia area, Doc had been chosen shop steward, just as his Philadelphia tower buddies had singled him out for this post one month before the strike. Personable, proud, and assertive, Doc had been highly regarded in PATCO pre-strike circles for his militancy and unswerving allegiance to the union.

With the 72-hour collapse of the strike, however, Doc went suddenly from front-page heroism to fugitive status of sorts. While he never went underground, his home was staked out nightly by a pair of plainclothes federal marshals, and FBI agents questioned him in his living room 2 weeks into the labor dispute. His later surrender to the marshals was carefully arranged to minimize adverse publicity, though TV portable crews nevertheless camped out on his home lawn to spotlight drawn shades.

Relieved never to have finally spent any time behind bars, as did other PATCO strikers, Doc and Donna both laughed over their tale of his one major arrest. After a 1981 Halloween party held by several ex-controllers and spouses, a few costumed couples decided to protest one last time out at the Philadelphia Airport. As they walked through the employees' parking lot toward the tower they intended to picket, they were challenged by security guards. Several of these officials thought Doc resembled a PATCO member suspected of having vandalized nonstrikers' cars in the same lot many weeks earlier.

Despite Doc's vehement denials, one loud word led to another, and he was soon tossed face down on the pavement, his hands cuffed behind his back. Donna was beside herself with rage, and sought the badge numbers of the policemen to charge them with "unnecessary brutality." Cooler heads prevailed, and Doc was released from the police station with an apology from policemen intent on minimizing their further involvement in PATCO zaniness. As Doc wanted no arrests on his record before his pending federal court appearance, he and Donna quickly agreed to drop their police brutality countercharges.

Far less humorous was the fight Doc came very close to losing with joblessness. Over the past 30 months his income had plummeted from over $40,000 gross before the strike to zero earnings for himself, and perhaps $15,000 annually for Donna in the preceding 2½ years. His income had been sporadic, except for 6 months of relief payments. A major insurance company had called, and, in response to his poststrike publicity, asked him to "give it a shot," which he did for a year, but gave up as "not for him." A half-year with a smaller insurance agency followed, though to no real gain. Frequent efforts were made to land an organizer's job with other unions friendly to PATCO's lost cause, but none were hiring. So, from the August 1981 strike to October 1983, Doc failed to earn any income at all.

In Fall 1983, however, Doc's luck took a turn for the better. He heard there were jobs open at the construction site of a nuclear power plant 1½ hours' drive away. Offered a position as an insulator's aide, at the pay level of a second-year apprentice, he seized the opportunity to rejoin the ranks of wage earners. Now, 4 weeks into the job as we talked, he shared his deep pleasure in the interest coworkers were paying his PATCO strike anecdotes, the frequency with which they sought his opinions on any and everything, and the good likelihood that this job might last a year or more.

Donna was visibly dismayed when Doc boasted that construction site overtime was now a distinct possibility. Earlier his daughter had cited his presence around the house as the single biggest benefit of the entire strike experience. And his wife had echoed that thought, recalling that when Doc had been putting in his 8 years as a controller the family had hardly ever seen him. Noting her failure to beam at his mention of his new overtime option, Doc reassured her he could and would turn it down if it seemed best to do so.

Much less amenable to compromise was the sorry state of poststrike contact with certain special relatives. Doc's mother, for example, had long since declined to hear her son's telephone efforts at explaining PATCO-related events. And whereas Doc, Donna, and the kids used to visit at least once or twice a year, he had not been home now in nearly 3 years. Similarly, Doc's younger brother, a controller in a midwest city, had declined to join Doc on strike. Despite the personal effort made to win him over, the brother had concluded that PATCO's demands went farther than anything he could support, and he crossed the picket line daily until the strike was broken. The two men subsequently found they had nothing to say to one another, and had not talked in many months. Doc had no idea when they might ever make contact again, and Donna silently nodded in sad concurrence.

On her side, the key relative had been Donna's father, and his early opposition to the strike had been quite considerable. His union, however, chose to invite Doc and his family to march as celebrities at the head of their "Solidarity Day" 1982 parade contingent in Washington, D.C. This remarkable display of pro-PATCO support persuaded Donna's father of the error of his opposition, and overnight he switched to offering strong support. His daily phone calls became a valued morale booster, especially when the rest of the world lost interest.

After the clamor died down and the spotlight of intense media attention turned elsewhere, the going got especially tough. Donna's strained voice recalled that they reached the point where they only paid bills that threatened a shutoff of an essential service: "We paid the electric when the man was at the door, and the gas and fuel bills, the same way—just one step ahead of losin' it. As soon as any money showed up, it went right into groceries."

Donna's anxiety reached back even before the actual 1981 strike itself: "I was uneasy when they had us wives out at their [1980 PATCO] Las Vegas convention, and conducted classes for us in what to expect. They handcuffed us behind our backs, so that we could get used to the feeling, and I hated it and swore no one would ever do that to me. They talked about federal marshals coming to the door to arrest our husbands, and they were certainly right about that. But when they urged us to begin stockpiling groceries, I sat there wondering, 'Why do that, if the strike is only going to last 48 hours?' But later, when at our wives' workshop they showed the film, *Harlan County, USA*, and I saw how vital the wives were in *that* strike, I knew what I had to do, and I knew how important the PATCO wives would become."

At the strike's outset, Donna was so excited she could not get any sleep, For over 90 consecutive days she picketed or protested someplace or other, usually with one of the children in tow, but seldom with Doc, who was busy elsewhere on PATCO business. She remembers now thinking briefly that PATCO *would* win—until she heard the President's return-to-work ultimatum. Then, fear took over, and she actually asked Doc if it wouldn't be better if he went back in.

But hesitant about undermining anyone else's morale she generally kept her own counsel, though her doubts and misgivings grew. When at a well-publicized PATCO picnic the crowd defiantly counted down the minutes left in the return-to-work offer and cheered loudly when the time elapsed, Donna privately felt something had changed for all time, and possibly not for the better.

Within a few weeks of the PATCO refusal of the President's terms, Donna knew the strike effort had begun to fall apart. Some of PATCO's solidarity gave way to fear-driven divisiveness, and former allies began a wave of vicious verbal attacks that often targeted Doc as the villain of the piece. Donna heard him accused at PATCO chapter meetings of every kind of vile behavior, and the false accusations hurt: "You wouldn't believe the name-calling that went on, much of it aimed at Doc—"

As if in partial response, Donna recalled the temptation to fight back with any means possible. At a dinner one night with other strikers' wives, they noticed several scabs in a nearby booth. Donna learned the name of one of the strikebreakers, located his phone number from information, and made a frightening call in the early morning hours to his wife. Her message was designed to upset that woman enough to possibly get her to force her husband to end his strikebreaking. Persuaded then and now that it was too low a blow, Donna felt compelled to mention it soon after at Confession, do Contrition, and recall (and relive) it nearly 2 years later as a prime example of how strike stressors can bring out the worst in one.

Far more satisfying to her was her conviction that the strike had brought Doc and her closer together than ever before. At the worst time, when the house was foreclosed and Doc came home and cried, she felt the strike threatened to rob him of his self-worth, his dignity. It tended to make men feel like failures, or slide into depression, and she was resolute about not letting that happen. At those bitter times Donna dwelled on her admiration for Doc: "He pulled himself out of it. A recovered alcoholic, he never once went back on the booze. He kept trying, and when the big blow came and we lost the house, I told him, 'We *didn't* lose, because it's just material, and we still have one another.'"

Without the help of the church, however, Donna wasn't sure it would have all turned out as bearable as it has. After Doc heard about a sermon the local priest had given doubting PATCO's morality in breaking its antistrike oath, Doc visited the clergyman and persuaded him to see PATCO's side of the matter.

From that point on the local parish was a mainstay of valued support. Each year at Christmas, a check for $200 or $300 dollars arrived unsolicited, with a note telling them that the parish did not want Doc and Donna's children to go without. The priest often dropped by unexpectedly to inquire into the family's well-being, and offer timely counsel. For the past 3 years, the parish had waived Catholic school tuition costs, explaining that no child should be deprived of a proper religious education because his or her parents were temporarily down on their luck. And, best of all, as "born-again" charismatic Catholics, Doc and Donna had turned to God, a joint decision that Donna credits with having saved the marriage.

Regrets were few and far between. Doc rues his decision at the outset not to engage in the sort of vandalism and "dirty tricks" that would have put enormous instant pressure on FAA to give in to PATCO demands. Donna regrets their choice not to sell their home before foreclosure, and use the receipts as a mortgage on a new and more secure property. Doc regrets the choice PATCO made before the strike not to seek support from the labor councils of America's 30 largest cities. Donna regrets the loss of friends she had among the wives of controllers, and the families of strikers and those of strikebreakers no longer stay in touch.

Above all, the couple regrets the loss of a way of work that Doc characterizes as "the most exciting part of my entire life." They have heard that tower work since PATCO's decertification has become more rigid and insufferable than ever before. Sick leave is harshly regulated, a dress code has been imposed, and no one has the role of handling employee grievances. Those who never struck shun any contact with returning former strikers, since the former condemn the latter as sniveling liars, eunuchs without integrity. Where the tower was once host to friendly banter and tight-knit solidarity, it is now said to house only carefully guarded shoptalk and grim divisiveness.

Doc believes that only a presidential pardon will ever enable him to work again as a controller, and he is convinced only a Democratic win in 1984 can do the trick. He knows that 18 controllers from his 54-man Philadelphia tower appealed their firing, and nine were reinstated. The fact rankles that the nine accused him of harassment and intimidation, the price the Review Board expects for such reinstatement. So he prays nightly for the nine "liars," and especially, for "all the controllers, and their families," hoping that they may soon achieve the peace of mind he feels he has earned.

Optimistic that a new Amway selling program the entire family has entered into will soon pay off, Donna agrees with Doc that the really bad times are behind them, and she is confident "the rewards are coming." Resigned to the possibility of soon having to move out of a home she loves, Donna insists "we're O.K. Our Amway business has taught us how to dream *big* again, and while I once used to pray that he'd go back someday to a tower, I see him more now than I used to, and I prefer it this way." Smiling at her, Doc closes our evening dialog with the thought, "I'd have to have a cause before I'd ever go back, a cause like organizing the whole place all over again, and putting it right this time. A man has got to have a cause, or else, what's it all about?"

2. Columbus Activist (Spring 1984)*

Ted, a controller for 13 years at the C. Center, grew up in southwest Pennsylvania, an area with a long history of labor strikes and union activity, He had been a "union man" since childhood, and at the time of the PATCO strike, was president of the local. Since the strike he has remained active as a vice president of a local labor council. Ted describes himself as an "even stronger union person than before." But, reflecting on the strains on a household whose income has dropped from annual earnings of $45,000 to ADC payments, he can't help but wonder about the serious negative effects of the PATCO strike on his family, particularly on his two daughters and two sons, now teenagers.

One of his young teenage daughers became pregnant about a year and a half ago; she decided to keep the baby. Ted and Maryanne have assumed responsibility for raising their grandchild. Although he doesn't believe his daughter's pregnancy happened only because of his work situation, Ted said he often wonders if "things would have been different" if the family had not been so disrupted by and preoccupied with the strike and its aftermath.

In describing the ATC job prior to the strike, Ted cites stressful working conditions, computer failures, and the negative effects of shift rotation on family and social life. He reserves most of his complaints, however, for the relationship between controllers and supervisors. Ted observes that the supervisors tended to be older men who accepted authority unquestioningly and who expected the same from the younger controllers. Stating emphatically that he would never want to be a supervisor, Ted frequently comments that to become a supervisor one had to undergo a "backbone removal operation and a lobotomy." Conditions were so stressful that, according to Ted, 90 percent of retirements were for medical reasons. Ironically, many of those who had gone out on medical disability were rehired after the strike.

The Center is responsible for air traffic over a portion of seven states and Canada. Of the 600 controllers who worked at the Center, 460 went out on strike; 50 of them returned when President Reagan issued his 48-hour ultimatum. Most of the remaining strikers appealed their firings; about 35 to 40, including the former vice president of the local, have been rehired, some going to other facilities. But, according to Ted, "the best controllers didn't go back." Most of the remaining fired controllers have found other jobs in the 3

---

*Conducted and transcribed by Edie Kligman (May 26, 1984).

years since the strike, including some who returned to college for 2-year degrees "in computers" and some who have opened their own businesses. A few have become house-husbands.

At the time a strike decision was reached, Ted realized that his leadership position made it very likely that, unless the strike was very short, he would be fired. After the 48-hour ultimatum he knew that his job was gone, but he assumed he would be able to find some kind of work in a reasonable amount of time. For the first year or so Ted didn't have time to look for a job. As president of the local, he felt that he had to stay around the local headquarters and assist his coworkers in whatever ways possible. (He still maintains a "headquarters.") During that time the family lived off Ted's past earnings. On occasion, Ted and other strikers would spend a few hours chopping wood to sell. Aside from some temporary, part-time jobs, Ted has not been employed since the strike. Before becoming a controller Ted had been a radio operator in the military, had worked in a bank, and for the United Parcel Service. He has no decent-paying job skills to fall back on.

Working as an ATC in a foreign country was not a real possibility, as Ted sees it. If he worked in a place like Saudi Arabia he wouldn't be able to take his family with him. Australia, on the other hand, hired American controllers only if their wives also had a critical skill.

Ted has a high school education and some college credits in labor studies. Although he has a great deal of experience in dealing with people, he lacks the "credentials" necessary for personnel management jobs and he can't afford to go back to college. He is hoping for any job that he can get at a "decent wage." Ted has submitted many job applications, but he wonders if anyone has even looked at them. He has had no job contacts or leads through his family or friends. His best hopes are pinned on his union contacts but, in the current state of the economy, they are in no position to help him.

Although he has no full-time paid job, Ted is out of the house most of the day, doing "missionary work, for no pay, to keep my sanity." His "missionary" work includes the maintenance of a small union headquarters and his active involvement with many local labor and CETA (now JTPA) organizations, attending approximately 33 meetings a month. One of his major activities is in assisting workers facing plant closings to anticipate and deal with the consequences of unemployment. Based on his own experiences, he makes available information and advice about such matters as preparing their families, setting aside money for future bills, and going to creditors to renegotiate loan repayments prior to actual layoff.

Ted enjoys working with labor, and thinks he would be able to work as a union organizer if the economy picks up. At the time of the interview he was hoping to land a paid position with a local private industry council if the council receives JTPA funding. Unlike corporations where the credentials are more essential, local labor leaders appear to recognize his ability and experience in dealing with people. They recently asked him to run for county commissioner. He declined, thinking he wasn't "ready for it now"—perhaps later. Nevertheless, no money is available for local labor to hire Ed in a permanent position unless JTPA funds come through.

(Ted says he is less active in politics now than he was before. But his anti-Reagan sentiments are obvious, and understandable. As I turned in to his street I quickly spotted his house by the Mondale sticker on the car in his driveway.)

The precipitous drop from $45,000 a year wage earner and union leader to welfare father has had, of course, serious consequences for the family's lifestyle, a change which Ted acknowledges but is reluctant to discuss. Without elaboration, Ted and Maryanne both agree that their marriage has had its "bumps." In the early days of their marriage Maryanne worked as a hairdresser. But she hasn't worked in almost 20 years and feels she now has no marketable job skills.

In preparation for the impending strike, the couple had paid off most of their bills and had set some money aside. They also toned down their style of living as much as possible, a fact that Ted credits with saving them from real financial disaster. "Those who didn't want to change their lifestyles," observes Ted, "got hit the worst." After the strike they lived off Ted's lump-sum retirement payment. They now receive welfare payments. Occasionally he earns some under-the-table money delivering pizza. Although they are usually a little behind in mortgage and utility payments, they don't appear to be in danger of losing their home.

One of the most difficult adjustments to a much reduced income for a family with two adults and five children, understandably, has been the inability to use private medical facilities. For instance, they have had to use Medicaid for the birth and pediatric care of their grandchild. Luckily, the family has not needed much medical care. Ted's health has not changed since the strike. He claims to have less mental stress now that he no longer has the pressures of the controller's job, but says he has other kinds of stresses instead. Acknowledging that many controllers had alcohol problems, Ted says he has never had a drinking problem—a few beers with the boys has always been his limit.

The family, especially the children, experienced relatively little harassment during the strike. On occasion, FBI agents came to the house and spoke with one of the teenage daughters. But, on the whole, they report little harassment by press, government agents, police, or acquaintances. One of the few such stories they related concerned the reaction they received while waiting in a line at the welfare office, where they were the object of invidious remarks about the amount of money they had earned before and against their strike action.

Family and friends have remained sympathetic throughout. Both Ted's

and Maryanne's families have been supportive. Ted's mother finally became a
U.S. citizen (after many years of eligibility) just so that she could vote against
Reagan. Although the children escaped harassing incidents for the most part,
Ted thinks they have learned a lesson from the whole ordeal. They have had
"their eyes opened and they have learned to question more."

Although there were many controllers with whom they chose not to so-
cialize, most of their friends, prior to the strike, were other ATCs and their
families, particularly as a result of the "crazy shifts" controllers work, which
make it difficult to plan social get-togethers with people who work more conventional hours. Many of his former friends, however, now avoid Ted. Looking back, he believes he had lots of acquaintances, but "you find out when
times are tough who your friends are. Now they turn their backs on me because I was president." Ted had maintained his friendship with the former
vice president of the local, a controller who appealed and has been rehired at
the Center.

The wives of the four main local union officials had been friends before
the strike and have maintained their friendship. During the strike the four
women alternated cooking for the strikers—one of the few strike activities in
which wives in the Columbus area were involved. Before the strike Ted had
met with the controllers' wives to discuss the objections some of them had
raised and to enlist their long-term support. The local, however, had decided
not to use wives and children on the picket lines; there were very few strike
activities that included families. For the first 2 months wives' groups held
sales to raise money to operate the strike headquarters. Otherwise, there was
little effort to involve families.

In response to the nagging question, "What went wrong?" Ted replies,
"We were battling the big one: the United States Government. We never
got a fair shake." Things would have worked out differently, Ted asserts, if
Reagan had *forced* Secretary Lewis and PATCO president Poli to mediate. But
the "anti-union and antiworker" Administration wanted to break PATCO
and, therefore, wanted the strike. He feels PATCO underestimated the government's ability to control the media and underestimated the extent to
which the airlines would allow the government to regulate their scheduling. It
was also unrealistic to assume that "safety" could be an issue around which to
rally public support. For 2 years prior to the strike the local had tried to enlist
the understanding and support of other area unions, sending out speakers
and appearing on local radio "talk" shows, to publicize the conditions on the
job. Although Ted feels they were "sold down the river" by the national AFL-
CIO, area unions did help out by picketing with the striking controllers and
by taking up a collection at the gate of a local Ford plant.

Unlike some of his former coworkers, Ted has no quarrel with the way
PATCO handled the strike. Many former controllers, he says, "blame the
union for where they are." But he adds, "Poli had no choice. We [local leaders

and membership] told him what to do." Although some of the controllers now say they should have taken over the facility, the members of the local, at the time of the strike, made it plain that they did not want to resort to "dirty tricks." Believing that the strike could succeed only if at least 80 percent of the controllers went out and stayed out, Ted says he laid the cards on the table as honestly as he could.

Prior to the strike Ted made sure that local members had access to information about food stamps, financial planning, and counseling services. He recalls, however, that "some people had to be dragged to some of the services offered." The controllers were told that they could be arrested, that they could be fired; they were warned in advance of all of the possibilities, with the exception of how long an appeals process would take (something PATCO officials could not anticipate). Even with that knowledge, Ted feels, many controllers continued to believe they could go out on strike and still "hold onto friendships"; they continued to hope that they would not have to be scabs, but would still be able to go back to work.

Would he ever be an ATC again? "Not under Reagan—not a chance! Maybe under someone else." Ted sees no possibility of going back if Reagan is reelected. He would not want to go back anyway, he says, under the present working conditions. His contacts at the Center tell him that personnel shortages have created conditions that are even worse than those that existed in the past. (Ted also feels that even though today's ATCs talk about needing a union, they do not want any PATCO/USATCO people involved.)

3. Boston Activist (Winter 1984)

"I really thought we could win when we started back in '78 to prepare, but by 1980 I began to get worried. I had a premonition we were heading for a loss, and when Poli and Leyden split, I wound up opposed to Poli and increasingly disillusioned with PATCO.

"I was an activist for 12 years before the '81 strike, but when I took Poli's measure I felt he just wasn't the guy to lead the 'big one.' Bob just didn't have it, to deal in the big leagues—so I knew a disaster was coming.

"With FAA pushing us harder and harder all the time I got back at 'em by serving as president of the PATCO local at my facility, and, as the strike drew closer, as the 'choirboy' for my area.

"When we took a strike vote, and found we honestly didn't have the numbers, it was one of the most emotionally draining experiences I'd ever had: When we got our numbers a month later, I felt better—but, it seemed suspicious that the FAA was behaving worse than ever! They seemed to *want* a strike, and they were forcing us—helping us organize our people by being such bastards.

"I now see that the FAA could only win, whatever the outcome: If our strike had been successful, we would have forced Congress to give the FAA more money, and, as our bosses, they would have gotten salary increases to keep them ahead of what we would have won. If the bastards beat us, and PATCO lost big, like I mean, *real* big, the FAA would be rid of a *real* thorn in its side.

"Once we had struck and took 80 percent out with us, I first worked as a 'missionary,' and tried to talk guys into not going back. Then, when our numbers settled I served as a liaison to the local AFL-CIO city labor council. Those guys were *very* cautious at the outset about helping us, because they were afraid the feds and the courts would lean on them—sue them, and draw them into our legal problems. But I soon calmed them down about that.

"We had several thousand dollars in the AFL-CIO Strike Relief Fund, but our guys jumped on it too soon. We depleted it quickly, with $200 and $300 grants, and really should have gone slower: A lot of the disappointment guys expressed in the labor relief was really *our* fault.

"From August through maybe November I still thought that somehow, someway, we could still win. But then the PATCO executive board surrendered, I guess for the third time, and indicated all of its efforts would now go into trying to win amnesty for us.

"At the outset we had blocked traffic at the airport and raised a ruckus, but it was only a token effort. When we learned that amnesty was the only hope left, the heart went out of a lot of guys—they still hoped to go back, however, and kept setting a day a few weeks or months ahead, a day before which they would not really stop believing they would never control air traffic again. Christmas 1981 and then New Year's Day, 1982, were the days I remember many guys pinned their hopes on; a Christmas amnesty was a big rumor in 1981.

"Our local, when we learned in November about the executive board surrender, was angry and confused and scared. We held one hell of a horror show at a meeting we called with the PATCO regional VP, and it went completely out of control. He tried to explain that all we could do was try to cut our losses and limit our casualties, but some of our guys went crazy and shouted for more than that.

"My family made it largely because my wife had gone to work in January of '81, and when I lost my paycheck she went on regular overtime. My fifteen-year-old boy and my daughters, ages nineteen and twenty, walked on the airport picket line with me, attended our local meetings, and gave me the backing I needed. Still, we all took the loss of the strike hard, *very* hard.

"I couldn't find any work for about 8 months, and even then it was only pickup work, 1 or 2 days a week as a substitute on a beer delivery truck. I was not in good shape for that sort of work, and would come home so sore and tired I'd flop into bed and sleep for hours and hours. Now I'm finally full-time, and have some job stability. I'm also fit and content—as a full-timer I can pick my load, while as a spare I couldn't, so work is much better, *much* better now.

"Our beer plant is with the Teamsters, so we've got a *good* contract, but even with that I've gone from about $48,000 with the FAA to making about $30 to $35,000 hauling beer. Still, I'm home on weekends and at night, and I'm fighting-trim, and I have no supervisors riding me hard once I pull out with my street load. The wife continues to enjoy her job, the kids are off at college, and we've come through okay . . .

"Three years of going without my FAA income has wiped out all our savings and my retirement money, so, except for owning our house, we've got nothing to fall back on—but 'bumping beer' is a helluva lot better job for me, because I really want less and less pressure on any job I do. Now I don't have to worry about killing anybody.

"You know, I was the Job Placement Counselor for PATCO in my area, and I have a Bachelor's degree in business and years of leadership experience in labor affairs, but I still couldn't find anything! I sent out scores of resumes, and pounded on doors, and followed up every lead, and came up dry. Finally, a contact I had made in the Teamsters Union gave me his card, and 2 days later I got called in as a spare, at $100 a day—and here I am. Now I've made the seniority list, and I've got it made.

"We hold an annual reunion, and every year the guys are more cheerful than the last. Less than 40 percent would go back if given a chance, and I wouldn't be among them. Hell, I've got a chance to become an officer with the Teamsters Union, and that makes a lot more sense.

"Up here controllers live in fairly small communities, and the FAA centers are a *big* employer in a small labor market, maybe 350 FAA controllers in a town of 60,000. So, everybody really knew everybody else, and the strike made it like a civil war. We had 80 percent go out, and we know who the scabs are, and know why they're no longer our friends. Controllers living on the same block no longer talk to one another. It got real mean there for awhile, but as guys move out to find work elsewhere, it will fade—like everything else about this, I suspect."

4. Ft. Lauderdale Activist (Summer 1984)

"I wanted to be a controller from the time I was twelve. I used to bicycle 20 miles out to the airport just to see the tower and watch the planes come and go. God, but I loved the idea of moving them around, telling 'em what to do and when—so I joined the military when I turned seventeen, and I've been controlling air traffic ever since.

"Now I choreograph air shows for warbirds, you know, vintage WWII beauties, and I control over 100 planes in a really good show. I get a lot of calls to work this show and that one, and I love it!

"That's my hobby, but my job isn't much different. I'm the operating manager of a small airline company, with 12 9-passenger aircraft and three 19-seaters. I set up the use we make of computer scheduling, and discovered the neat things you can do with that little machine. I never thought I would do this sort of job, but I never doubted that I could.

"If you want to know what I am *really* proud of, it is that I choreograph, design, explain over the loudspeakers, and completely control the largest air shows in the world—with no interference whatsoever from the munchkins who run the FAA!

"I really love those old warbirds, and I used to do as many as 26 shows a year, but I've cut back now to about three or so. The FAA, they hate my planes, and call them a thorn in the side of safe airways! Bullshit! Those beauties are a significant part of aviation history, and should not have their engines torn out, and get hung like rusting hulks in a tomb of a museum. They should be kept up, and flown! The FAA has a lousy attitude, and I fight 'em here, as an airshow controller, just like I've fought 'em everywhere else!

"When I'm doing a show it is more than 3-dimensional chess; it is 6-dimensional! I've got 105 to 110 'crowd-killers' doing about 500 mph closing speeds; maybe 40 to 50 ft apart; in the bomb runs and flying formations they used to use, passing in opposite directions, and, best of all, I get to go flying in some of the best—like the P-51 Mustang that started me on this in 1974—that's a picture of it over there; I've given this diner scores of pictures that they put up all over; warbirds, real beauties.

"I started at a Navy base in Georgia when I turned seventeen, and got to be in charge of training B-25 crews how to land on aircraft carriers. I only joined so I would get ATC experience before I went to the FAA on my twenty-first birthday.

"I aced every test! I 'made out' as a controller. You do the best there is, everyone worth a shit does! You *must* retire at fifty-six, and ATCs have an average lifespan of 47 years, nine years shorter than most people. So, you do your best while you're around!

"In April of 1979 we had a midair, and two men died, one a friend of mine. I gave the FAA boss here 1 year's warning. Either he straightened this shit out, and fixed the radar, and put on runway lights, or I would unload 6 years' documentation of his mistakes on the media. He said, 'You can't hurt me. You can't reach me!' I kept giving him warnings, 6 months, 3 months, 1 month, 1 week, 1 day. On Friday I said, 'If you don't give me something in writing I unload today!' He said I had no credibility, and insulted me to the max. So, I went on TV and let him have it! We may doze, but we never close!

"Everybody knew better than to mess with me. There are four things you don't do: French-kiss with alligators, piss into the wind, arm wrestle with eskimos, or fuck with me!

"Before the strike I was one cocky S.O.B., an alligator mouth, and I went on national TV and crucified one of those FAA feds as an incompetent fuck. He should not have been allowed anywhere near aviation! I researched and documented the last 6 years of changes at my airport, and a lot of money earmarked for improvements was missing and unaccounted for. This guy was pocketing the funds, and delaying expansion here at least 10 years. His wife and friends buy up land cheap, and when it triples in value they sell it back to the airport. I said all of this on national TV, and they didn't say boo; not a word!

"Before the strike, while I was not an officer or choirboy, I was one of the rowdies who kept the local jumping: Saying our people were militant was like saying Idi Amin had a bad temper!

"When the strike came down I was out on vacation, so I never officially 'struck.' But the FAA says they called me to come in. They have no proof, so I have them in court, even though the MSPB sided with them.

"I picked up work doing air shows, and helped deliver boats and airplanes, till the FAA stopped me by cancelling my physical permit to fly! The bastards refused to give me a legal medical certificate, so I got the job I now have and settled down.

"I got involved in the strike over one issue, and only one: *Safety!* That was where it was at! We never should have let the public think money was the issue. We got hell on our informational picket lines, because we never got our safety ideas across: I used to hear—'How much do you guys want *this* time? Fuck you!'

"So I had a bad feeling, like I knew it was going to be a disaster. We never should have struck; we just should have gone by the FAA book—because it sucks!

"PATCO could have been better prepared, like with facts to prove FAA faults, and a profile of FAA authorities. And some ability to use knowledge to intimidate the FAA. Here, at my facility, the FAA told the media it expected sabotage and PATCO efforts to blow up the radar, so armed guards went up everywhere. But we did nothing, and got no credit for doing that. There was no way for us to squeeze the FAA's balls when 4 weeks after us the feds were scheduled to bargain with 650,000 postal employees: We should have gone after, not before them.

"We needed more preparation, and we needed longer time to make a walkout work. A lot of guys did not go out for good reasons, like over safety —so a few went back real soon. Some never came out, and I have nothing against them if their reasons were really good.

"We could have won if only we knew about 'collating feces'; that is, if only we really knew about *Power* and how to win with it. We also should have known how to approach the public.

"Now, the system is not safe: I fly, and it's *not* safe! I talk with a lot of people inside, and they don't like it any better than we did. Some of the FAA munchkins are trying to kill them with overwork, and the system sucks!

"USATCO has my respect, and I regret I can't contribute any money to it. They give us valuable information, and serve as a knowledgeable watchdog—it was a logical evolution from PATCO.

"Had the FAA used 50 percent of what it cost to kill PATCO to improve the system we never would have struck. Nobody wanted to go out, because we all knew *nobody* wins! If I had been in charge, there wouldn't have been a strike; I'd have solved our problems. PATCO had the power of threat, but not the power to make it work. When Poli didn't get a strike vote in June, it was an omen. He should have known it could not work later in August. The FAA had run a 'war game' trial on how to operate with fewer people, by spreading out the traffic, and they knew they could whip our ass.

"Overall, I've made out O.K. Before the strike I was earning $40,000 from the FAA and another $60,000 from the air shows. Now, I earn a helluva lot less. But I no longer grind my teeth or feel ready to explode, ready to fight any FAA munchkin who looks at me cross-eyed. My time is my own, even if I choose to work 20-hour days every so often. My hours are of my own making, and I feel much better, *much*, much better.

"Would I go back? Shit, yeah! But I've never stopped controlling planes, warbirds or my little passenger line, and I'll never stop—with or without the blessings of the FAA. I've fought to improve the design of this airport since the strike, and I'll always 'make trouble' to improve the system. I love it too much to turn it over to the munchkins. I really don't like anyone to get into my basket, so someday I'll be back in that FAA tower, in my seat, doing the best goddamn job they've ever seen!"

5. CHICAGO ACTIVIST and WIFE (SPRING 1983)

Husband

"We might have won—the FAA should have folded. But, one week before our strike, the FAA got a radical new plan of flow control, and it was *good*! We knew about it, but confused it with the previous plan, which would *not* have worked. Oh me, David should never tangle with Goliath. When you have 1,500 returnees, flow control, the refusal of the media to focus on safety risks, and the need to 'send a message' to the postal workers, you can't win . . .

"In my heart, before we struck I felt it wouldn't work. But I was a leader, and I couldn't say it. The FAA wanted the strike, and encouraged it. They fully intended to kill us, and did; USATCO may have no future as it is too closely tied to what was a plot on our lives! I knew a lot about government hanky-panky, and that sort of thing before, but I never dreamed of lies as cold and calculating as those aimed at us after the strike came down.

"The government fed so much bullshit to the public! It was Russian roulette up there, and the FAA *knew* it was unsafe. The new people are not trained in the Academy, but on the job, and that is cockeyed! They are much less versatile and knowledgeable than the job requires. We used to wheel and deal, using split-second timing, and when the computer went down, you felt your way through. The new people can't do any of that—and the supervisors, at least at the outset, were incompetent.

"What was learned? Hell, we wrote the book on how to call a strike! My unit had 95 percent go out, and 90 percent stay out! In 11 weeks I put 12,000 miles on my car speaking and doing TV shows to help raise $24,000 in strike aid. There isn't a union anywhere that can't learn something useful from our example—like, expect those yelling the loudest and showing the most bravado before the strike to fold first!

"It all meant so much to me that I stuck with PATCO for over a year, paying my own expenses, and driving all over the state to do media work, coordinate appeals, and cover any FAA deficiencies I heard or read about. I had helped John Leyden prepare the original PATCO strike plan, and it was a beaut! One of the best ever put together. A *real* beaut!

"Why did we fail? The biggest sole reason is that 1,500 went back in during the first month. But that did not surprise me. I knew my coworkers, and I knew a few would buckle. After about 2 months I knew it was over, and while I still support USATCO, I hope it does not keep alive false hopes . . .

"For 13 years PATCO had won every confrontation, and we had momentum. We had no reason to fear a total defeat, and it will always remain still a bit hard to accept, to believe—like a really bad dream I really want to shake off.

"As for Poli, he did all and more than we asked of him. I think the world of the man, and always will! PATCO was right, the system *was* unsafe—before and after the strike. FAA officials admitted there was chaos in the first month, as Poli had said there would be . . .

"But the stress of the strike was so bad I had to have $2,000 worth of peridenture surgery. It was emotionally gut-wrenching, and I'm fortunate to be out of it. I'll never ever put my heart and soul into anything again! When you get the shit kicked out of you, you cannot get reinvolved. It was my cause, and I'd do it over again, but there was *too* much human suffering. I regret the emotional roller coaster and the hardships my family suffered, when everything went down the shitter. I just hate to see something like this happen.

"I'm still in litigation over my back pay, and, in the long run, maybe 7 or so years, I feel we will win—because we were *right*!

"Now, I'm left with pure unadulterated hatred for the scabs, for those PATCO members who only came out because of peer pressure, and went back as soon as they could. FAA supervisors do not upset me, as they were only doing their jobs, but the scabs drive me up a wall!

"The AFL-CIO did not do diddly-shit, except to walk our picket line in week 3. But they did get us money or jobs. We got *real* help only from the Operating Engineers, who gave us a free office and some financial aid. If labor had backed our strike, *really* backed us up, it would not be in its death throes now . . .

"Since I had never worked at anything else, and I only had 2 years of college, I had it kind of hard. I read the Richard Bolles' book, *What Color Is Your Parachute?*, and did all the exercises in it. Then I searched everywhere, including some labor unions, but couldn't get anything. Finally I learned about 12 ex-controllers in Denver who had bought a business. They modified a carpet-cleaning machine and sold it to others, like me. I went in with another striker, then bought him out after 1½ years, and now am my own boss.

"I would not go back, even with 17 years invested. I like running my own business, and working my own hours! No more bullcrap from supervisors! And, some of my old buddies who stayed aboard tell me it's *much* worse now inside than ever before.

"We see some other strikers and their families on occasion, and no one has any regrets. Everyone sees themselves as survivors, with the wives holding the same point of view as their husbands. Most of us, however, are pretty disillusioned with the government, the media, and some of our neighbors. Maybe 50 to 60 percent would cheer the news of reinstatement openings, but only one in three of us would actually go back, 'cause we all know life is better off without the FAA!

"We've done fine, and my boys now tell me the FAA job had me in a rut. I've gotten to know them a helluva lot better, and feel great about that. But I do feel bad for those who couldn't cope. Many families broke up, and there is a lot of emotional wreckage. Many marriages went down the drain, and I'll always regret the human suffering our strike caused."

Wife, Mother of 2

"Do you want to know what they were like, *really* like, before the strike? Before it all ended?

"They were like gods! Gods! They felt like heroes, like men in charge. Nothing fazed them! Nothing could rattle them! And nothing was allowed to get in their way, nothing—not family, children, illness, wife—nothing! They were like—gods.

"Now, it's all different, and even better in some ways. . . .

"That job he used to have, it was something else! It really separated a man from his family. Those men, they had to be *very* self-confident, very self-centered! They had to feel on top of things—they were, you know, almost like gods.

"You know, from the very beginning, in my heart, I knew it couldn't be won. He felt it had an 80 percent chance of going our way, but I felt no chance at all even before they went out.

"'You fool,' I thought to myself, 'the federal government is *too* powerful.'

"Now, I have no trust left in government officials. They're all a bunch of politicians, who promise you the world, but crucify you later!

"I was a bit of a skeptic about government before the strike, but not like I am now. I always believed people before, but I'm not as willing to walk away from trouble and bad faith as before. They hurt us *bad*, and I'm not willing to have it ever happen again.

"I still find it hard to believe how little regard they have for our money, our tax money! Why, the government spent $1 to $2 billion to break PATCO and the strike, and then shifted the cost to us, as taxpayers! It is absolutely astonishing to me, what they can do and get away with.

"As for Bill, for a while he was really down. This whole thing depressed him terribly, and he didn't joke much about it—or anything else.

"You see, many other controllers had other jobs on the side before the strike. They'd do different things when they weren't on duty, and so they were prepared to start new vocations when they were fired.

"But Bill only had tower work and PATCO—with just 2 years of college, not even his 17 years as a controller seemed enough to get him work, certainly not at the $40,000 he had worked up to.

"Still, we've had no family problems, none to speak of. We saved a lot of money before, and that saw us through. I worried more about its disappearance than Bill, and it has kept me so *mad*! We had to spend it all, every last bit of it. I'm not very materialistic, so we had no big debts. But still, to see all our savings go was very hard on me.

"The whole thing has made us a better, much closer family. Bill has gotten to know his sons all over again, and they really like that. He has had time to rejoin our family, and we know now how little of him we saw when he was in the tower. We are like a *new* family, and a much better one, for all of it.

"I've always worked part-time, 6 hours a day, as a secretary to a VP, so my earnings came in very handy. Plus, when the strike cost Bill all of his health fringes, I got them, and covered our family that way.

"You want to know what was the hardest part? Not his losing his job. That was no shock, as I was expecting it. No, the *hardest* part was the fear that built up in me concerning our future. I grew more and more apprehensive as months went by and our savings dwindled away. I felt like I was no longer in control of my life. Although I was doing everything I could to keep us above water, to hold everything together, I began to feel I was not in control at all: *That* was the hardest part."

6. STEVE O'KEEFE (APTOS, CALIFORNIA, SUMMER 1985)

"As I wanted to be a pilot, with 2 years of college behind me I enlisted in the Marine Corps with a guarantee of aviation training. I believed I could enter Officer Candidate School and receive pilot training, if I was lucky, but I wasn't! The pilot training program was closed when it was time to assign me to training, so I was offered air traffic control training instead. It seemed a relatively safe occuaption to hold during the Vietnam war. In fact, I was sent overseas, but only as far as Okinawa and Japan, so I never saw combat. While I was in Japan in 1968–1969, PATCO was born in the U.S., and I followed every news item with great interest, anticipating that I would eventually play a role in this new organization.

"The hype of air traffic control was good for me for several years but it started wearing me down. I wanted the system to be safer, and so I became Chairman of PATCO's Safety Committee in Honolulu. The FAA resisted almost every suggestion PATCO ever made about safety. They always maintained they couldn't afford new equipment, more personnel, etc. I became very frustrated and angry with the FAA as an employer. The strike was an exercise of that frustration and anger.

"I feel the strike was unavoidable. Controllers held the opinion that they were the special people behind the scenes who made the air traffic system work in spite of the FAA's mismanagement. They wanted the public to know how important they were to maintain air safety and to keeping the nation's economy functioning, through air commerce. The FAA ignored controllers' efforts to improve the system, opposed legislation to increase controllers' salaries, and publicly humiliated them when Administrator Langhorne Bond compared controllers' responsibility for safety to that of bus drivers. [Bond was a Jimmy Carter appointee and controllers' contempt for him helps to explain PATCO's fateful endorsement of candidate Ronald Reagan.]

"I walked the picket lines at San Francisco International, Oakland Airport, and at my own facility, the Oakland Bay TRACON. I had transferred to Oakland after 7 years at Honolulu Airport and was nearing completion of my training when the strike occurred. The controller who trained me at Oakland used to boast about being the last controller to return to work after the 1971 sick-out. He was one of the first to cross our picket line and go back in 1981.

"I expected Congress or organized labor to work out a 'return to work' compromise with the Reagan Administration. Realization came very slowly that we were finished, and that Reagan's firing us all was not just a bluff. I honestly could not believe he would risk the safety of the flying public by replacing 12,000 seasoned professionals with completely inexperienced replacements and experienced but burned-out supervisors.

"Most of my friends and family called to express their support during the strike, but some were critical of my action or simply pretended it wasn't happening. One blowup with a family member was particularly ugly, and now, 4 years later, the wounds have still not healed. Another friend wrote to say 'We love you, but a $10,000 raise . . .?' I have avoided all contact with that person ever since.

"I walked into a coffee shop during the first week of the strike wearing a PATCO T-shirt. Sitting nearby, two couples were having lunch. 'I'm glad Reagan fired them,' one of the women said in a loud voice. Unable to decide whether to go over and try to explain the PATCO position, or go over and punch out her husband, I left in frustration. That reaction was my admission that the public was unalterably opposed to PATCO and solidly behind Reagan.

"I continued writing letters to Congress until January 1, 1982, when I finally started looking for work. I didn't find a job until August of 1982, and that turned out to be a disaster. So I entered school the following spring, and received my degree in Human Relations a year later. Throughout that time my wife was extremely supportive, yet the strain of my unemployment, its associated alienation and depression, created numerous problems in our marriage. Eventually we separated.

"I pounded the pavement, visiting as many labor union offices as possible. I had studied Bolles' *What Color is Your Parachute* and followed his advice on getting the job you want. I found out who in each union did the hiring and firing and went to meet him or her personally. I was persistent in seeking appointments with labor people, and found them sympathetic to my PATCO experience. Finally, I landed a job as a field representative with a public employee union. I have never worked such long hours or handled so many complex problems, but it is the most fulfilling work I have ever done. It's not just a job, it's a cause and a way of life.

"The 1981 strike became an end in itself, instead of the means to an end. Most controllers felt that the strike would finally educate the public and the government as to who they were and how vital they were to this country. It hardly mattered what happened as a result of the strike, as long as the strike happened. People would stand up and take notice at last!

"My own participation in the strike can be attributed to this, to support of PATCO since its inception, a belief that the cause was a just one, and the confident expectation that the strike would succeed. This expectation was partly attributed to my brief experience as a postal worker in 1971–1972. Letter carriers had struck illegally in 1970 and their strike was an overwhelming success. I worked daily with people who had participated in that strike, and they frequently remarked that their standard of living had improved significantly since that illegal action. They were federal employees who walked off the job, violated their no-strike oath under a Republican Administration, and won. I expected the same results as a PATCO striker.

"Even in unemployment or underemployment, I could appreciate the fact that, at the end of the workday, my stomach was not tied up in a knot as it always was after 8 hours of controlling airplanes. I am delighted to be able to say I would never go back to FAA (or any government) employment again, but I have the liberty of saying so because I have found fulfillment in working to improve the lot of the working person.

"If I were still struggling financially and unhappy with my current employment, I might feel the longing to return to the last challenging (and financially rewarding) job I held. Nevertheless, my bitterness toward scabs, FAA, and airline pilots (not necessarily in that order) would make me a rotten employee. My morale would be terrible and I would affect everyone who had to work with me, so it's far better that I never go near another control tower or radar facility again.

"Another reason why I would decline to work as a controller again is the loss of esteem suffered by the air traffic controller image. PATCO-era controllers held a fierce pride in their work, considered themselves professionals, and frequently received praise for the high-pressure, highly responsible nature of their work. One frequently heard that it took "a special kind of person" to be a controller.

"The Reagan Administration used the media during the PATCO strike to advertise for replacements, then boasted of the vast number of applicants which came forward. To me, this was a message to the public which said "controllers are a dime a dozen"; i.e., anyone with a high school education could do this work. The special image of controllers was gone forever. I don't think working controllers can consider themselves special, nor could I if I were to return and join their ranks.

"As a person working within the labor movement, I frequently hear how labor's problems really began with the PATCO dismantling by the Reagan Administration. It reversed the general feeling in this country that strikebusting, use of scab labor, and harsh, punitive treatment of striking employees was wrong. Employers took the cue from Reagan and began their policy of takeaways. Labor acknowledges that turning point, but I don't see what could have been done that would have made a real difference. The American people did not support PATCO, therefore workers would not have participated in a labor-initiated general strike. There was plenty of negotiating behind the scenes, but there wasn't much organized labor could have done to avert PATCO's demise.

"I'm afraid the FAA learned that gross mismanagement was acceptable, that they could treat controllers with no respect and not be held accountable, and they could risk lives and get the backing of the media and the American public. I wouldn't expect to see much change for the better within that quasi-military bureaucracy.

"Finally, the working controllers would have to be pushed to incredible extremes before they would dare to take action. They witnessed (presumably applauded) the massacre of their predecessors, thus they should have a realistic estimate of how little regard the FAA has for controller concerns. Perhaps the next generation of controllers will rebel, but not this acquiescent group.

"Without the benefit of hindsight, I would, naturally, strike again if it were scheduled for tomorrow. On the other hand, when asked if I would do it all again, knowing the outcome, I feel like someone who has been struck by a locomotive being asked if he would cross the tracks again, knowing that the train was coming."

7. SAN ANTONIO ACTIVIST (SUMMER 1984)

"We knew the strike was inevitable, and we *really* got an emotional high out of it. Shift work had kept us from ever getting more than two-thirds of us together, but we got 89 percent to go out! The mood was *very* positive, and when all of us were together, we were *high*—only later, when we were apart from each other, some began to doubt, and some began to have reservations. Poli called and told us he saw 'light at the end of the tunnel,' and that helped —for a while.

"My wife is a schoolteacher, so she went right into a job. Other guys were not so lucky, and many of the men had to go into construction or common labor—that sort of thing. By now, though, almost all have moved up, and are foremen or lead men—maybe one in three have gone into sales, and prefer it because they are free to make a lot of their own decisions. A small number, smaller all the time, are still waiting for a Supreme Court decision to vindicate us, but everybody else is heading in other directions. Me, I'm a bit different, as I've won reinstatement. I had gone out on vacation leave to fly to a Wisconsin air show just before the strike, so I won my hearing case, even though the FAA had doctored my papers to make it appear like I was AWOL.

"It was a victory to be reinstated, so I went back for a while. But I left soon after because I didn't want to be hypocritical. When I saw our strike had accomplished nothing inside, that the FAA was worse than ever, I resigned. Sometimes I think now maybe we all should have done that, rather than strike.

"Don't get me wrong. It was the right thing for us to do. If we had not been going into the recession, we just might have done it. The strike might have been illegal, but it was necessary. Some of the controllers feel we lost control of it, and there is a lot of bitterness out here aimed at Poli. We let the public think we were only money-hungry power brokers, and that hurt us bad. But it was still the right thing for us to do . . .

"My own family came through strong, with my kids of six and eight learning to sing *Solidarity Forever*. But we had bad problems with our neighbors, an ultraconservative couple that stopped talking to us, and shouted insults whenever they saw us. The wife was a controller, and she didn't come out with the rest of us. She had been real close with my wife, but all of that is over now. Her husband was also a controller, and his FAA chief called him and warned he might lose his VA benefits if he struck with us, so he went back in. We continued to get PATCO dues from him for 3 or 4 months afterwards, but now—real bitterness has set in.

"My mother was worried about it, since my father had been fired in the 1950s for union activities as a schoolteacher. He had to slip into a manufacturing job, and then he went into the army, so mom was concerned about what was happening to me. My wife's folks were *cool* to the whole matter.

"My sister, who works in computers in Canada, thinks the strike was part of a big campaign to replace us with third generation computers. She tells me the computer magazines have articles in which the FAA represents computers as their salvation. They used them during our strike to 'flow' the traffic better than ever before, so they grabbed power we thought we could keep from them. The computers really took charge of the small aircraft, and all of that undercut the strike.

"You know, when I graduated in '68 none of my friends went to 'Nam. So, all of us feel guilty about doing nothing patriotic, nothing that involved risks. In a way the '81 strike was *my* cause, one that I felt strongly about. I actually hid out for 5 days at the start, because I heard the feds were looking for me.

"For the first month of the strike we ran 24-hour picket shifts, and we expected to be called back to work at any time. Rumors were our biggest problem, so we started some of our own to help relieve tension. The best part of it was making new friends, really *good* friends, and some from among guys I didn't care about as controllers. I joined when I turned twenty, and spent 10 years 'moving traffic,' so I knew a lot of guys, but the strike brought us together like nothing before.

"When I went back in I found we had a new dress code: The chief now insisted our sport shirts had to have buttons, and a tie was encouraged. We couldn't wear denim or boots anymore, and our slacks had to be neat. Before the strike I handled 75 or 80 aircraft an hour; after, 45 was considered busy. In the old days you had time to fine-tune your technique, and you had flexibility in the 'little things' in your assignment. But I found rigidity in the new regs, and I hated it. No animosity from the 'sprinters' and scabs, but too much rigidity from the chief.

"So, I only stayed in a month, just enough time to collect about $25,000 in back pay. Then I resigned, and we had 30 strikers attend my 'coming out' party, one helluva good time! The chief was very upset, I'm told. We took a 3-week vacation up north, and I got a chance to thank the controllers in British Columbia for all the help PATCO got from the Canadian controllers.

"People ask me whether I think a new union is possible. I found the facility was understaffed, nervous, and really had no unified voice to bitch for the men. Still, I don't expect much from any effort to unionize those guys. The older men only want to qualify for retirement, and the new guys don't know enough to protect themselves.

"When I think back on it all and ask what we've learned I think it is clear that working controllers will not gain any useful power for years to come. PATCO should have told us all to go back, and thereby demonstrated its power and our loyalty to it. It should also have used publicity specialists *before* the strike. USATCO should put its money into lobbying, and resist any talk of a strike soon again by controllers. And the labor movement should have made good on its promise to provide financial help—because our loss now may cost the labor movement *everything*! It may not last another few years, and is due for a great transition under Reagan. One more thing; USATCO should *not* try and get us reinstated unless that also means real improvements *first* in the job. Without changes there, the job is just not worth going back to.

"As for me, I've let it go. The FAA has not learned anything, so it is lousy inside. The supervisors see '81 as a match only they won, and they are pushing their advantage. The old-timers pray for retirement, and the new kids have no knowledge of what PATCO won from the FAA before '81. They regard a 6-day week as normal, and do not know yet what burnouts are about. The worst of the scabs are brown-nosing for supervisory posts since there are so few people with higher seniority than theirs: It's bad, and gonna get worse.

"Me, I've rediscovered my family, make my own hours as a crafts maker, have weekends free, and only regret that we lost—I'm better off now than *ever* before."

CHRONOLOGY: 1981–1982

February 12, 1981:	PATCO and the FAA began negotiating, with the union putting 96 issues on the table (41 of which were negotiable, and nearly 50 of which would have required congressional action).
March 10, 1981:	PATCO concluded the fifth and final survey of the contract and strike preparation attitudes of its members (the survey series had begun in July, 1980).
March 15-16, 1981:	Led by the PATCO "choirboys," hundreds of PATCO members manned informational picket lines at airports across the country to protest the March 15 expiration of the PATCO-FAA contract without any progress in stalled negotiations.
April 1, 1981:	Over 730 PATCO members and spouses rallied on the Hill to lobby for passage of the "Air Traffic Controllers Act of 1981" (introduced on Feb. 3 in Congress by Representative William Clay).
April 28, 1981:	Negotiations were broken off, as agreement had been reached on only four of 41 directly negotiable items.
May 20, 1981:	The FAA sent a letter home to every controller warning of the penalties attendant on breaking the law against striking. The FAA also had every super-

	visor deliver an oral message to every controller about the liabilities entailed in an illegal strike.
May 22, 1981:	At PATCO's Annual Convention (New Orleans) Poli set a June 22 strike deadline.
June 15, 1981:	Bargaining between PATCO and the FAA resumed under the auspices of the Federal Mediation and Conciliation Service.
June 18, 1981:	The FAA complained to a congressional subcommittee that controllers were being intimidated by pro-PATCO militants, though firm evidence was not available.
	Judge Platt of the Eastern District of New York ruled that the 1970 injunction against PATCO ever striking again remained in effect; the Judge "gently reminded" PATCO's members of their duty to obey the law.
June 19, 1981:	Secretary of Transportation Drew Lewis became directly involved in the PATCO-FAA negotiations. By June 22, a tentative agreement had been reached, and proponents hailed it as a breakthrough—for PATCO had successfully bargained for wages outside of the civil service regulations, an unprecedented event in federal labor relations.
June 22, 1981:	PATCO failed to get the 80 percent vote needed to call a strike; Poli agreed to a new contract with the FAA, pending a vote of endorsement from PATCO members.
June 28, 1981:	A congressional subcommittee was disturbed by a "letter of understanding" PATCO had sent in late October 1980 to a Reagan-Bush campaign official; the White House denied any "deal" was entailed.
July 2, 1981:	The PATCO board met in Chicago and voted unanimously (with Poli abstaining) to reject the Lewis-Poli June 22 agreement.
July 5-7, 1981:	A bloc of "choirboys" met to assess the June 22 agreement. They voted to reject it, and PATCO agreed to send five of their ranks out to campaign against it with PATCO locals across the country. They also decided to modify the "'81 Strike Plan" to make a prostrike vote more attainable than it had been on June 22.
July 12, 1981:	Congressman Clay introduced a substantially scaled down version of his "Air Traffic Controllers Act of

1981," a revision with lower salary ceilings and a pledge not to strike against the government.

July 28, 1981: A letter signed by 55 U.S. senators was sent to every controller reminding them of their legal duty not to strike.

July 29, 1981: A letter signed by 17 U.S. congressmen was sent to every controller warning against the penalties for an illegal strike by federal workers.

PATCO announced that its members had rejected the June 22 agreement, and asked an immediate resumption of negotiations.

July 31, 1981: PATCO scaled down its bargaining demands by $285,000,000 below its initial February proposal ($775 million); the FAA refused to budge from its June 22 offer of $40,000,000.

August 3, 1981: Negotiations broke down, and at 7 a.m., PATCO began the first large-scale strike of its kind against the FAA.

(4:35 a.m.) The government obtained a temporary restraining order from the District Court for the District of Columbia enjoining PATCO, its officers, and its members from commencing the threatened strike.

The Federal Labor Relations Authority issued an unfair labor practice complaint against PATCO, and sought and received a temporary restraining order barring PATCO's strike activity.

(11 a.m.) President Ronald Reagan issued a televised warning that controllers on strike 48 hours from that time would be fired.

(4:30 p.m.) The District Court found PATCO and Robert Poli in contempt, and created a series of fines to be imposed if the strike continued. Eventually, ATA obtained a judgment of $4,500,000 and attached most of PATCO's funds, including the $3,000,000 amassed since 1978 in the union's strike fund.

AFL-CIO president Lane Kirkland called a press conference to express strong support for PATCO, and condemn the "brutal and repressive" acts of the White House. The entire AFL-CIO executive council then went out to a nearby airport to march in sympathy with cheering PATCO pickets.

August 5, 1981: After only 1,300 strikers went back to work, the FAA fired 11,345 remaining PATCO strikers (or 90 percent of those who had struck on August 3), a group equal to 75 percent of the FAA's entire controller labor force.

Scores of union officials, including Gary Eads, Steven L. Wallart, Bill Taylor, and others, were jailed for violating back-to-work orders, as the Justice Department moved against PATCO in 57 federal courts across the country (criminal complaints were issued against 39 PATCO grass roots leaders).

AFL-CIO president Lane Kirkland urged the White House to appoint a special mediator to find a face-saving way out of a no-win impasse for both PATCO and the White House.

Drew Lewis indicated the government would not consider binding arbitration, an option PATCO also turned down.

Drew Lewis declared the firing of 11,345 strikers had effectively ended the PATCO job action: None of the strikers, Lewis noted, would ever be permitted back.

August 8, 1981:   A Gallup Poll found 60 percent of the public approved of the White House decision to fire the strikers, and 67 percent felt the strikers had been wrong to leave their jobs.

August 10-11, 1981:   Canadian controllers called work stoppages in sympathy with PATCO, but were forced to end their job action by a threat of harsh reprisals from the Canadian government.

August 14, 1981:   John Fenron, the Chief Administrative Law Judge for the FLRA, held that PATCO had committed an unfair labor practice with its strike. He recommended revocation of PATCO's status as the exclusive bargaining representative.

August 20, 1981:   The Air Transport Association estimated losses during the first 2 weeks of the strike at $210,000,000 to $315,000,000. Mutual of Omaha reported its sales of flight insurance policies had jumped 25 percent.

Labor Day, September 7, 1981:   PATCO strikers were the guests of honor at local parades and rallies of unionists from coast-to-coast.

September 9, 1981:   The first long-term airline schedules drawn up since the August 3 strike were put into effect.

September 17, 1981:   PATCO sought to avoid decertification by arguing at an FLRA hearing that punishment be put aside in favor of an order that the parties start negotiating by September 23, and, after 30 days, an independent arbitrator resolve any remaining differences.

October 17, 1981: AFL-CIO president Lane Kirkland allegedly called Poli to a private meeting to discuss a surrender deal that *might* avoid decertification and secure the rehiring by strict seniority of the strikers.

October 22, 1981: PATCO's executive board rejected the Kirkland terms on the grounds that all the strikers were returned or none would go back; the board also wanted the offer in writing and on the signature of a federal bureaucrat with the power to uphold its terms.

The FLRA voted to decertify PATCO (Chairman Ronald Houghton indicated he would join the other two voters if PATCO did not immediately call off its strike and promise to obey the no-strike provisions of the law).

October 27, 1981: The Court of Appeals for the District of Columbia lifted its stay of the October 22 FLRA decertification judgment. The FAA ended dues collection from 3,228 PATCO working controllers, and froze $350,000 in dues collected by the FAA for PATCO since August 3.

November 19, 1981: Poli received a standing ovation at the AFL-CIO convention, but the delegates declined to call for a nationwide 1-day sympathy strike.

November 1981: Five prominent union leaders, including the head of AFGE, joined with Ralph Nader and the head of the Consumer Federation of America, in filing suit to require the FAA to rehire the fired strikers.

PATCO filed for protection under Chapter 11 of the Federal Bankruptcy Act, and indicated its intention to reorganize, not to liquidate.

December 9, 1981: The White House indicated that the fired strikers could now apply for any federal job opening, except that of controller.

December 1981: PATCO agreed to pay 14 airlines $28,900,000 in damages for the August 3–5 period, and thereby avoid the legal costs of a trial in the matter.

December 31, 1981: A group of working controllers who called themselves CATCO (Concerned Air Traffic Controllers) indicated their intention to win control over

$3,500,000 in PATCO assets frozen since the strike. CATCO accused PATCO of having breached the labor-management contract by calling the August 3 strike.

Robert E. Poli resigned as PATCO president, and expressed his hope that reinstatement could now begin.

January 1, 1982:   Gary Eads defeated Dave Siegal in a close vote to become the fourth PATCO president.

May 1982:   The NLRB held that Poli and PATCO had committed unfair labor practices in refusing to negotiate with a now defunct union of PATCO office employees.

July 2, 1982:   PATCO declared bankruptcy, as its fines amounted to $33,400,000, and it had only $1,000,000 left in assets.

July 1982:   The Circuit Court of Appeals upheld the PATCO decertification decision of the FLRA.

REFERENCE NOTES

Foreword

1. Interviews were held with Ed Curran, Director of Personnel and Technical Training, and Joseph Noonan, Director, Office of Labor and Employee Relations, on January 31, 1986 at the FAA headquarters in Washington, D.C. Both held the same posts during the 1981 strike.

Introduction

1. Severo, R. Controller-FAA clash tied to personalities. *New York Times*, August 9, 1981, p. 23.
2. Psychiatrist R. M. Rose, as quoted in Van Riper, F. Doc: Controllers don't hate jobs. *New York Daily News*, August 7, 1981. p. 20.
3. Witkin, R. Controller Training Academy set to triple output. *New York Times*, August 7, 1981, p. A-11.
4. Paden, D.L. Air traffic control. Unpublished Ph.D. dissertation. Bloomington, IN: Indiana University, Graduate Schoool of Business, 1962, p. 463.
5. Severo, R. Controller-FAA clash . . . *New York Times*, op. cit.
6. As quoted in Arena, S., & Gentile, D. His future up in the air. *New York Daily News*, August 9, 1981, p. 23.
7. Weil, H. Those ultracool, death-defying air-traffic controllers. *Cosmopolitan*, May 1976, p. 230.

8. Serrin, W. "Air controllers, still defiant, compete for jobs in tight market." *New York Times*, November 8, 1981, p. 22.

Chapter 1

1. Much of the history that follows is drawn from Paden, D. L. Air traffic control. Unpublished Ph.D. dissertation. Bloomington, IN: Indiana University, Graduate School of Business, 1962. See also Mannix, G. K. The history of PATCO. Unpublished manuscript, 1981.
2. See Searls, H. *The crowded sky.* New York: Harper & Bros., 1960.
3. Paden, D. L. Air traffic control, op. cit., p. 392.
4. U.S. Congress, Senate. *Air Traffic Controllers.* (Corson Report) S. Rept. 91-1012, 91st Congress, 2nd Session, July 9, 1970.

Chapter 3

1. I draw here on an unpublished manuscript, The history of PATCO, by G. K. Mannix. Lent to me by PATCO activist Jack Seddon, the manuscript should earn full-scale publication in its own right at the earliest possible time.
2. Helpful in the entire Bailey saga in his own reconstruction of events: Bailey, F. L. *Cleared for the approach.* Englewood Cliffs, N.J.: Prentice-Hall, Inc., 1977.
3. Gordon and others were astonished and awed by the response, as it fulfilled their highest hopes for the occasion and got PATCO off to an exhilarating start.
4. Bailey, F.L., op. cit., p. 94.
5. Anonymous. Stack-up, danger, and confusion of the air traffic jam. *Life*, August 9, 1968, pp. 38-47.
6. U.S. Department of Transportation. *The career of the air traffic controller—A cause of action.* Washington, DC: Government Printing Office, 1970. See also *PATCO Newsletter*, December 3, 1969, pp. 1-2.
7. See in this connection, *PATCO Newsletter*, October 2, 1969, p. 3. See also *Government Employee Relations Report*, No. 370, October 12, 1970, p. G-2.
8. Mannix notes that Rock pleaded it be written on a matchbox cover, but get it in writing. Mannix, G.K. op. cit., p. 222 (Footnote #57).
9. It should be noted that the Federal Mediation and Conciliation Service was "irate with the Department of Transportation. They tried in vain to have DOT live up to the agreement, but were unsuccessful," ibid., p. 112.
10. *Government Employee Relations Report*, October 12, 1970. No. 370, G-4. Col. 1.
11. Ibid., G-5, Col., 1, No. 6.
12. *PATCO Newsletter*, January 30, 1978, pp. 2-4.
13. *Government Employee Relations Report*, October 12, 1970. op. cit., G-4, Col. 2.
14. As cited in Witkin, R. White House warns flight controllers. *New York Times*, June 19, 1981, p. A-12.
15. As recalled with pride by Stan Gordon and another PATCO activist, Jack Seddon.

Chapter 4

1. As noted in the primary source for this entire chapter, Mannix, G. K. The history of PATCO. Unpublished monograph, 1981.
2. The intermediary was Helen Bentley, a Chairperson of the Federal Maritime Commission, and the writer of a daily transportation column for the *Baltimore Sun*. ibid., p. 140.
3. Founded in 1897, MEBA reached its peak membership in 1921, and in 1985 had fallen to 12,280 members (or 60 percent of the 1921 tally). Troy, L. & Sheflin, N. *U.S. union source book*. West Orange, NJ: Industrial Relations Data and Information Services, 1985, p. 42.
4. It should be noted that despite the earlier overtures from various unions, "the failure of the 1970 strike had alienated all other sources of aid. It was an easy decision for Leyden to reach, since only MEBA had confidence in PATCO, and only MEBA was offering tangible assistance." Mannix, G. K. op. cit., p. 142.
5. Personal interview with Stan Gordon at the AFL-CIO George Meany Center for Labor Studies, Silver Spring, MD. July 1985.
6. "Each and every department, or individual involved in aviation, has responded favorably to the changes we have made in the past months in PATCO. . . . We have illustrated honesty, integrity, and responsibility in our approach to solutions." *PATCO Newsletter*, September 14, 1970, p. 1.
7. Personal interview with John F. Leyden at the AFL-CIO George Meany Center for Labor Studies, Silver Spring, MD. July 1984.
8. Mannix, G. K. op. cit., p. 174.
9. When the Civil Service actually attempted to downgrade a facility, PATCO secured an injunction delaying this action for 18 months. Ibid., p. 182.
10. This doctrine of "as much as possible for as many as possible" was emphatically rejected in 1981 when the PATCO Board insisted on reinstatement for all strikers or the return of none: Two of nine Board members consistently voted the other way.
11. *PATCO Newsletter*, January 1980, p. 3. (As recorded on February 14, 1978.)
12. I lean heavily in this section on a personal interview with Jack Seddon at the AFL-CIO's George Meany Center for Labor Studies, Silver Spring, MD, July 1984 (and, several phone discussions thereafter).
13. This appears a rare instance where the FAA actually was sympathetic to PATCO, as "the FAA was being embarrassed by the refusal of ATA to honor the overseas FAM agreement." Mannix, op. cit., pp. 193-194.
14. Leyden, John F., in *PATCO Newsletter*, June 12, 1978, p. 6.
15. Doyle, Pat, in *PATCO Newsletter*, August 1979, p. 13. "We have survived that defeat, the fiber of our organization tested, and after a few steps backward we are ready to proceed on the new course of PATCO" (p. 13).
16. *PATCO Newsletter*, December 31, 1978, p. 3.
17. *PATCO Newsletter*, April 23, 1979, p. 1.

18.   *PATCO Newsletter*, August 1979, p. 2.
19.   FAA administrator Langhorne Bond grew fond of repeating that thought, a sentence lifted out of context from the Rose Report, and entirely out of keeping with its major findings. See The Rose Report, *PATCO Newsletter*, August 1979, pp. 5-7.
20.   *PATCO Newsletter*, April 23, 1979, p. 4.
21.   Ibid., p. 6.
22.   Ibid.
23.   Magnuson, E., et al. Turbulence in the tower. *Time*, August 17, 1981, p. 18.
24.   Personal interview with John F. Leyden, op. cit.
25.   *PATCO Newsletter*, January 1980, pp. 4-5.
26.   Ibid., p. 3.
27.   Allegations about "high living" misuse of PATCO funds were a mainstay of the anti-Poli campaign, and remained to alienate certain PATCO members from the entire 20-month Poli administration. Poli vigorously denied and bitterly resented this line of attack.

Chapter 5

1.   Private correspondence with a PATCO activist who prefers anonymity, August 1985. In a September 1985 phone conversation with me, Poli judged this the single biggest mistake of his PATCO presidency, and the act he most regretted and wished he had managed differently. He attributed his actions to exhaustion, undue haste, the distraction of strike preparation matters, and bad advice.
2.   Hurd, R. How PATCO was led into a trap. *The Nation*, December 26, 1981. p. 698.
3.   Feazel, M. FAA files new charges against PATCO. *Aviation Week and Space Technology*, June 23, 1980, p. 34.
4.   Ibid. PATCO officer Robert Myers, Executive Vice President, was the source.
5.   Ibid.
6.   Ibid.
7.   Poli, R. E., in Air traffic control. *Hearings*, op. cit. pp. 17-22.
8.   From his testimony in U.S. Congress Hearings: Aviation Safety, Subcommittee on Investigations and Oversight, 97th Congress, June 19, 1981, p. 83. Washington, DC: U.S. Government Printing Office, 1982.
9.   The text appeared in the *New York Times*, August 16, 1981. p. 69, in a full-page pro-PATCO ad taken out by the International Association of Flight Attendants, a gesture of support PATCO activists continue to hold in very high regard. (Reagan's letter is dated October 20, 1980.)
10.   Poli, R. E. FAA is to blame in air strike. *Philadelphia Inquirer*, August 14, 1981, p. 27-A.
11.   Ibid. See also R. E. Poli in *The MacNeil/Lehrer Report*, August 5, 1981. (Transcript, p. 6)
12.   Aviation safety. *Hearings*, op. cit., p. 107.
13.   *PATCO Press Release*, February 3, 1981, pp. 1-2.

14. Anonymous. The air controllers lobby for more pay. *Business Week*, May 4, 1981, p. 56.
15. *PATCO Negotiations Update*, April 10, 1981, p. 1. "... we require the continued support of all PATCO members by allowing the negotiating team to exhaust the bargaining process."
16. Anonymous. Bring the controllers down to earth (Editorial). *New York Times*, June 19, 1981, p. A-26.
17. As quoted in Anonymous. Air pact termed trash. *Philadelphia Evening Bulletin*, June 23, 1981, p. A-4.
18. On the July 28, 1981 letter from 55 senators and 19 congressmen, see Northrup, H. R. The rise and demise of PATCO. *Industrial and Labor Relations Review*, January, 1984 37(2), p. 177. See also Hebert, H. F. Air controllers reject Pact 20-1: Strike hinted. *Philadelphia Inquirer*, July 30, 1981, p. 2-A.
19. Anonymous. The air traffic controllers (Editorial). *The Washington Post*, July 28, 1981, p. A-12.
20. Moody, J. P. Controllers rejecting contract offer. *Pittsburgh Post-Gazette*, July 29, 1981, p. 10. See also Anonymous, The air controllers ..., *Business Week*, op. cit.
21. Rose, R. M., et al. *Air traffic controller health change study.* Boston: Boston University, School of Medicine, 1978. For the PATCO rebuttal, see the *PATCO Newsletter*, August 1979, pp. 5, 7. (It tried to accomplish too much, and offered only vague and familiar recommendations.)
22. Keisling, P. Money over what really mattered: Where the air traffic controllers went wrong. *The Washington Monthly*, September 1983, p. 14. "What the union didn't mention were the tremendous incentives for controllers to leave as 'disabled'." See also Staten, M. E., & Umbeck, J. Information costs and incentives to shirk: Disability compensation of air traffic controllers. *American Economic Review*, (December 1982), 72(5), pp. 1023-1037.
23. Royko, M. Controller stress? Yes, but. . . . *New York Daily News*, August 10, 1981, p. 21.
24. Anonymous. The air controllers. . . . *Business Week*, op. cit. p. 58.

Chapter 7

1. Witkin, R. Controllers strike, halting 7,000 flights: Reagan gives 48-hour notice of dismissal. *New York Times*, August 4, 1981, p. 1.
2. Raines, H. Reagan warns controllers to return or face dismissal. *New York Times*, August 4, 1981, p. B-8.
3. Ibid.
4. Magnuson, E., et al. Turbulence in the tower. *Time*, August 17, 1981, p. 14.
5. Witkin, Controllers strike. . . . *New York Times*, op. cit., p. 1
6. Magnuson, E. Turbulence. . . . *Time*, August 17, 1981, p. 15.
7. Dickinson, D. S. The unmaking of a union. *Journal of Collective Negotiations*, 1983, 12(4), p. 268. The number later reached 225,000 for 7,000 openings.

8. Keisling, P. Money over what really mattered: Where the air traffic controllers went wrong. *The Washington Monthly*, September 1983, p. 14.
9. Serrin, W. Kirkland defends decision by controllers to strike. *New York Times*, August 4, 1981, p. B-8.
10. Magnuson, E. Turbulence. . . . *Time*, op. cit., p. 20.
11. Ibid.
12. Witkin, R. Accord in Canada reopens air lanes crossing atlantic. *New York Times*, August 13, 1981, p. 1.
13. As cited in a letter from Helms to Northrup, dated July 26, 1983. In Northrup, H. R. The rise and demise of PATCO. *Industrial and Labor Relations Review*, January 1984, *37*(2), p. 181.
14. Anonymous. No room for compromise. *Wall Street Journal*, August 6, 1981, p. 22.
15. Anonymous. Firings, jailings as strike spreads. *New York Post*, August 6, 1981, p. 4.
16. Gearty, R. U.S. steps up flight fight. *New York Daily News*, August 8, 1981.
17. Anonymous (Editorial). Reagan drops the other shoe. *New York Daily News*, August 6, 1981. p. 28.
18. UPI. Most in poll approve of Reagan's actions. *New York Times*, August 9, 1981, p. 22. See also *Newsweek*, August 17, 1981, p. 21.
19. Anonymous. Striking controllers lose support. *New York Times*, August 16, 1981. p. 4-1.
20. Lublin, J. S. Air controllers' union loses a round on decertification, gets Portuguese aid. *Wall Street Journal*, August 14, 1981. p. 2.
21. As quoted in Raines, Reagan warns. . . . *New York Times*, op. cit.
22. Bennetts, L. An uneasy time for strikers. *New York Times*, August 13, 1981, p. 1.

Chapter 9

1. Gearty, R. Hold air skeds at half. *New York Daily News*, August 7, 1981, p. 2.
2. Anonymous. PATCO says U.S. acted improperly on decertification. *Wall Street Journal*, February 19, 1982, p. 11.
3. Witkin, R. No new move on controllers. *New York Times*, November 10, 1981, p. A-18.
4. Leyden, J. G. The dangers of rehiring fired air controllers. *St. Petersburg Times*, December 26, 1981, p. 21-A.
5. Mac Avoy, P. W. An FAA mistake. *New York Times*, September 16, 1981, p. A-27.
6. Anonymous. Controllers will pay $29 million in strike. *Philadelphia Inquirer*, December 8, 1981, p. A-5.
7. Anonymous. Poli resigns post with controllers. *New York Times*, January 1, 1982. p. 7.
8. Meyers, D. Poli resigns as president of air controllers. *Philadelphia Inquirer*, January 1, 1982, pp. 1-A, 4-A.
9. As quoted in Fuerbringer, J. Militant controller chief. *New York Times*, August 4, 1981, p. B-8.

10. Anonymous. Controllers' union, $40 million in debt, files for bankruptcy. *New York Times*, August 4, 1981, p. B-8.

Chapter 15

1. Northrup attributes the union's total loss to PATCO ineptitude and personnel immaturity; Dickinson, to PATCO ineptitude and FAA intransigence; Keisling, to PATCO ineptitude and public hostility: Northrup, H. R. The rise and demise of PATCO. *Industrial and Labor Relations Review*, (January 1984), *37*(2), pp. 167-184; Dickinson, D. S. The unmaking of a union. *Journal of Collective Negotiations*, 1983, *12*(4), pp. 259-270; Keisling, P. Money over what really mattered: Where the air traffic controllers went wrong. *The Washington Monthly*, September 1983, pp. 10-18.
2. Typical of numerous media accounts is this one: "Management consultant Richard I. Lyles, author of *Management Boom II*, says that the [anti-labor] turning point was the disastrous air traffic controllers' strike of 1981. 'Never in history has a union so misread public sentiment. The air traffic controllers made demands much of the public felt unreasonable at a time when an overpowering concern was to get federal spending under control. They struck, the President fired them, and their union went out of business. Little sympathy was generated for the controllers—and none for the unions.'" As quoted in Donleavy, T., *American Business*, Summer 1984, p. 4.
3. Meyers, D. Poli resigns as president of air controllers. *Philadelphia Inquirer*, January 1, 1982, p. 4-A.
4. Ibid.
5. Kerr, A. Lewis complains about FAA approach. *Wall Street Journal*, February 7, 1983, p. 17; Anonymous. Lewis "regrets" ATC strike, criticizes FAA mgt. *USATCO Newsletter*, February 1983, p. 8.
6. Committee on Public Works and Transportation. Rebuilding of the nation's air traffic control system: Has safety taken a back seat to expediency? *Report* of the Subcommittee on Investigations and Oversight. Washington, DC: Government Printing Office, 1985, p. 82.
7. For a forecast of the inevitable unionization of the working controllers, see Keisling, P. Money over what really mattered. *Washington Monthly*, op. cit., p. 12. ". . . even FAA officials concede another union is inevitable. . . ."
8. Stuart, R. F.A.A. to increase air controllers. *New York Times*, September 20, 1985, p. A-16.
9. Helms, J. L., as quoted in Witkin, R. Revamping of air control system in next 20 years proposed by U.S. *New York Times*, January 29, 1982, p. A-14.
10. Committee on Public Works and Transportation: Rebuilding of the Nation's air traffic control system: Has safety taken a back seat to expediency? *Report* of the Subcommittee on Investigations and Oversight. Washington, DC: Government Printing Office, 1985.

11.   Ibid., p. 43.

12.   Ibid., p. 36.

13.   Aronowitz, S. *Working class hero: A new strategy for labor.* New York: Adama Books, 1983, p. 67.

14.   As quoted in Jackman, F. Flight safety: A question left hanging in midair. *New York Daily News,* August 12, 1981, p. 34.

15.   Poli was cheered at an ALPA Convention before the strike when he discussed PATCO's goals in the forthcoming negotiations. ALPA's president was one of the first to attempt to mediate between PATCO and the White House (he carried word of Kirkland's endorsement of Bill Usery as an independent mediator to the White House). Within two days of the strike's start, however, ALPA had publicly sided with the FAA in insisting the system remained safe . . . thereby exacerbating old and deep-set strife between controllers and pilots.

16.   Committee on Public Works and Transportation. Rebuilding. . . . *Report,* op. cit., pp. 4, 50-55. Before the strike controllers trained 50 percent of the time; afterwards, 20 percent.

17.   Ibid., p. 5.

18.   Ibid., p. 6. In a government survey in 1984 of 4,200 controllers, 86 percent felt there were too few experienced controllers at work.

19.   Ibid., p. 21.

20.   Ibid., p. 24.

21.   Ibid., p. 26. The Director, John Galipault, added: "I still believe the FAA did a masterful job managing information since 1981. And I think that if they could manage people as well as they have managed information, then I think we would have a fantastic system."

22.   Nussbaum, P. Renewed concern about air safety: Controllers cite overwork understaffing, poor tools. *Philadelphia Inquirer,* August 23, 1985, p. 1.

23.   Ibid., p. 32.

24.   Ibid., p. 24.

25.   Ibid., p. 55.

26.   Ibid., Jones, L., pp. 55-56.

27.   Ibid., Bowers, D., p. 58.

28.   Ibid., p. 59.

29.   Ibid., p. 73-74.

30.   Ibid., p. 71

31.   Ibid., p. 81.

32.   Ibid., p. 10.

33.   Invaluable here is Aronowitz, S. *Working class hero,* op. cit., p.67.

34.   Ibid., p. 71.

35.   Bowers, D. G. What would make 11,500 people quit their jobs? *Organizational Dynamics,* Winter 1983. p. 16.

36.   Ibid., p. 18.

37.   Aronowitz, S. *Working class hero,* op. cit., p. 72.

Chapter 16

1. See in this connection, Galante, M. A. Right to strike. California Supreme Court backs public employees in labor disputes. *The National Law Journal*, June 3, 1985, p. 6.

2. Hanslowe, K. L., & Acierno, J. L. The law and theory of strikes by government employees. *Cornell Law Review*, 1982, *67*, p. 1077.

3. As quoted in Anonymous. Management vs. labor. *ISR Newsletter*. University of Michigan, Ann Arbor, Michigan, Summer 1982, p. 3. See also Bowers, D. G. What would make 11,500 people quit their jobs? *Organization Dynamics*, Winter 1983, pp. 16-21.

4. See in this connection, Walsh, J. Air controllers unite. In *These Times*, January 9-15, 1985, p. 2; Anonymous. Why air controllers are talking union again. *Business Week*, May 27, 1985, pp. 124-126. ". . . the agency has managed to alienate many of the strikebreakers it has used to keep the system going." (p. 124) See also Witkin, R. Controllers find organizing snags. *New York Times*, October 27, 1985, p. 37.

5. See here, Shostak, A. Coping with blue collar stress: A solvable challenge for management. *Occupational Health & Safety*, November 1985, *55*(11), pp. 19-28; Shostak, A. *Blue-collar stress*. Reading, MA: Addison-Wesley, 1980.

6. For details, albeit from a hostile perspective, see Northrup, H. R. The rise and demise of PATCO. *Industrial and Labor Relations Review*, (January 1984), *37*(2) pp. 167-184.

7. On the FAA's automation plans, see Anonymous. FAA plans to automate air traffic control. *Science*, August 21, 1981, *213*, pp. 845-846; Anonymous. Revamping air traffic control. *Business Week*, January 18, 1982, pp. 100-101.

8. " . . . the single greatest discomfort to those who design, develop, and apply technology is caused by the demand of ordinary people to exercise the right to know." Reinecke, I. *Electronic illusions*. New York: Penguin, 1984, p. 243. See also Hirschhorn, L. *Beyond mechanization: Work and technology in a postindustrial age*. Cambridge, MA: MIT Press, 1984.

9. Nevins, B. How safe are the skies? *Sunshine (Ft. Lauderdale Sun-Sentinel)*, December 15, 1985. p. 8.

10. "There is ample evidence that the USA's air traffic control system is still under significant strain. Its controllers are less experienced than those who were fired in the 1981 strike, and heavy traffic and fatigue have taken their toll. . . ." Editorial, Air travel still isn't as safe as it must be. *USA Today*, August 20, 1985, p. 8-A. See also Carroll, J. R. Controller overload: A safety compromise? *The Miami Herald*, October 6, 1985, p. 8-A.

11. Nussbaum, P. Lawmakers ask U.S. to rehire some air controllers. *Philadelphia Inquirer*, November 15, 1985. p. 10-A. Three more signed in February of 1986.

12. This is not, of course, to imply that the full story has in any way been told in this thin volume. We need a book-length account from the FAA's perspective, a book-

length account from White House insiders, and some fresh writing about White House plans to transfer much ATC work to the private sector . . . and even then, the story will remain incomplete. We hope, however, to have helped make a good start on the task with this volume.

13. U.S. General Accounting Office. *Aviation safety: Serious problems concerning the air traffic control workforce.* Washington DC: GAO 1986, p. 1.
14. Ibid.
15. Ibid., p. 93.
16. Ibid., pp. 9,20.
17. For details, contact the Honorable Guy Molinari, 208 Cannon Building, Washington, DC 20515.
18. John O'Brien, ALPA Engineering and Safety Director, in an appearance on CBS TV Morning News, March 11, 1986.
19. U.S. GAO, *Aviation safety,* op. cit. pp. 21,2.

Appendix I: Bibliography for Fischer Essay

Blum, B. & Lobaco, G. Why the skies are unfriendlier. *The Nation,* June 1985: *240,* 668-672.
Boston Globe. Skies still turbulent in wake of controllers' strike. November 10, 1981, 1.
————. New careers and lingering memories. February 28, 1982, 74.
Braverman, H. *Labor and monopoly capital.* New York: Monthly Review Press, 1974.
Business Week. Revamping air traffic control. January 18, 1982, 100-101.
Fischer, B. & Offe, C. Unemployment of scientists and engineers. *Science for the People,* 1970, *2*(4): 5-9.
Fischer, B. *Engineers in the salaried petty bourgeoisie.* Ph.D. Dissertation, Washington University-St. Louis, 1980. Ann Arbor, MI: University Microfilms.
————. Unemployed engineers and air traffic controllers: A systematic comparison. *New England Sociologist,* Winter 1985: 15-22.
Newsweek. PATCO strikers find going tough. June 1982, 12.
New York Times. Air controllers turn to a wide variety of jobs. October 18, 1981, 24.
————. Air controllers still defiant, compete for jobs in tight market. November 8, 1981, 22.
————. Air controllers scan new vistas. October 24, 1982, 1,4.
Rose, R.M., Jenkins, C.D. & Hurst, M.W. *Air traffic controller health study.* Washington DC: U.S. Department of Transportation, Federal Aviation Agency, 1978.

Appendix I: Hurd Essay

1. Poli, R. E. *PATCO educational package.* April 15, 1980; Taylor, B. Telephone interviews, April 3, June 6, 7, 10, 1985; Vacca, J. Telephone interview, March 20, 1982; Martin, M. Personal interview, September 21, 1983.
2. Leyden, J. Personal interview, June 24, 1982.

3. Corson, J. J. *The career of the air traffic controller—A course of action.* U.S. Department of Transportation, Washington, DC, 1970; Rose, R. M. *Air traffic controller health change study,* U.S. Department of Transportation, Washington, DC, 1978.
4. Poli, R. E. Why controllers' strike failed. *New York Times,* January 17, 1982, p. F2.
5. *New York Times.* August 16, 1981, p. 69.
6. Christy, M. PATCO's Robert Poli on life after the fall. *Boston Globe,* March 28, 1982, p. A23.
7. Hershow, S. Law firm helped DOT control air strike. *The Federal Times,* August 30, 1982.
8. Reinhold, R. Enigmatic FAA chief. *New York Times,* August 11, 1981, p. B9.
9. Hurd, R. W. How PATCO was led into a trap. *The Nation,* December 26, 1981, pp. 696-698.
10. Ibid.
11. AFL-CIO. *The changing situation of workers and their unions.* Washington, DC, 1985, p. 23.

INDEX

NOTES ON THE AUTHORS

Skocik   Shostak

Arthur B. Shostak is a Professor of Sociology at Drexel University, where he teaches courses in industrial sociology, management and technology, futuristics, and the social implications of 20th century technology. He also teaches as an adjunct sociologist at the AFL-CIO George Meany Center for Labor Studies, Silver Spring, MD. He is the co-editor of *Blue-Collar World* (Prentice-Hall, 1965), *New Perspectives on Poverty* (Prentice-Hall, 1968), and *Privilege in America: An End to Inequality?* (Prentice-Hall, 1970). He is also the author of *Blue-Collar Life* (Random House, 1969) and *Blue-Collar Stress* (Addison-Wesley, 1980), along with scores of contributed chapters to volumes on working-class issues. A consultant on futuristics to the AFL-CIO Council of Union Secretary-Treasurers, he has also taught for District 65, RWDU-AFL-CIO; the Steelworkers Union (Lindenhall Education Center); the Postal Workers' Union; and others. Art earned a B.S. in Industrial and Labor Relations at Cornell University in 1958, and a Ph.D. in Industrial Sociology at Princeton University in 1961.

David Vincent Skocik is a teaching assistant at Philadelphia's Temple University, working toward a doctorate in mass communication. He enlisted in the Air Force in 1965 after graduating from high school and was trained as an air passenger specialist, but after being assigned to DaNang AB, Vietnam, was cross-trained into the air freight field. He requested and was accepted for retraining into air traffic control in 1969 at Dover Air Force Base, Delaware.

He later served as control tower training and certification official and temporary tower chief at Sondrestrom Air Base, Greenland. He was discharged in 1976 and hired by the FAA a year later, being assigned to the LaGuardia sector of the New York Common IFR Room, then located at JFK airport. In 1978, he became co-editor of PATCO Local 160's newsletter and was later elected to that local's executive board. After the strike, he was asked to become a spokesman for the union, working with the New York and national media. In January 1982 he was appointed executive press aide to incoming union president, Gary Eads. He left PATCO in March 1982, and started a small business as a vehicle to pursue higher education. After completing a B.A. at Delaware's Wilmington College, he was accepted for an assistantship at Temple University. He currently resides in Dover, Delaware, with his wife, Roseann, and their three children.

Britta Fischer is an associate Professor and Chairperson of the Department of Sociology at Emmanuel College in Boston, Massachusetts. She teaches courses in the sociology of work, urban sociology, and anthropology, and is a founding member of and contributor to the journal *Science for the People*. She received a B.A. from Barnard College in New York in 1964 and a Ph.D. in Sociology from Washington University in St. Louis in 1980.

Rick Hurd is an associate Professor of Economics at the University of New Hampshire. He has written two other pieces on the PATCO strike, How PATCO Was Led Into a Trap, *The Nation*, December 26, 1981, and The Rise and Demise of PATCO Reconstructed, with Jill Kriesky, which is scheduled to appear in *The Industrial and Labor Relations Review* in 1986. Professor Hurd has also written several other articles on unions, and is currently researching organizing activity among clerical workers. Hurd earned his Ph.D. in Economics from Vanderbilt University in 1972.